LBC FAMILY GUIDE TO LONDON

Vanessa Miles comes from a theatrical family and before the birth of her children was herself a successful actress, appearing in many stage and television productions. She began broadcasting in 1979 with Capital Radio and wrote *A Capital Guide for Kids*, *What Can I Do?* and *Castles and Dungeons*. Her other broadcasting activities have included book reviewing, presenting Listen with Mother for BBC Radio 4 and reading children's stories on television. She is Sky TV's folklore expert and has been with LBC since 1987.

LBC Family Guide to London

Vanessa Miles

Drawings by Stephen Wiltshire

HEADLINE

First published in 1994
by HEADLINE BOOK PUBLISHING

10 9 8 7 6 5 4 3 2 1

ISBN 0 7472 4044 2

Typeset by
Letterpart Limited, Reigate, Surrey

Printed and bound in Great Britain by
HarperCollins Manufacturing, Glasgow

HEADLINE BOOK PUBLISHING
A division of Hodder Headline PLC
Headline House
79 Great Titchfield Street
London W1P 7FN

For Michael, Luke and Ned

Special thanks to Susan Haynes, Elsa Petersen-Schepel, Jacqueline Danks and all on the Steve Jones show.

Contents

1

Introduction

London is one of the greatest cities in the world. Its diverse history is reflected not only in its layout and architecture but in street names, museums, parks, art galleries and, of course, in its people. There are so many different aspects to the capital that it can seem like an impenetrable maze. With a mission to make London accessible and interesting to everyone, residents and visitors alike, whatever their age, my family and I became tourists, seeking out the best the city has to offer. London is extremely accommodating, and the search for new and stimulating ideas produced surprising results and rarely disappointed. We learnt to plan our expeditions carefully, taking into account travelling expenses as well as costs of admission. Even with reduced-price family tickets our trip to the Tower of London, for instance, cost £19 for two adults and three children (the under-5-year-old went free), plus £7.60 in rail fares. Contrary to popular belief, however, there are a great many enjoyable activities in London which are completely free.

There is so much to see and do that it would be impossible to include everything in a single volume. The *LBC Family Guide to London* is by definition a personal look at the capital and what it has to offer, incorporating a cross-section of ideas which I hope will make London more exciting to people of all ages and tastes. In the eighteenth century Dr Samuel Johnson declared, 'When a man is tired of London he is tired of life.' His statement still holds true today. London is for everyone.

To the best of my knowledge the information in this book is correct at the time of going to press – but please let me know of any errors or omissions so that they may be corrected in future editions. I would also like to hear of any facilities or amusements in London that might interest a broad range of children and parents but have so far escaped my attention.

Vanessa Miles

2

Travel and transport

PUBLIC TRANSPORT

Do not be daunted by the thought of travelling around London with children. London Transport buses and underground services cover a wide area, offering easy access to many places of interest, even those further out of town. Under-5s travel free on buses and tubes, and, generally, older children pay at a reduced rate, either in the form of a flat fare (bus) or a fare graduated according to the distance travelled (tube). Always check whether cheap day-return tickets are available for a journey.

Travelling can be an expensive business, but there are special tickets available which cost less than normal fares. For unlimited travel ask for a Travelcard (daily, weekly or monthly). This covers journeys after 9.30a.m. Mon.–Fri. and at any time over the weekend. It applies to trains, tubes and buses and gives unconditional travel within one or more specified 'zones'. There are six zones in London and prices vary according to which ones you travel within.

Although under-5s go free and older children travel at reduced fares, 14- and 15-year-olds need a Child-rate Photocard (obtainable from London post offices or Travel Information Centres) before they can use a child's ticket. Proof of identity must accompany an application. Over-15s pay the full adult fare.

If you need to travel before 9.30a.m. Mon.–Fri., ask for the LT Card, but note that this does not cover mainline rail services and is economical only if you are making multiple journeys. For groups of ten or more, London Transport's Group Travel Cards are excellent value.

London Transport Headquarters, at 55 The Broadway, SW1 (tel. 071–222 1234 – 24 hours) will help with any travel queries and provide free bus and tube maps, as well as other useful leaflets, to help make your travelling as problem-free as possible.

London Transport Travel Information Centres can be found at:

Euston station, NW1 (mainline).
Open daily 8.30a.m.–9.30p.m.

King's Cross, NW1 (underground station).
Open daily 8.30a.m.–9.30p.m.

Liverpool Street station, EC2 (mainline).
Open Mon.–Sat. 8.15a.m.–6.00p.m.; Sun. 8.30a.m.– 4.40p.m.

Oxford Circus, W1 (underground station).
Open Mon.–Sat. 8.30a.m.–9.30p.m.; Sun. 8.30a.m.– 6.00p.m.

Piccadilly Circus, W1 (underground station).
Open daily 8.30a.m.–9.30p.m.

St James's Park, SW1 (underground station).
Open Mon.–Fri. 8.30a.m.–6.30p.m.

Victoria station, SW1 (mainline).
Open daily 8.30a.m.–9.30p.m.

Heathrow airport (underground station and at Terminals 1, 2, 3 and 4).
Open daily 7.30a.m.–9.30p.m.

West Croydon bus station.

The Docklands Light Railway (DLR) links the docklands area with London's underground system and the British Rail network. The two DLR routes connect docklands with the City of London (at Bank or Tower Gateway) and east London (at Stratford). The service operates Mon.–Fri. only, but there will be a weekend service from April 1994. Trains have no drivers, but 'train captains' are aboard to check tickets. DLR information centres can be found at Tower Gateway and Island Gardens. Docklands Travel Hotline (071–918 4000 – 24 hours) will help you find the quickest routes.

London's underground system is ideal for getting anywhere fast. Maps detailing the different routes can be obtained from all stations. However, if time is on your side and you can travel at a more leisurely pace, the best way to get around is by bus. There is no better way to view the sights of London than from the top of a double-decker.

London Transport's two-hour Round London Sightseeing Tour takes you past most of London's major tourist sights. There are no bookable seats, but buses leave from Piccadilly Circus, the forecourt of Baker Street underground station and Victoria (Grosvenor Gardens). Services operate daily (not Christmas Day) between 10.00a.m. and 4.00p.m. at hourly or half-hourly intervals.

The official London Transport Guided Tour takes you by coach around the major sights for a whole or part of a day. Lunch or tea is provided and there are reduced prices for under-14s. Trips run throughout the year. Bookings can be made at Travel Information Centres (see page 2) or at Victoria Coach Station (tel. 071–730 3499).

London Plus Bus Tours are more expensive but have the advantage of allowing you to get on and off wherever and whenever you please. The service operates daily from April to October, leaving Tobacco Dock at half-hourly intervals between 10.30a.m. and 4.00p.m. and covering the City and the West End.

London Docklands Tours (tel. 071–512 1111) operate regular two-hour coach trips which depart from the visitor centre on the Isle of Dogs, Tues. 2.00p.m., Thurs. 10.30a.m., Sun. 11.30a.m.

Cityrama (tel. 071–720 6663) offers good-value coach tours covering all the major sights of London. Trips last 1½ hours and leave from Coventry Street (off Piccadilly Circus) every 30 minutes from 9.30a.m. to 6.00p.m. daily.

For details of other coach trips such as Evan Evans Tours, telephone 071–828 6449 or 081–877 1722.

TRAVEL NEWS

A good way to avoid traffic jams and keep up to date with tube and bus information is to tune into LBC radio, which operates on 97.3FM and has all the latest travel news. There are travel updates every 10 minutes at peak times and at half-hourly intervals during the day.

PARKING

To the question 'Where should I park in London?', the short answer is: don't attempt it! Like most big cities in the world, London is at the mercy of the car, plagued by traffic jams, pollution and parking problems. If you feel tempted to travel into the city centre by car for the sake of convenience, weigh up the pros and cons before leaving home. Designated parking spaces are scarce and, if you break any of the strict parking regulations, you may have to pay a heavy fine or suffer the indignity and expense of having your car wheel-clamped or towed away. The best option is a car park. National Car Parks (distinguished by bright yellow NCP signs) now operate in most parts of the city and they will send on request a city map with their car parks marked. For more details about NCP, telephone 071–499 7050.

ELDERLY OR DISABLED TRAVELLERS

Anyone who has travelled on the London underground system will know how frustrating it is to find an escalator out of order. Suddenly, what had been envisaged as an unimportant part of your journey becomes a major obstacle. For elderly or disabled people – or for those with young children and pushchairs – such problems are particularly hard to cope with.

Shops, buses, the underground, cinemas, the street – all can present a challenge. If you use a wheelchair or have impaired sight, or you are simply not as young as you feel, getting around a city takes special planning. In recent years, a growing awareness on the part of town planners, developers and transport companies has meant a significant improvement in service for disabled city-dwellers. London Transport's Carelink and Mobility bus schemes, 'Talking Maps' and 'Helping Hand' notepads reflect some of the ways in which the needs of people with disabilities are being taken seriously. London Transport's Unit for Disabled Passengers operates special services and provides advice and information regarding routes, underground stations, trains and concessionary fares. If you would like a free information pack telling you more about what they do, telephone 071–918 3312 or write to the Unit for Disabled Passengers, London Transport Headquarters, 55 Broadway, SW1H 0BD.

3

Information services

The London Tourist Board's main information centre is at Victoria station (mainline). It has all the up-to-the-minute details of what is happening in London, plus free information sheets such as *Children's London* and *Entrance Fees to Attractions in London*. This is a good place to make tour reservations or book theatre tickets, for example. It is open Mon.–Fri. 9.00a.m.–6.00p.m.; Sat. 9.00a.m.–5.00p.m.

TELEPHONE INFORMATION SERVICES

Visitorcall is the London Tourist Board's comprehensive range of recorded information services. Available 24 hours a day and updated daily, Visitorcall is menu driven so that you can quickly and easily select the answer to your question or, if you prefer, listen to up-to-date listings of current and forthcoming events. Just dial 0839 123 plus the last three numbers as shown (e.g. for information on what's on this week call 0839 123 400).

What's on

What's on this week	400	Major sporting events	405
Sunday in London	407	Rock and pop concerts	422
Current exhibitions	403	Summer in the parks	406

Special events

Changing the guard	411	Lord Mayor's show	413
State opening of Parliament	413	Trooping the colour	413
Christmas and Easter	418	London marathon	414

Theatre

Comedy and thrillers	415	Plays	425
Musicals	416	Non West End productions	434
Shakespeare	419	New productions and how to book	438

Places to visit

Popular attractions	480	Military and maritime history	482
Museums	429	Famous houses and gardens	483
Palaces, Royal and State	481	Day trips from London	484

Where to take children

What's on 404

Places to visit 424

Out and about

Getting around London	430	Shopping in London	486
Guided tours and walks	431	Street markets	428
River trips	432	Pubs and restaurants	485

Weather

Met Office forecast for Greater London 0839 500 951.

If you would like to make an inquiry in writing, contact the London Tourist Board and Convention Bureau, 26 Grosvenor Gardens, SW1W 0DH.

Tourist information is also available from:

Bloomsbury Tourist Information Centre
35–36 Woburn Place, WC1.
Tel. 071–580 4599.
Open daily 7.30a.m.–7.00p.m.

City of London Tourist Information Centre
St Paul's Churchyard (by St Paul's Cathedral), EC4.
Tel. 071–260 1456.
Open May–Oct. daily 9.30a.m.–5.00p.m.; Nov.–April half-day Sat., closed Sun.

Greenwich Tourist Information Centre
Cutty Sark Gardens, SE10.
Tel. 081–858 6376.
Open daily to personal callers 10.30a.m.–4.30p.m.; July–Aug. 10.00a.m.–5.00p.m. Telephone inquiries 11.00a.m.–12 noon and 3.00p.m.–4.00p.m.

Heathrow airport Terminals 1, 2 and 3.
Tel. 071–730 3488.
Open Mon.–Fri. 9.00a.m.–6.00p.m.

HM Tower of London (including docklands information)
West Gate, Tower of London, EC3.
Tel. 071–730 3488.
Nearest tube: Liverpool Street.
Open April–Oct. daily Mon. 8.15a.m.–7.00p.m., Tues.–Sat.
8.15a.m.–6.00p.m., Sun. 8.30a.m.–4.45p.m.

London Docklands Visitor Centre
3 Limeharbour, E14.
Tel. 071–512 3000.
Open Mon.–Fri. 9.00a.m.–6.00p.m.; Sat. and Sun. 10.00a.m.–
4.30p.m.

Selfridges
400 Oxford Street, W1.
In person only.
Open Mon.–Fri. 9.00a.m.–5.30p.m. (Thurs. until 8.00p.m.).

There are some useful telephone services offering information on specific areas of interest:

Artsline (071–388 2227) provides good advice for those with special needs who want to find out about access to cinemas, theatres, arts centres and music venues. Mon.–Fri. 10.00a.m.–5.00p.m.

Circusline (0891 313 455) gives information on circuses performing in and around London. Although not listed on Circusline, you can catch Zippo's Circus touring around the London parks between May and August when they perform their animal-free show. It is aimed at those who enjoy the more traditional kind of family outing, and introduces a completely new line-up of international acts from all over the world. A virtuoso balancing performance, dare-devil BMX riding stunts and the first independent Chinese troupe to appear outside China all guarantee a good time out, proving that a circus line-up can work even without animals. For dates of current venues telephone 0962 868092.

Great Days Out (0891 335 533) gives up-to-the-minute information on the current week's selection of events and attractions, plus travel information.

Kidsline (071–222 8070) has an enormous fund of information covering all aspects of children's London. School holidays Mon.–Fri. 9.00a.m.–4.00p.m.; termtime Mon.–Fri. 4.00p.m.–6.00p.m.

Sportsline (071–222 8000) has the latest information on everything from abseiling to skiing, including where to go and how much it will cost, and offers helpful ideas for those who feel like being energetic but are unsure how to get started. This service also covers sporting activities for under-5s and crèche facilities. Mon.–Fri. 10.00a.m.–6.00p.m.

4

Annual events and regular ceremonies

London's diary is full of traditional events, some of which were established centuries ago. Many are held out of doors and are free, which makes them ideal family entertainment. Listed below are some which might be fun to attend. As dates may vary from year to year, check these with your nearest Tourist Information Centre (see page 7).

JANUARY

Lord Mayor of Westminster's New Year's Day Spectacular

At noon on New Year's Day a fantastic parade of marching bands from Europe and America swings into action and marches along Piccadilly, up Regent Street and into Oxford Street. Cheerleaders, circus animals, clowns, floats, veteran cars and horse-drawn carriages make up the colourful procession, after which there is a concert at the Royal Albert Hall involving many thousands of musicians, dancers, acrobats and clowns.

Nearest tube: Piccadilly Circus.
Nearby buses: 3, 6, 9, 12, 13, 14, 15, 19, 22, 23, 38, 53, 88, 94, 139, 159.

Chinese New Year

Since the Chinese calendar is based on the lunar cycle, which varies from year to year, the Chinese New Year is a movable feast that may fall in late January or early February. Chinese New Year is celebrated in Soho's China Town, when the area around Newport Place, Gerard Street and Lisle Street comes to life with music and dancing. The celebrations take place between 11.00a.m. and 6.30p.m., starting with the famous 'lion dances'. Streamers, decorations and garlands hang from the buildings lining the route as the colourful procession weaves its way through the streets. The 'lion' receives gifts of food and money from local residents and restaurants to help ward off evil spirits for the coming year. The celebrations attract large crowds throughout the day. For more information, contact the China Town Association (tel. 071–439 3822).

Nearest tubes: Leicester Square, Piccadilly Circus.
Nearby buses: 3, 6, 9, 12, 13, 14, 15, 19, 22, 23, 38, 53, 88, 94, 139, 159.

King Charles I Commemoration

The commemoration of the execution of King Charles I in 1649 takes place each year on the last Sunday in January. The march starts at 11.30a.m., when a body of men representing the king's army and dressed in seventeenth-century costume, proceeds from St James's Palace down the Mall through Horse Guards Parade to the Banqueting House – the route of Charles I's final walk. A short service is held and a wreath laid beneath the window through which the king stepped onto the scaffold. The parade then returns to St James's Palace via Trafalgar Square and the Mall.

Nearest tube: Green Park.
Nearby buses: 8, 9, 14, 19, 22, 38.

International Boat Show

The International Boat Show, which takes place at the Earls Court Exhibition Centre, Warwick Road, SW5 (tel. 071–385 1200), is one of London's most popular exhibitions. Hundreds of boats, from rubber dinghies to ocean-going yachts, are on display, as well as all types of boating equipment. The major feature is a central marina, where naval cadets perform various feats and exercises on rigging and in small boats. The exhibition starts during the first week of January and runs for two weeks. To find out more, telephone 0784–473377.

Admission charge; two children enter free with each paying adult.
Nearest tube: Earls Court.
Nearby buses: 31, 74, C3.

Holiday on Ice

The Holiday on Ice, held at Wembley Arena, Wembley, Middlesex, starts at the end of January and runs for six weeks. It is a lavish skating spectacular, with a different theme each year, featuring dancers, clowns and acrobats performing incredible feats on the ice. This is an enjoyable New Year treat for all the family, but wrap up well, as it can be chilly sitting near the ice rink. Take snacks and drinks with you. For more details, telephone the Wembley Arena box office on 081–900 1234.

Admission charge.
Nearest tubes: Wembley Central, Wembley Park.
Nearby buses: 83, 92, 182, 297.

FEBRUARY

Pancake Day

Shrove Tuesday, or Pancake Day, marks the last day before Lent; it traditionally represents the last chance to eat, drink and make merry before the serious business of fasting begins. The 'shriving' or pancake bell used to be rung to herald the start of the holiday and to call everyone to church to confess their sins and be 'shriven' or cleansed. Pancake Day is still celebrated today in London, when people take to the streets with frying pans for annual pancake races at Lincoln's Inn Fields, WC2, and Covent Garden Piazza, WC2. Both events start at 11.00a.m.

Nearest tubes: Covent Garden, Holborn.
Nearby buses: 1, 4, 6, 9, 11, 13, 15, 23, 26, 76, 77A, 168, 171, 171A, 176, 188, 196, 501, 505, 521.

See also Chinese New Year (page 10).

MARCH

Oranges and Lemons Service

A special service takes place at St Clement Dane's Church in the Strand, WC2, on the third or fourth Thursday in March, at 3.00p.m., when fruit is distributed to children to celebrate the arrival of the first oranges and lemons in London. The well-known nursery rhyme 'Oranges and Lemons' is played on handbells.

Nearest tube: Temple.
Nearby buses: 1, 4, 6, 9, 11, 13, 15, 23, 26, 30, 68, 76, 77A, 168, 171, 171A, 176, 188, 196, 501, 505, 521.

Head of the River Race

This is a race for boats with a crew of eight rowed over the Oxford and Cambridge course (see next entry) from Mortlake to Putney. More than 400 different crews may take part and the race lasts for 1½ hours. It is best viewed from the Surrey bank above Chiswick Bridge. The starting time varies according to the tides, so check this with the London Tourist Board. To make the most of the event, walk along the towpath towards Putney. For further details, telephone 071–730 3488.

Nearby buses: 190, 290.

Oxford and Cambridge Boat Race

One of the most popular sporting events on the Thames, the Oxford and Cambridge Boat Race takes place at the end of March or in early April. Teams from Oxford and Cambridge row at break-neck speed from Putney to Mortlake, a distance of 4 miles. Good views can be had from the riverside and Putney Bridge. The starting time varies according to tides, so check this by telephoning 071–730 3488.

Nearest tube: Putney.
Nearby buses: 14, 22, 74, 93, 220.

EASTER

Maundy Money

The distribution of Maundy Money by the sovereign dates back to the twelfth century, when money was given to the poor. Today each Maundy Thursday (the Thursday before Easter) the Queen hands out specially minted coins to a chosen group of children and those who have given special service to the church. The ceremony takes place at a different church each year. For further details, telephone 071–730 3488.

Easter Parade

The highlight of a full day's family entertainment at Battersea Park, SW11, is the Easter Sunday Parade, which begins at 3.00p.m. A grand procession of floats, colourful costumes, bands and dance groups makes its way around the park. Crowds line the route, so get there early to be sure of a good view. Stalls and sideshows operate in the park all day.

BR: Battersea Park.
Nearest tube: Sloane Square.
Nearby buses: 19, 37.

London Harness Horse Parade

This event, held on Easter Monday, offers a chance to see magnificent working horses at their best as they parade around the Inner Circle of Regent's Park, NW1, competing for top prizes in various classes. The day begins at 9.30a.m. with a veterinary inspection, followed by the main display. The grand parade of winners starts at noon.

Nearest tube: Regent's Park.
Nearby buses: 18, 27, 74, 135, C2.

Fairs

Fairs spring into action all over London during the Easter weekend. Look out for them at Blackheath, Ealing Common, Finsbury Park and Hampstead Heath.

Kite Festival

On both Easter Sunday and Monday the kite festival at Blackheath, SE3, lifts off at noon, when kite enthusiasts from all over the world display their latest flyers.

BR: Blackheath.
Nearby buses: 54, 89, 108, 178, 202.

APRIL

London Marathon

Some 30,000 runners participate in the London Marathon, which covers a distance of 26 miles from Greenwich Park, Blackheath, to Westminster Bridge. It is an exciting and enjoyable event for both spectators and participants, who raise millions of pounds each year for charity. Anyone brave enough to attempt the course can enter. For further details, telephone 081–948 7935.

BR: Greenwich.
Nearest tube: Island Gardens DLR, then Greenwich foot tunnel.
Nearest buses: 65, 371.

See also Oxford and Cambridge Boat Race (page 12) and Easter events (page 13).

MAY

Punch and Judy Festival

The tyrannical pair have their own special festival at St Paul's Churchyard, Covent Garden, WC1. It is held on the nearest Sunday to 9 May, to commemorate the date on which Samuel Pepys watched the first recorded Punch and Judy Show in 1662.

Nearest tube: Covent Garden.
Nearby buses: 1, 4, 6, 9, 11, 13, 15, 23, 26, 76, 77A, 168, 171, 171A, 176, 188, 196, 501, 505, 521.

Spring Bank Holiday Fairs

Over the Bank Holiday weekend, funfairs are in full swing in many London parks. For further details, telephone the London Tourist Board on 071–730 3488.

JUNE

Beating the Retreat

In the first week of June, the Guards and massed bands of the Household Division, which includes the Household Cavalry, perform Beating the Retreat. During the second week of June, the Light Division, including massed bands and bugles of the Light Infantry and Royal Green Jackets, perform Sounding the Retreat. These spectacular displays of marching and drilling, accompanied by rousing military music, take place in Horse Guards Parade, SW1. Certain performances are held in the evening by floodlight. Tickets are available from February. For further details, telephone 071–839 6815 or 071–836 4114, or write to Premier Box Office, 1b Bridge Street, London SW1A 2JR.

Nearest tubes: Charing Cross, Westminster.
Nearby buses: 3, 6, 9, 11, 12, 13, 15, 23, 24, 29, 30, 53, 77A, 88, 94, 109, 139, 159, 176, 184, 196.

Covent Garden Festival of Street Theatre

A ten-day theatre festival held in the Covent Garden Piazza, WC1 when street artists perform a variety of acts ranging from trapeze to mime shows. Dates vary annually; for more information contact 071–836 9136.

Nearest tube: Covent Garden.
Nearby buses: 1, 4, 6, 9, 11, 13, 15, 23, 26, 76, 168, 171, 171A, 176, 188, 196, 501, 505, 521.

Greenwich Festival

Each weekend in June, the borough of Greenwich, SE10, celebrates summer by hosting a variety of local arts events and community activities. These include street theatre, jazz, the International Wooden Boat Show and open-air art exhibitions. For more information contact 081–317 8687.

BR: Greenwich.
Nearest tube: Island Gardens (DLR) then foot tunnel.
Nearby buses: 47, 53, 177, 188, 199.
River boats from Charing Cross, Tower Pier and Westminster.

Trooping the Colour

The Queen's official birthday is celebrated on the Saturday nearest 11 June with a spectacular military display known as Trooping the Colour. The Queen and other members of the royal household leave Buckingham Palace on horseback and proceed along the Mall to arrive at Horse Guards Parade at 11.00a.m., when a gun salute is fired, the national anthem is played and the Queen inspects her troops. Each year a different battalion parades its colours. On her return to Buckingham Palace, the Queen appears on the balcony at 1.00p.m. for a flypast by the Royal Air Force, which coincides with another gun salute at the Tower of London. Tickets for the ceremony must be applied for before the end of February by writing to the Brigade Major (Trooping the Colour), Headquarters, Household Division, Chelsea Barracks, London SW1 8RS. They are allocated by ballot and limited to two per application, for which there is a small charge.

Nearest tubes: Green Park, Hyde Park Corner.
Nearby buses: 2A, 2B, 8, 9, 10, 14, 16, 19, 22, 36, 38, 52, 73, 74, 82, 137.

Wimbledon Lawn Tennis Championships

This is the highlight of the tennis calendar, when the world's best players compete for the most prestigious titles in the game. The championships run for a fortnight, starting in the last week of June. Application forms for tickets can be obtained by sending a stamped addressed envelope between October and December of the preceding year to the All England Lawn Tennis and Croquet Club, PO Box 98, Church Road, Wimbledon SW19 (tel. 081–946 2244). London Transport provides special buses during the championships from Southfields and Wimbledon tube stations. For more details, telephone 071–222 1234.

Lord's Test Match

The Lord's Test Match takes place over a five-day period in June when England entertains various teams from around the world. You can apply for tickets any time after January. Write to Lord's Cricket Ground, St John's Wood Road, London NW8 8QN. See also page 153.

Nearest tube: St John's Wood.
Nearby buses: 13, 82, 113, 274.

JULY

Swan Upping

Throughout the third week in July the ancient ceremony of Swan Upping takes place, when all the swans on the river Thames – more than 1000 of them – are checked, marked and counted. Three pairs of skiffs, representing the Dyers' Guild, the Vintners' Guild and the Queen, set off from Sunbury-on-Thames in Surrey and work their way along the river to Wargrave in Berkshire. Brought to England by King Richard I 'the Lionheart' (1157–99), swans were owned by successive reigning monarchs until the fifteenth century, when the king granted rights of ownership to local city guilds. The best place to view the ceremony is from the riverbank at Romney Lock below Windsor Castle. For more details, telephone 071–236 1863.

BR: Windsor.
Bus: 702 Green Line from Victoria station.

National Festival of Music for Youth

Founded in 1971, the National Festival of Music for Youth is the largest such event in Europe, involving more than 8000 young musicians each year. It takes place at the South Bank Centre (see page 25). Throughout July, school-based and independent instrumental ensembles from all over the country present a varied programme covering all types of music, from jazz and brass bands to pop and rock. For more details, write to 4 Blade Mews, Deodar Road, London SW15 2NN. Tickets for the festival can be bought from the South Bank box office (tel. 071–928 8800).

BR: Waterloo.
Nearest tubes: Embankment, Waterloo.
Nearest buses: 14, 26, 68, 76, 77, 149, 168, 171, 176, 188, 501, 507, 511, 521, D1, P11.

Royal Tournament

The Royal Tournament, held at the Earls Court Exhibition Centre, Warwick Road, SW5, is a thrilling, action-packed evening involving 2000 members of the armed forces. It includes mock battles, motorcycle displays, artillery demonstrations, dog-handling exhibitions and marching military bands, and is often attended by the Queen and other members of the royal family. Tickets are available from the beginning of January from the Royal Tournament box office (tel. 071–373 8141).

Nearest tube: Earls Court.
Nearby buses: 31, 74, C3.

City of London Festival

This festival consists of two weeks of musical events at various venues in the City of London, such as churches, museums and the Guildhall School of Music and Drama. There are also talks and organised walks. Tickets for the concerts are available from the City of London Tourist Information Centre, beside St Paul's Cathedral (tel. 071–260 1456).

'Proms'

Mid-July sees the start each year of the world-famous series of Henry Wood Promenade Concerts ('Proms') at the Royal Albert Hall, SW7. There are nightly concerts seven days a week until mid-September, covering every type of music from jazz to symphonies. Details are available from early May. Tickets can be obtained from the Promenade Concerts box office (tel. 071–589 8212).

Nearest tube: High Street Kensington.
Nearby buses: 9, 9A, 10, 52, C1.

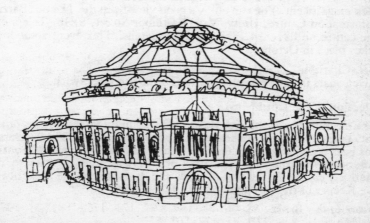

AUGUST

The Oval Test Match

For five days during August, the sixth Cornhill Insurance Test Match
– the last of any cricket series taking place in England – is played at
the Oval in Kennington, SE11 (see also page 153). Apply for tickets
any time after January by telephoning 071–582 7764.

Nearest tube: Oval.
Nearby buses: 36, 185.

Notting Hill Carnival

Bank Holiday Sunday and Monday, at the end of August, would not
be the same without the Notting Hill Carnival, the largest street
festival in Europe. The area around Ladbroke Grove, W11, comes
alive to the exhilarating sounds of steel, brass and calypso bands
playing their own special brand of music – reggae, rap, hiphop and
jazz. The carnival parade, made up of more than 100 spectacular
costumed bands, weaves its way through the streets. The event is loud
and exciting and the atmosphere can be electric, but be prepared to
cope with huge crowds.

Nearest tubes: Ladbroke Grove, Notting Hill Gate.
Nearby buses: 12, 15, 23, 27, 28, 31, 52, 70, 94, 302.

SEPTEMBER

Annual Closing of the Thames Barrier

The Thames Barrier floodgates (see page 121) are raised each month
for a two-hour test at low tide, but the annual full tidal closure blocks
off the river for a whole day. Raised up from the riverbed, the gates
look magnificent. You can enjoy a good view from the Thames Barrier
Information Centre, Unity Way, Eastmoor Street, SE18. Telephone
the centre on 081–854 1373 for more details. This event sometimes
takes place in October.

BR: Charlton.
River boats from Westminster, the Tower and Greenwich.

Election of the Lord Mayor

The election of a new Lord Mayor of London by the liverymen of the
City takes place each Michaelmas Day at the Guildhall. The ceremony
has been a major event in the City's calendar for more than 400 years.
After the swearing-in, the new Lord Mayor rides in state to the
Mansion House. For details of times and dates, telephone the office of
the Keeper of the Guildhall on 071–606 3030.

Nearest tube: Bank.
Nearby buses: 4, 8, 22B, 25, 172, 501, 521.

Great River Race

This 22-mile Thames marathon between Richmond and docklands is one of the most colourful events on the river. Boats taking part include skiffs, Chinese dragonboats, Viking longboats, whalers, Hawaiian war canoes and a 200-year-old boat from Northern Ireland, reputed to be the oldest surviving rowing boat in working order in the world. The race begins from below Ham House, Richmond, at 9.30a.m. and finishes at Island Gardens, opposite Greenwich Pier, at about 1.00p.m. To find out about dates and best viewing positions along the river, telephone Stewart Wolf on 081–398 9057.

OCTOBER

Horse of the Year Show

The most popular horse show of the year takes place at the beginning of October at Wembley Arena, Wembley, Middlesex. Top riders compete in a full programme of events which includes show jumping, dressage, and Pony Club competitions. For details and tickets, telephone the box office on 081–900 1234.

Nearest tubes: Wembley Central, Wembley Park.
Nearby bus: 83.

Punch and Judy Festival

Professor Percy Press, king of Punch and Judy performers and a member of the famous 'inner magic circle', comes to Covent Garden, WC1, on the first Sunday in October to host this event, bringing with him guest artists from different European countries and their Punch and Judy counterparts – the French Polichinelle, the German Kasper, the Italian Pulcinella. Shows take place throughout the day.

Nearest tube: Covent Garden.
Nearby buses: 1, 4, 6, 9, 11, 13, 15, 23, 26, 76, 77A, 168, 171, 171A, 176, 188, 196, 501, 505, 521.

NOVEMBER

London to Brighton Car Run

The most famous of all veteran car runs, the London to Brighton began in 1896, when a law requiring a red flag to be carried in front of every car was abolished. To celebrate its abolition, a group of London motorists destroyed their flags and drove to Brighton – and the London to Brighton Car Run was born. On the first Sunday in November up to 400 entrants from different countries set off between 8.00a.m. and 9.00a.m. from Hyde Park Corner, following the A23 to Brighton at an average speed of 20 m.p.h. The oldest cars leave first and youngest last. Only half the thirty-nine starters on the original run reached the coast. Today the event is restricted to veteran cars built between 1895 and 1904. Many drivers add a touch of fun to the occasion by dressing in period costumes. Although the run is not classed as a race, in order to qualify for a brass car badge, all entrants must arrive in Brighton by 4.00p.m.

Nearest tube: Hyde Park Corner.
Nearby buses: 2A, 2B, 6, 7, 10, 12, 15, 16, 16A, 23, 36, 73, 74, 82, 88, 94, 98, 135, 137, 137A, 274.

Fireworks Night

The unsuccessful 'Gunpowder Plot' of 1605, when the conspirator Guy Fawkes attempted to blow up King James and the Houses of Parliament is remembered each year on or around 5 November, when bonfires are lit in London's parks and effigies of Guy Fawkes are burnt. Many boroughs organise terrific firework displays, which sometimes include funfairs. Gates generally open between 6.00p.m. and 7.00p.m. *Firework Displays in the London Boroughs*, a leaflet produced by the London Tourist Board (see page 6), gives comprehensive listings.

Lord Mayor's Show

The City of London comes into its own for the Lord Mayor's Show on the second Saturday in November, when the mayor travels in a gilded coach to the law courts for his official inauguration. This glorious pageant, complete with colourful floats, dates back to the thirteenth century, and all the major City companies and institutions take part, as well as the armed services. The procession starts at 11.00a.m. from the Guildhall, arriving at St Paul's Churchyard (south side) before moving on to the Royal Courts of Justice in the Strand. It then returns via Temple Place and Victoria Embankment to Queen Victoria Street and the Guildhall. Occasionally the date varies, so check this by telephoning 081–882 1083.

Nearest tubes: Bank, St Paul's.
Nearby buses: 4, 8, 22B, 25, 172, 501, 521.

State Opening of Parliament

The State Opening of Parliament is usually in November. Although this ceremony is not open to the public, it still provides an opportunity to see the Queen splendidly attired in state robes. She and the Duke of Edinburgh travel by horse-drawn coach in a royal procession along the Mall through Horse Guards Parade and Whitehall to Parliament Square. The procession leaves Buckingham Palace at 11.00a.m. For details, telephone 071–332 1456.

Nearest tubes: Green Park, Hyde Park Corner.
Nearby buses: 2A, 2B, 8, 9, 10, 14, 16, 19, 22, 36, 38, 52, 73, 74, 82, 137.

Christmas Lights

Oxford Street, Bond Street, Jermyn Street and Regent Street take on the spirit of Christmas when spectacular decorative lights are switched on along their length in mid-November. A well-known personality or member of the royal family performs the lighting-up ceremony; in the last few years these celebrities have included the pop singer Elton John, the Olympic gold medallist Linford Christie and the Princess of Wales. For more information, telephone 071–332 1456.

Nearest tube: Oxford Circus.
Nearby buses: 3, 6, 7, 8, 10, 12, 13, 15, 16A, 23, 25, 53, 55, 73, 88, 94, 98, 113, 135, 137, 137A, 139, 159, 176, C2.

DECEMBER

Christmas Tree

Each Christmas the city of Oslo presents a Norwegian spruce to Londoners in thanks for help given by Britain in the Second World War. The tree is put up in Trafalgar Square at the beginning of December. Decorated according to Norwegian custom with thousands of white lights, it is lit up daily from 3.00p.m. to midnight, until the twelfth night after Christmas. Every evening, up until Christmas Eve, carols are sung around the tree. For details, telephone 071–332 1456.

Nearest tube: Charing Cross.
Nearby buses: 3, 6, 9, 11, 12, 13, 15, 23, 24, 29, 30, 53, 77A, 88, 94, 109, 139, 159, 176, 184, 196.

Inspection of the Yeoman Warders at the Tower of London

On the Sunday before Christmas the Yeoman Warders parade in front of the Queen's House at the Tower of London and are inspected by the Governor of the Tower, who is then escorted into St Peter's Chapel for a service. Members of the public who wish to attend should arrive at the front gates of the Tower at 10.45a.m. You can check details by telephoning 071–709 0765.

Nearest tube: Tower Hill.
Nearby buses: 15, 25, 42, 78, 100, D1, D9, D11.

GUARD-CHANGING CEREMONIES

These ceremonies take place at Buckingham Palace, Horse Guards Parade and the Tower of London. They are cancelled during very wet weather or when there is an important state event.

Buckingham Palace

There is nothing quite like the Changing of the Guard at Buckingham Palace. At 11.30a.m. every day during summer, and alternate days in winter, the Queen's guards, brilliant in their smart uniforms and accompanied by a regimental band, march to the palace from Chelsea or Wellington barracks to relieve the old guard. The ceremony, which takes place in the palace courtyard and lasts for 30 minutes, is an absorbing display of soldierly precision. For a good view, stay close to the palace railings or stand by Queen Victoria's Memorial. This is one of the most popular events in London, so aim to arrive in good time. It gets very crowded, especially in summer. (See also Buckingham Palace, page 77).

Nearest tubes: Green Park, Hyde Park.
Nearby buses: 2A, 2B, 8, 9, 10, 14, 16, 19, 22, 36, 38, 52, 73, 74, 82, 137.

Horse Guards

At 11.00a.m. across St James's Park from Buckingham Palace, another colourful spectacle takes place when the Queen's Life Guard is changed in front of the clock tower at Horse Guards Parade. The eighteenth-century building is now home to the Commander-in-Chief of the Combined Forces. It stands on the site of a guard house that was part of the Palace of Whitehall, which burnt down in 1698. Soldiers have kept watch here for nearly 300 years. Today, resplendent in their plumed hats and crimson uniforms, the Horse Guards sit on their beautifully groomed horses and carry out their duties with great aplomb. As the new guard takes over from the old, a trumpet sounds the royal salute. The ceremony takes place an hour earlier on Sundays.

Nearest tubes: Charing Cross, Westminster.
Nearby buses: 3, 6, 9, 11, 12, 13, 15, 23, 24, 29, 30, 53, 77A, 88, 94, 109, 139, 159, 176, 184, 196.

Tower of London
The guard at the Tower of London is changed at 11.30a.m. on days when there is also a Changing of the Guard at Buckingham Palace.

Nearest tube: Tower Hill.
Nearby buses: 15, 25, 42, 78, 100, D1, D9, D11.

OTHER CEREMONIAL EVENTS

Ceremony of the Keys

This famous ceremony at the Tower of London first took place more than 700 years ago and is still carried on today. Each evening at 9.30 the gates of the Tower are locked by the Chief Yeoman Warder accompanied by a small escort. The group then makes its way back to the Bloody Tower and the main guardroom. On the stroke of 10.00p.m. a bugler plays 'The Last Post' and the keys are returned to the Queen's House for the night. Free permits to watch the ceremony can be obtained from the Resident Governor, Queen's House, HM The Tower of London, Tower Hill, EC3N 4AB.

Nearest tube: Tower Hill.
Nearby buses: 15, 25, 42, 78, 100, D1, D9, D11.

Gun salutes

A 41-gun salute is fired at noon on 21 April in Hyde Park (opposite the Dorchester Hotel) to mark the Queen's birthday. In preparation for the event, a company of soldiers gallops through the park, pulling the heavy gun carriage used to fire the salute. Other gun salutes take place on the following dates:

6 February	Accession Day
2 June	Coronation Day
10 June	Prince Philip's birthday
4 August	Queen Mother's birthday

If any of these dates fall on a Sunday, the salute is postponed until the following day.

Nearest tubes: Hyde Park Corner, Marble Arch.
Nearby buses: 2A, 2B, 6, 7, 8, 9, 10, 12, 14, 15, 16, 16A, 19, 22, 23, 36, 73, 74, 82, 88, 94, 98, 135, 137, 137A, 274.

5

Music and arts centres

There is a wealth of family entertainment in London, including music for all ages, indoor and outdoor theatre and special shows for pre-school children. An increasing number of concert halls are putting on family concerts suitable for young children. The programmes are short – essential for those who find it difficult to sit still for a long time – and the material is varied.

THE BARBICAN CENTRE AND THE SOUTH BANK

Barbican Centre
Silk Street, EC2.
Tel. 071–638 4141.

A concrete jungle on the northern fringe of the City of London, the Barbican Centre has been the target of much undeserved criticism since it opened in 1982. This ambitiously conceived arts complex has two theatres, a studio theatre, an art gallery, three cinemas, a lending library and children's library, which holds free monthly events for over-5s, and two restaurants. Exhibitions are held in the main foyers and there are free musical performances, many of which are suitable for children. Annual events include a Children's Fun Day during the Easter holidays for under-10s. Starting at 10.00a.m., this is an action-packed event with jugglers, magicians, egg hunts and puppet shows, and it draws large crowds.

In August the Barbican's annual week-long children's jamboree, Summer in the City, provides a non-stop programme of activities for 2–10s, most of which are free. Games, competitions, storytelling, puppet shows, poetry readings, giant inflatables, mechanical sculptures and boating on the lake are usually on the agenda. If you have time to spare while the children are being entertained, relax at the Waterside café by the Lakeside Terrace, which has outdoor seating, or enjoy one of the temporary foyer exhibitions.

Annual Teddy Bears' concerts take place on two Sundays during December in the Barbican Hall, starting at 3.00p.m. Although the tickets are expensive, £1 is deducted for each child who brings a teddy bear. Seasonal songs such as 'Rudolph the Red-nosed Reindeer' and other well-known favourites such as 'Nellie the Elephant' are played by the London Concert Orchestra, and Father Christmas makes an appearance. There is also a prize for the biggest and best bear.

The Barbican's series of special weekend events for children are always popular. In past years they have included storytelling for the under-5s, team activities using Lego for over-7s and lessons in how to perform magic tricks. There is a limited number of places for these, so you need to pre-book; there is usually a charge.

For up-to-the-minute details of what is happening at the Barbican, telephone 071–638 4141 (ext. 218) and ask for a free copy of the centre's monthly diary. For films at the Barbican, see page 37.

Open Mon.–Fri. 9.00a.m.–11.00p.m.; Sun. 12.00 noon– 11.00p.m.

BR: Blackfriars, City Thameslink, Farringdon, Liverpool Street.
Nearest tubes: Barbican, Moorgate.
Nearby buses: 4, 8, 25, 141, 172, 226, 501, 521.

South Bank Centre
South Bank, SE1.
Tel. 071–928 3002.

The South Bank Centre is part of an arts complex that occupies 27 acres along the south bank of the river Thames. The largest such complex in the world, it lies midway between the Houses of Parliament and St Paul's Cathedral on the opposite bank. The centre – made up of the Royal Festival Hall, the Queen Elizabeth Hall, the Purcell Room and the Hayward Gallery – shares the site with the independently managed National Theatre, National Film Theatre and Museum of the Moving Image.

The education department at the South Bank was set up to promote understanding and enjoyment of the arts, and in particular to encourage awareness of the wide range of performances, exhibitions and special events which take place at the centre throughout the year. In cooperation with artists and art organisations, educational institutions and local education authorities, the education department runs a variety of projects designed to involve people of all ages, abilities and backgrounds, including teachers, schools, youth and community groups and the general public. Its programme provides resource materials and offers courses, talks, study days and workshops, plus a whole range of special projects and events to help people get the most out of the centre. To join the department's free mailing list, write to the Education Department, South Bank Centre, Royal Festival Hall, London SE1 8XX.

BR: Waterloo.
Nearest tubes: Embankment, Waterloo.
Nearby buses: 1, 4, 26, 68, 76, 77, 149, 168, 171, 176, 188, 501, 505, 507, 511, 521, D1, P11.

Royal Festival Hall
South Bank, SE1.
Tel. 071–928 8800.
Information: 071–928 3002.

Built in 1951 to mark the Festival of Britain, the Festival Hall is the headquarters of the South Bank Centre (see page 25). Its resident symphony orchestra, the London Philharmonic, gives regular one-hour family concerts throughout the year, usually at weekends. A programme of light classical music might include Ravel's *Mother Goose*, Tchaikovsky's *Sleeping Beauty* or Rimsky-Korsakov's *Capriccio Espagnol*. Specially priced family lunches are sometimes available after the concert. From mid-December there are a number of excellent family Christmas evenings focusing on music by well-known composers and carols for choir and audience. The concerts are extremely popular, so book well in advance.

Orchestral concerts specifically aimed at families are given by the Ernest Read organisation during the concert season, which runs from September until July. Aimed at 7–12s they offer a cross-section of music from the great masterpieces to marches. Active involvement by the children is encouraged – there may be an audience song to be learnt and performed or a quiz to keep everyone on their toes. A typical programme lasts for just over an hour. The Ernest Read series consists of five morning concerts and four afternoon concerts; season tickets at 20 per cent discount can be booked by post from May until 1 September or by telephone after 1 September. Details can be obtained from the box office at the Royal Festival Hall or from Erma Tickets, 9 Cotsford Avenue, New Malden, Surrey (tel. 081–336 0777).

There are free musical programmes every day at the Festival Hall between 12.30p.m. and 2.00p.m., performed in the foyer on level 2. A children's leaflet called *Things to See and Do* is available from the information desk on level 1.

For transport details, see South Bank Centre, page 25.

Purcell Room
South Bank, SE1.
Tel. 071–928 8800.
Information: 071–928 3002.

Afternoon musical stories for 5–8s are performed throughout the year at the Purcell Room. They include songs for everyone and plenty of audience participation. There are also entertainments for over-6s such as musical mystery tours and poetry set to music.

For transport details, see South Bank Centre, page 25.

Queen Elizabeth Hall
South Bank, SE1.
Tel. 071–928 8800.
Information: 071–928 3002.

Children's concerts are held at the Queen Elizabeth Hall throughout the year, with special family evenings at Christmas, when the audience can join in recitals given by the National Children's Orchestra.

For transport details, see South Bank Centre, page 25.

MUSICAL EVENTS

Fairfield Halls
Park Lane, Croydon, Surrey.
Tel. 081–688 9291.

Saturday morning concerts are held at Fairfield Hall once a month throughout the year, except for a short break during the summer. Designed to appeal to all ages, the repertoire has included many favourite ballet classics, as well as Saint-Saëns' *Carnival of the Animals* and Benjamin Britten's *Young Person's Guide to the Orchestra*. Performances begin at 11.00a.m. Family season tickets are good value but need to be booked well in advance.

BR: East Croydon.
Nearby buses: 197, 250, 264, 353, 354, 356, 357.

Morley College
61 Westminster Bridge Road, SE1.
Tel. 071–928 8501.

Every two weeks during the autumn and spring terms, plus once a week for three weeks in July, Morley College holds Saturday morning family music sessions where adults and children over 5 can play music together. Enjoying music is the starting point from which the group learn the basic principles of how instruments work and explore a variety of musical forms and arrangements. People are encouraged to bring their own instruments if they have any. The college also puts on good-value Saturday morning concerts which give families a chance to listen and work together with different types of music, including opera, jazz, pop and steel bands. The atmosphere is relaxed, informal and fun. Most important of all, you do not have to be musical to join in. Performances take place at 10.30a.m. on six Saturdays during the concert season, which runs from September to June.

Nearest tube: Lambeth North.
Nearby buses: 12, 53, 109, 184, 196.

Music in the open air

Brass bands perform in the Royal Parks during the summer months. The best place to hear them are Hyde Park, Regent's Park, Greenwich Park and St James's Park (see Royal Parks, pages 84–88). Certain London boroughs – including Camden, which holds an annual Summer Funsplash event involving various musical entertainments – arrange holiday treats in the parks which include musical items, such as Sunday afternoon jazz sessions in August. Contact your local borough's arts and entertainment department for more information. Alternatively, English Heritage produces a useful free booklet called *Music on a Summer Evening*. This gives information on open-air concerts and opera recitals taking place in the grounds of some of their historic properties, such as Kenwood and Marble Hill (tel. 071– 973 3401).

Lunchtime music

Some City of London churches put on free organ recitals. While grand music is not everyone's cup of tea, children may enjoy the unexpected volume. Tourist Information Centres (see pages 6–8) and libraries have all the details in a leaflet called *Events in the City of London*.

ARTS CENTRES

Battersea Arts Centre
Old Town Hall, Lavender Hill, SW11.
Tel. 071–223 2223.

There is always something interesting happening at Battersea Arts Centre. Saturdays are given over to children's arts and crafts workshops covering such subjects as drama, music, circus skills, art and mime. Theatre productions are usually aimed at over-4s (see page 30), although during the summer holidays pre-school children are also catered for. Workshops are divided into different age groups: under-5s, 5–9s, 9–14s and 15–25s. A typical programme for under-5s might consist of five mornings devoted to activities such as movement and dance, led by experienced, professional artists. Parents are always welcome and the centre also provides extended workshops for older children. A free monthly diary of forthcoming events is available from the centre. The Puppet Centre Trust at the Battersea Arts Centre provides all kinds of advice on puppetry and has listings of current events, exhibitions, courses and workshops.

BR: Clapham Junction, Victoria, Waterloo.
Nearby buses: 19, 45, 49, 77.

John Peel Children's Arts Centre
Factory Yard, The Green, Hanwell, W7.
Tel. 081–579 4789.

The John Peel Children's Arts Centre is the only arts centre in Britain to provide activities exclusively for children and young people. The schedule of events is coordinated to fit in with the academic year and covers a wide range of subjects for all ages. Saturday afternoon live performances range from Punch and Judy shows and storytelling to mime and magic. Environmental workshops in craft and design are worth investigating; they are aimed at 8–13s, who are encouraged to create 'pretend' environments using junk materials. The Youth Theatre Group is for over-11s. There are also plans to establish a permanent theatre group in west London and tour schools in the area. There are no workshops during the Christmas holidays.

BR: Hanwell.
Nearest tube: Boston Manor.
Nearby buses: 207, E8.

Lauderdale House Community Arts Centre
Waterlow Park, Highgate Hill, N6.
Tel. 081–348 8716.

Numerous activities are organised at Lauderdale House throughout the year for children of all ages. Twice weekly during termtime there are lively toddler dance sessions, at which under-3s and their parents can practise movement to music. Creative dance classes for 3–6s are held every Thursday. There are arts and crafts sessions after school for 5–11s and children's theatre on Saturdays. On the last Sunday of each month, except August, the lunchtime family cabaret at 12.30p.m. is a mixture of music, poetry and fun for all. John Hegley, Otiz Cannelloni and friends take charge of the proceedings and entertain everyone. A café at the centre is open every day except Monday, 9.30a.m.–5.30p.m.

Nearest tube: Archway.
Nearby buses: 210, 271.

Waterman's Arts Centre
40 High Street, Brentford, Middlesex.
Tel. 081–847 5651.

Overlooking the Thames only a short distance from Kew Bridge, this relatively new arts centre organises all kinds of workshops for children, throughout the year. These include music sessions for under-5s and sculpture and mask-making for 6–13s. Free live music is performed after 7.00p.m. The café is open every day except Monday – Tues.–Thurs. 10.30a.m.–9.00p.m., Fri. 10.30a.m.–4.00p.m. and 6.00p.m.–9.00p.m., Sat. and Sun. 10.30a.m.–9.00p.m. For theatrical events at the centre, see page 33, and for films see page 38.

BR: Kew Bridge.
Nearest tubes: Gunnersbury, South Ealing.
Nearby buses: 65, 117, 203, 237, 267, 391, E2, E8.

6

Theatres

Battersea Arts Centre
Old Town Hall, Lavender Hill, SW11.
Tel. 071–223 2223.

Various theatre companies perform at the Battersea Arts Centre during the school holidays and at weekends. Recent shows have included a musical adaptation of Oscar Wilde's famous short story *The Selfish Giant* and others that particularly encourage audience participation. For more details about the centre, see page 28.

BR: Clapham Junction, Victoria, Waterloo.
Nearby buses: 19, 45, 77, 77A, 156, 160, 219, 249, 337.

Bubble Theatre Company
9 Kingsford Street, NW5.
Tel. 081–485 3420.

Set up in 1972, the Bubble is Britain's only fully mobile theatre, touring the parks and commons of London during the summer with its gaily coloured 'bubble' tent. The company spends up to two weeks at each site. Venues have included Greenwich, Ealing, Peckham Rye and Wandsworth. Shows change each year and attract considerable acclaim from both the public and critics. Plays in the parks are aimed at under-11s, but during the past few years the company's activities have expanded and it now runs two popular youth theatres, for 14–25s in Southwark and 12–16s in Bexley.

Little Angel Marionette Theatre
14 Dagmar Passage, Cross Street, N1.
Tel. 071–226 1787.

The Little Angel Marionette Theatre is one of the best children's theatres in London. Among the few permanent puppet companies providing regular weekend entertainment for children, it is housed in a tiny converted church in the heart of Islington. In addition to the resident company, many visiting puppeteers perform here. The short shows on Saturday mornings are aimed at under-5s, who sometimes find it difficult to sit still through a full-length play. Afternoon performances are designed for slightly older children. The programme of plays, ranging from traditional folk stories to Christmas pantos, is changed regularly. Extra shows are put on during Christmas, Easter and half-term holidays, but the theatre is closed for part of the summer. Telephone to reserve seats before you go.

Nearest tube: Angel.
Nearby buses: 4, 19, 30, 38, 43, 56, 73, 171A, 196, 279A.

Lyric Theatre
King Street, Hammersmith, W6.
Tel. 081–741 2311.

The studio theatre upstairs at the Lyric offers a mixed bag of children's entertainment at weekends, including puppet shows, jugglers, music, dance sessions and the occasional clown. There are extra performances during the school holidays and occasional shows especially for under-5s. Apart from an excellent craft fair held in the main foyer on Saturdays, the Lyric also holds lunchtime jazz sessions. It is worth stopping off here for a bite to eat and catching some good music at the same time.

Nearest tube: Hammersmith.
Nearby buses: 27, 190, 267, 391, H91.

Molecule Theatre of Science
First Floor, 12 Mercer Street, WC2.
Tel. 071–379 5045/5093.

The Molecule Theatre has an uncanny knack of making the most unlikely subjects engrossing. Through drama, the sciences are brought down to earth, proving that even such achievements as splitting the atom have their funny sides. Entertainments are aimed at over-6s and range from scientific adventures to dramas about the internal workings of the human brain. The company spends much of the year touring the country, returning to London for performances during school holidays.

Movingstage Marionette Company
Puppet Theatre Barge, Little Venice, Blomfield Road, W9.
Tel. 071–249 6876.

The Moving Stage Marionette Company has successfully converted an old Thames barge into a delightful floating theatre. During the summer the company tours the upper Thames between Richmond and Oxford, but from November to early June it is based at Little Venice. The mini-theatre below deck makes an ideal setting for a variety of productions, which have included Aesop's *Fables* and *Babushka Baboon* for under-5s, as well as slightly longer plays for over-6s. Performances take place every day at 3.00p.m. during school holidays and on Saturday and Sunday during termtime.

Nearest tube: Warwick Avenue.
Nearby buses: 6, 8, 16, 18, 46.

Polka Theatre for Children
240 The Broadway, SW19.
Tel. 081–543 4888.

The resident theatre company at the Polka stages high-quality productions involving magic, music and mime which are tailor-made for children of all ages, including the under-5s. The theatre also houses a permanent museum of puppets and toys, plus an adventure room, workshop and café. They organise a summer school for children, too (see page 157).

BR: Wimbledon.
Nearest tube: Wimbledon.
Nearby buses: 93, 155, 156, 163, 164, 200.

Riverside Studios
Crisp Road, Hammersmith, W6.
Tel. 081–748 3354.

The Riverside provides plenty of good entertainment for children during school holidays and half-terms. There is something ultra-modish about this venue. It would come as no surprise to see an entire circus troupe sitting at the Riverside's self-service café complete with make-up! Check with the box office for details of events.

Nearest tube: Hammersmith.
Nearby buses: 9, 10, 11, 27, 33, 72, 220, 266, 267, 295.

Theatre Museum
Russell Street, WC2.
Tel. 071–836 7891.

Apart from a pantomime at Christmas, the Theatre Museum stages occasional plays for children during the rest of the year. Check with the box office for details.

Nearest tube: Covent Garden.
Nearby buses: 1, 4, 6, 9, 11, 13, 15, 23, 26, 76, 77A, 168, 171, 176, 188, 196, 501, 505, 521.

Tricycle Theatre
269 Kilburn High Road, NW6.
Tel. 071–328 1000.

Shows for 3–12s take place every Saturday at the Tricycle, at 11.00a.m. and 2.00p.m. Many of Britain's major theatre companies perform here. The youth theatre, for 16–25s, meets twice weekly and mounts two productions a year. During termtime the Tricycle's after-school workshops cover such activities as dancing, improvisation, mask-making and circus skills.

Nearest tube: Kilburn.
Nearby buses: 16, 16A, 28, 31, 32, 98.

Unicorn Theatre for Children
Great Newport Street, WC2.
Tel. 071–836 3334.

Founded in 1947, the Unicorn is the oldest children's theatre in the country. It aims to introduce live theatre to all children and promote their enjoyment of it. There are always two productions running at the theatre, one for 4–7s and the other for 8–12s. Many well-known authors are commissioned to write for the theatre and the plays are of a high standard. In recent years playwrights have included Andy Rashleigh, Fay Weldon and Ken Campbell. From Tuesday to Friday the company performs for school groups, but at weekends the theatre is open to the general public. Performances take place on Saturday at 11.00a.m. and 2.30p.m. and on Sunday at 2.30p.m.

At least twice a year the theatre opens its doors to anyone who wants to find out more about the theatre. Visitors are invited to take part in an afternoon of free workshops, chats with the actors and face painting.

Nearest tube: Leicester Square.
Nearby buses: 14, 19, 24, 29, 38, 176.

Warehouse Theatre Company
Dingwall Road, Croydon.
Tel. 081–680 4060.

The Warehouse Theatre puts on regular Saturday morning shows for 3–7s. Productions range from well-known favourites such as *Jack in the Beanstalk* to pantomimes at Christmas.

BR: East Croydon.
Nearby buses: 54, 60, 64, 68, 75, 109, 119, 130, 154, 250, 255, 301.

Waterman's Theatre
Waterman's Arts Centre, 40 High Street, Brentford, Middlesex.
Tel. 081–568 1176.

In addition to the many other activities organised by Waterman's Arts Centre (see page 29), there is a regular Saturday afternoon theatre for over-3s which includes puppet shows, music and magic from top theatre companies. Performances start at 2.30p.m.

BR: Kew Bridge.
Nearest tubes: Gunnersbury, South Ealing.
Nearby buses: 65, 117, 203, 237, 391, E2, E8.

PANTOMIMES

Not long ago Christmas pantomimes could be found only in the West End. Now many fringe and local theatres also mount productions, often with great success. Some shows open early in December while others start just before Christmas. For details of current productions, consult the *Evening Standard* newspaper or *Time Out* magazine. Your local newspaper should also run theatre listings. It is always advisable to book early.

Listed below are the addresses and box-office numbers of theatres that offer pantomimes and Christmas shows during the holiday season. Under-5s, who do not necessarily appreciate the finer points of pantomime, may prefer shorter shows; theatres that cater for the very young are marked with asterisks.

Aldwych Theatre
Aldwych, WC2.
Tel. 071–836 6404.

Ashcroft Theatre, Fairfield Halls
Park Lane, Croydon, Surrey.
Tel. 081–688 9291.

Battersea Arts Centre
Old Town Hall, Lavender Hill, SW11.
Tel. 071–223 2223.

Beck Theatre
Grange Road, Hayes, Middlesex.
Tel. 081–561 8371.

Bloomsbury Theatre
15 Gordon Square, WC1.
Tel. 071–387 9629.

Drill Hall Arts Centre
16 Chenies Street, WC1.
Tel. 071–637 8270.

Fortune Theatre
Russell Street, WC2.
Tel. 071–836 2238.

Hackney Empire
291 Mare Street, E8.
Tel. 081–985 2424.

Latchmere Theatre
503 Battersea Park Road, SW11.
Tel. 071–228 2620.

Lewisham Theatre
Rushey Green, Catford, SE6.
Tel. 081–690 0002.

*Little Angel Marionette Theatre
14 Dagmar Passage, Cross Street, N1.
Tel. 071–226 1787.

*Mayfair Theatre
Stratton Street, W1.
Tel. 071–495 1760.

Mermaid Theatre
Puddle Dock, Blackfriars, EC4.
Tel. 071–410 0000.

Millfield Theatre
Silver Street, N18.
Tel. 081–807 6680.

National Theatre
South Bank, SE1.
Tel. 071–928 2252.

*Nomad Puppet Studio
37 Upper Tooting Road, SW17.
Tel. 081–767 4005.

Piccadilly Theatre
Denman Street, W1.
Tel. 071–867 1118.

*Polka Children's Theatre
240 Broadway, SW19.
Tel. 081–543 4888.

*Puppet Theatre Barge
Little Venice, Bloomfield Road, W9.
Tel. 071–249 6876.

Richmond Theatre
The Green, Richmond, Surrey.
Tel. 081–940 0088.

Riverside Studios
Crisp Road, Hammersmith, W6.
Tel. 081–748 3354.

Shaw Theatre
100 Euston Road, NW1.
Tel. 071–388 1394.

Theatre Museum
Russell Street, WC2.
Tel. 071–836 2330.

Theatre Royal, Stratford East
Gerry Raffles Square, E15.
Tel. 081–534 0310.

Tower Theatre
Canonbury Tower, Canonbury Place, N1.
Tel. 071–226 3633.

Tricycle Theatre
269 Kilburn High Road, NW6.
Tel. 071–328 1000.

*Unicorn Theatre
6 Great Newport Street, WC2.
Tel. 071–836 3334.

Waterman's Arts Centre
40 High Street, Brentford, Middlesex.
Tel. 081–568 1176.

Wimbledon Theatre
The Broadway, Wimbledon, SW19.
Tel. 081–540 0362.

Young Vic
60 The Cut, SE1.
Tel. 071–633 0133.

7

Cinemas

REGULAR EVENTS

Consult *Time Out* and other publications with listings sections for films showing in your area. Some arts centres and cinemas regularly show children's films during school holidays and at weekends. Telephone before you go for details of programmes.

Barbican Centre
Silk Street, EC2.
Tel. 071–638 4141.

The Barbican Centre runs a Children's Cinema Club with activities each Saturday. Members enjoy live shows and the best children's films, plus cartoons and special entertainments. It costs £3 to join, for which a child receives a badge, membership card and details of forthcoming events. Two friends can accompany a member to the club as guests.

BR: Farringdon, Liverpool Street.
Nearest tubes: Barbican, Moorgate, Liverpool Street, Bank.
Nearby buses: 4, 8, 25, 141, 172, 226, 501, 521.

Battersea Arts Centre
Old Town Hall, Lavender Hill, SW11.
Tel. 071–223 6557.

Saturdays are set aside for family entertainment and films are often shown in the afternoons.

BR: Clapham Junction, Victoria, Waterloo.
Nearby buses: 19, 45, 49, 77.

Institute of Contemporary Arts (ICA)
12 Carlton House Terrace, SW1.
Tel. 071–930 0493.

Although the ICA has discontinued its children's cinema club, it occasionally shows children's films, usually at weekends and half-terms.

Nearest tube: Charing Cross.
Nearby buses: 3, 6, 9, 11, 12, 13, 15, 23, 24, 29, 30, 53, 77A, 88, 94, 109, 139, 159, 176, 184, 196.

National Film Theatre
South Bank, SE1.
Tel. 071–928 3232.

The National Film Theatre sets aside certain times for children's films, usually at weekends.

BR: Waterloo.
Nearest tubes: Embankment, Waterloo.
Nearby buses: 1, 4, 26, 68, 76, 77, 149, 168, 171, 176, 188, 501, 505, 507, 511, 521, D1, P11.

Rio Cinema
107 Kingsland High Street, E8.
Tel. 071–249 2722.

The Children's Saturday Picture Club at the Rio offers films at 11.00a.m. each week, with repeat shows, known as Play Centre matinees, on Tuesdays at 4.15p.m. Membership is free.

Nearest tube: Dalston Kingsland.
Nearby buses: 30, 38, 149, 236.

Riverside Studios
Crisp Road, Hammersmith, W6.
Tel. 081–748 3354.

The Riverside offers children's matinees on Saturday at 2.00p.m. The programmes include old favourites as well as new movies.

Nearest tube: Hammersmith.
Nearby buses: 9, 10, 11, 27, 33, 72, 220, 266, 267, 295.

Waterman's Arts Centre
40 High Street, Brentford, Middlesex.
Tel. 081–568 1176.

Waterman's cinema programme changes monthly and includes old and new PG and U certificate films. It regularly shows children's films during the school holidays, half-term and at weekends.

BR: Kew Bridge.
Nearest tube: Gunnersbury, South Ealing.
Nearby buses: 65, 117, 203, 237, 267, 391, E2, E8.

FREE FILMS

The museums listed below show free films during half-term and school holidays.

British Museum
Great Russell Street, WC1.
Tel. 071–636 1555.

Nearest tubes: Tottenham Court Road, Russell Square.

Nearby buses: 7, 8, 10, 14, 19, 22B, 24, 25, 29, 38, 55, 73, 98, 134, 176.

Commonwealth Institute
Kensington High Street, W8.
Tel. 071–602 3252.

Nearest tube: High Street Kensington.
Nearby buses: 9, 9A, 10, 27, 28, 31, 49.

Imperial War Museum
Lambeth Road, SE1.
Tel. 071–416 5000.

BR: Waterloo.
Nearest tubes: Lambeth North, Elephant and Castle.
Nearby buses: 1, 3, 12, 53, 63, 68, 109, 159, 171, 184, 188, 344.

Museum of Mankind
6 Burlington Gardens, W1.
Tel. 071–437 2224.

Nearest tube: Green Park.
Nearby buses: 8, 9, 14, 19, 22, 38.

National Army Museum
Royal Hospital Road, SW3.
Tel. 071–730 0717.

BR: Victoria.
Nearest tube: Sloane Square.
Nearby buses: 11, 19.

National Maritime Museum
Romney Road, Greenwich, SE10.
Tel. 081–858 4422.

BR: Greenwich, Maze Hill.
DLR: Island Gardens, then Greenwich foot tunnel.
River boats from Westminster, Charing Cross, Tower Pier.
River buses run from most piers, including London City airport.

Science Museum
Exhibition Road, SW7.
Tel. 071–589 3456.

Nearest tube: South Kensington.
Nearby buses: 14, 45A, 49, 74, 249, 349, C1.

8

Art galleries and exhibitions

GALLERIES

Most of London's major art galleries have items of interest to young people, and many organise special activities for children during the school holidays.

Courtauld Institute Galleries
Somerset House, Strand, WC2.
Tel. 071–873 2526.

Once the base of the Royal Academy of Arts, Somerset House is now the permanent home of a superb collection of Impressionist and Post-Impressionist paintings bequeathed to the nation by Samuel Courtauld. Compared with some of the larger London galleries, it is often fairly empty. There is also a temporary exhibition programme that changes monthly and includes subjects as varied as *British Abstract Art of the 1950s* and *Medieval Manuscripts from Merseyside*. A worksheet for children, 'Different Kinds of Paintings', takes 7–12s on a picture trail around the galleries, highlighting particular paintings and asking questions about them. There is a good coffee shop on the lower ground floor.

Open Mon.–Sat. 10.00a.m.–6.00p.m.; Sun. 2.00pm– 6.00p.m.
Admission charge; free for under-10s.
BR: Charing Cross, Waterloo.
Nearest tubes: Covent Garden, Temple.
Nearby buses: 1, 4, 9, 11, 13, 68, 77.

Dulwich Picture Gallery
College Road, SE21.
Tel. 081–693 6911.

Dulwich offers a good introduction for older children to some of the Old Masters. One of the first purpose-built picture galleries in Britain, it houses some 300 works of art, including paintings by Canaletto, Rubens, Van Dyck and Gainsborough, as well as an interesting private collection belonging to an actor called William Cartwright. Cartwright was an enthusiastic collector, and his paintings, many of which are by English artists, indicate the kind of works a moderately wealthy man might have bought in the seventeenth century. The gallery's education programme is designed for school groups only.

Open Tues.–Fri. 10.00a.m.–1.00p.m. and 2.00p.m.– 5.00p.m.; Sat.
11.00a.m.–5.00p.m.; Sun. 2.00p.m.–5.00p.m.
Admission charge; free for under-16s.
BR: West Dulwich, North Dulwich.
Nearby buses: 3, 12, 37, 78, 176, 185, P4.

Hayward Gallery
South Bank, SE1.
Tel. 071–921 0876.

One of London's major art venues, the Hayward mounts exhibitions
from all over the world. Many of them are suitable for older children;
recent examples of these have featured the work of Van Gogh, Warhol
and Leonardo da Vinci (complete with flying machine). The gallery is
closed between exhibitions, so check details before you go. There is a
coffee shop in the upper galleries. A good-value family ticket is
available.

Open daily 10.00a.m.–6.00p.m.
BR: Waterloo.
Nearest tubes: Embankment, Waterloo.
Nearby buses: 1, 4, 26, 68, 76, 77, 149, 168, 171, 176, 188, 501, 505,
507, 511, 521, D1, P11.

National Gallery
Trafalgar Square, WC2.
Tel. 071–839 3321.

The National Gallery boasts one of the finest collections of paintings
in the world, featuring examples of work by numerous famous artists
through the ages. Before entering the gallery, pause by the balustrades
to enjoy one of the finest views of London, over Trafalgar Square and
Whitehall towards the Houses of Parliament and beyond. The
building itself has been criticised for its 'pepper-box turrets', odd

proportions and general misshapenness, but to the untrained eye at least it has a certain charm. The new Sainsbury Wing, opened in 1991, has been designed specifically to contain the older, more fragile works of art, some of which date back to the thirteenth century. If an excess of masterpieces proves too much for children, light relief is available during school holidays in the form of quizzes, tours and slide shows.

Open Mon.–Sat. 10.00a.m.–6.00p.m.; Sun. 2.00p.m.– 5.00p.m.
Admission free.
Nearest tubes: Charing Cross, Leicester Square.
Nearby buses: 3, 6, 9, 11, 12, 13, 15, 23, 24, 29, 30, 53, 77A, 88, 94, 109, 139, 159, 176, 184, 196.

National Portrait Gallery
St Martin's Place, WC2.
Tel. 071–306 0055.

The National Portrait Gallery's collection covers a broad spectrum of subjects, from kings and queens to poets, inventors, philanthropists and politicians. Look out for Henry VIII and Elizabeth I in the Tudor Gallery. Both are magnificently dressed in jewel-encrusted robes, while the playwright William Shakespeare (room 1), wearing a single golden earring, looks quite rakish. There are also several portraits of the modern royal family, some of which do not do them justice. The gallery organises special children's events during the holidays.

Open Mon.–Fri. 10.00a.m.–5.00p.m.; Sat. 10.00a.m.– 6.00p.m.; Sun. 2.00p.m.–6.00p.m.
Admission free.
Nearest tubes: Charing Cross, Leicester Square.
Nearby buses: 3, 6, 9, 11, 12, 13, 15, 23, 24, 29, 30, 53, 77A, 88, 94, 109, 139, 159, 176, 184, 196.

South London Art Gallery
65 Peckham Road, SE5.
Tel. 071–703 6120.

Six temporary exhibitions are mounted annually by the South London Art Gallery, each complemented by a range of workshops. Some of the workshops are for adults and others for school groups. A few are organised during school holidays and at weekends especially for children; activities include painting and drawing sessions for under-5s, papier-mâché mask-making for older children and occasional Punch and Judy shows. The gallery devotes certain Sundays throughout the year to making art accessible and enjoyable for everyone. Drawing materials are available for children of all ages and the staff are on hand to assist. Southwark borough arts service, which organises the events, can be contacted on 071–732 3232. Leisure centres and main libraries in Southwark also have details.

Open Mon.–Sat. 10.00a.m.–6.00p.m.; Sun. 3.00p.m.– 6.00p.m.
Admission free.
Nearest tube: Elephant and Castle, then buses 12, 171, P3. Oval, then
bus 36.
Nearby buses: 12, 36, 36A, 36B, 171.

Serpentine Gallery
Kensington Gardens, W2.
Tel. 071–402 6075.

The Serpentine enjoys a splendid location and mounts many fine
exhibitions, with an emphasis on modern art. Opening times vary
from one exhibition to another, so telephone the gallery for details.
The Serpentine Restaurant across the road has a cafeteria.

Admission free.
Nearest tubes: Knightsbridge, South Kensington.
Nearby buses: 9, 9A, 10, 52, C1.

Tate Gallery
Millbank, SW1.
Tel. 071–821 1313.

The Tate is an ideal introduction to the world of art. It has an
unstuffy, friendly atmosphere and houses paintings dating from the
sixteenth century to the present time. On a first visit, you might like
to see some Impressionist works or Andy Warhol's pop art, and to
investigate the Clore Gallery, which is full of paintings by one of
Britain's most famous and prolific artists, J.M.W. Turner. Children
may enjoy the surrealist art at the Tate such as Salvador Dali's picture
of a telephone receiver in the shape of a lobster. If you plan to visit the
Tate during the school holidays, inquire about special activities for
children. Their junior tours, trails and quizzes help breathe new life
into the business of looking at paintings. The gallery has a good coffee
shop. See also Millbank Gardens on page 94.

Open Mon.–Sat. 10.00a.m.–5.50p.m.; Sun. 2.00p.m.– 5.50p.m.
Admission free.
Nearest tube: Pimlico.
Nearby buses: 2, 3, 36, 77, 88.

Queen's Gallery
Buckingham Palace, Buckingham Palace Road, SW1.
Tel. 071–930 4832.

One of the smallest but perhaps most interesting of London's galleries
is the Queen's Gallery. Housed in part of Buckingham Palace, it
contains pictures and works of art from the Queen's private collection.
The exhibits are changed at regular intervals, so there is usually
something new and different to see.

Open Tues.–Sat. 11.00a.m.–5.00p.m.; Sun. 2.00p.m.– 5.00p.m.

Admission charge.
BR: Victoria.
Nearest tubes: St James's Park, Victoria.
Nearby buses: 2, 2A, 2B, 8, 11, 16, 24, 36, 38, 52, 73, 82, 185, 239, 507, 511, C1, C10.

Wallace Collection
Hertford House, Manchester Square, W1.
Tel. 071–935 0687.

This extraordinary and extremely diverse collection of art treasures was put together by successive generations of the Hertford family, who were passionate collectors. By the time Lady Wallace donated it to the nation in 1900, the Wallace ranked as the largest and most valuable private collection ever given away by one person. It includes fine porcelain, ivories, French eighteenth-century furniture, bronzes, armour and some exquisite paintings by, among others, Rembrandt, Van Gogh and Rubens; perhaps its most famous painting is Frans Hals's *Laughing Cavalier*.

Open Mon.–Sat. 10.00a.m.–5.00p.m.; Sun. 2.00p.m.– 5.00p.m.
Admission free.
Nearest tubes: Bond Street, Baker Street.
Nearby buses: 2A, 2B, 6, 7, 8, 10, 12, 13, 15, 18, 23, 27, 73, 74, 82, 88, 94, 98, 113, 135, 139, 159, 274.

Whitechapel Art Gallery
Whitechapel High Street, E1.
Tel. 071–377 0107.

The Whitechapel is a great place to go if you want to keep up with the latest in modern art. The gallery does not have a permanent collection of paintings but specialises in exhibitions of contemporary and early twentieth-century art which are held throughout the year. News sheets list the different events organised by the gallery. These include tours, lectures and special family days during school holidays or at half-terms, when children can paint their own masterpieces.

Open Tues.–Sun. 11.00a.m.–5.00p.m. (Wed. 8.00p.m.).
Admission charge; free admission on certain days.
BR: Fenchurch Street, Liverpool Street.
Nearest tubes: Aldgate, Aldgate East.
Nearby buses: 5, 15, 15A, 25, 40, 67, 78, 253.

ART IN THE OPEN AIR

A number of open-air exhibitions are held in London at weekends at which less well known artists can display and sell their works. Prices and styles vary considerably, but there is no lack of choice. Choose a fine day and wander to one of the venues listed below.

Green Park (on the pavement by Hyde Park corner).
Nearest tubes: Green Park, Hyde Park Corner.
Nearby buses: 2A, 2B, 8, 9, 10, 14, 16, 19, 22, 36, 38, 52, 73, 74, 82, 137.

Bayswater Road (next to the park).
Nearest tubes: Lancaster Gate, Marble Arch.
Nearby buses: 2A, 2B, 6, 7, 10, 12, 15, 16, 23, 36, 70, 73, 74, 88, 94, 98, 135, 137, 274.

Hampstead Pond
Heath Street, NW3
Nearest tube: Hampstead.
Nearby bus: 210.

9

Museums and attractions

A great deal has been written about the changing face of London's museums. No longer the dusty, musty, forbidding places they once were, the museums have altered their image and now show great imagination in their reflection of exciting new discoveries and developments in many spheres. Pre-school children may treat museums as glorified toyshops, places to wander through and have fun in. Older children will have clearer ideas about what interests them. But beware: only a certain amount can be absorbed in a single visit and it is easy to overdo things. The age guidelines given are only a rough indication of suitability because every child is different. Most museums are closed on Christmas Day, Boxing Day and New Year's Day. Not all remain open during Bank Holiday periods, so telephone to check before setting off.

Bank of England Museum
Bartholomew Lane, Threadneedle Street, EC2.
Tel. 071–601 5545.

Housed inside the Bank of England, the museum covers the history of the bank from 1694 to the present day. It has the world's finest collections of Bank of England notes, from simple handwritten receipts to sophisticated twentieth-century notes. Among the exhibits are a small armoury of pikes and muskets which were once used to defend the bank; a reconstruction of an eighteenth-century banking hall, complete with mahogany counter-tops and oak ledger-rests; and a fine display of gold, including Roman bars. An inter-active video outlines the work of the bank today and tests the operator's knowledge of money and banking. There is also a replica dealing desk with up-to-the-minute information and telephone commentary explaining the work of dealers. Not suitable for under-6s.

Open April–Sept. only. Mon.–Fri. 10.00a.m.–5.00p.m.; Sun. 11.00a.m.–5.00p.m.
Admission free.
BR: Fenchurch Street, Liverpool Street.
Nearest tube: Bank.
Nearby buses: 6, 8, 9, 11, 15, 21, 22, 43, 76, 133.

Bethnal Green Museum of Childhood
Cambridge Heath Road, E2.
Tel. 081–980 2415.

Although slightly off the beaten track, this light, airy museum in the heart of London's East End has the advantage of being small enough to cover in one visit. It contains one of the finest collections of dolls' houses in the country, antique dolls older than Queen Victoria and plenty of puppets, trains and teddy bears. Nineteenth-century optical toys demonstrate unexpected visual tricks and illusions and there are miniature theatres and games to look at, as well as some splendid children's costumes. The museum would benefit from more 'hands-on' displays for younger children – many of the exhibits are behind glass – but the excellent toyshop and children's workshops compensate for this lack. Activities throughout the school holidays range from storytelling for under-5s to classes in how to make your own puppet, hat or optical toy. Art workshops for over-3s are held on Saturday mornings and afternoons. A new café is planned for the museum; in the meantime take your picnic to nearby Victoria Park.

Open Mon.–Thurs. and Sat. 10.00a.m.–5.50p.m.; Sun. 2.30p.m.–5.50p.m.
Admission free.
Nearest tube: Bethnal Green.
Nearby buses: 8, 106, 253.

Bramah Tea and Coffee Museum
The Clove Building, Maguire Street, SE1.
Tel. 071–378 0222

This unusual museum traces the history of two great trades carried on in this area for 350 years. Its fine collection of over 1000 coffee makers and teapots – including the world's largest – demonstrate the many ways tea and coffee have been made and served since they were introduced to this country in the seventeenth century. The museum also explains how the British became a nation of tea drinkers. The café is open to everyone; even if you don't visit the museum. The museum is not suitable for children under 10.

Open daily 10.00a.m–5.30p.m.
Admission charge. Family ticket available.
Nearest tube: Tower Hill, London Bridge.
DLR: Tower Gateway.
Nearby buses: 15, 42, 47, 78, P11.

British Museum
Great Russell Street, WC1.
Tel. 071–636 1555.

The first thing you notice about the British Museum is the grandeur and size of the place. With a building covering 17 acres, this is the largest museum in the world, housing the most remarkable collection of antiquities ever assembled under one roof.

With so many things to see, it can be difficult to know where to begin. The tallest exhibit in the museum is the giant North American

Indian totem pole beside the north-east stairway. Highly decorated with carved and painted images and over 11 metres high, it soars up through two complete floors. The Sutton Hoo Treasure (room 41) was found much closer to home and is a good deal older, dating back to the seventh century. This incredible collection, retrieved in Suffolk in 1939, belonged to an Anglo-Saxon king. The jewellery, sword, helmet and shield represent one of the most astounding archaeological finds of the century. The famous Rosetta Stone (room 25), discovered in 1799 by Napoleonic soldiers fighting in Egypt, enabled scholars to decipher for the first time the mysteries of ancient Egyptian hiero-glyphs. The museum's collection of mummies is also worth a visit. Thousands of years ago Egyptian kings and queens were carefully preserved and bandaged after death. Embalming could take up to ten weeks and involved removing those parts of the corpse which were likely to decompose first. The body was then stuffed, perfumed, dressed and finally bandaged. A mummy was sometimes wrapped in many hundreds of metres of material. One of the best statues in the museum can be found in the Oriental Gallery. This is the Judge of Hell, a Chinese figurine dating from the fourth or fifth century. He is a grim, green-faced character created to remind people how important it was to behave well in life, as this would reflect how they would be judged after death. The large book under the judge's arm is supposed to contain bad deeds. The museum also has one of the finest collections of clocks in the world; it is fascinating to go to room 44 just to hear them chime. The Congreve Rolling Ball Timepiece, an extraordinary-looking instrument, works with the help of a steel ball which takes precisely 30 seconds to complete its rolling movement from side to side. The insides of the seventeenth-century domestic wall clocks look as complicated as those of Big Ben, and some of the miniature pocket watches are so intricately designed that it is difficult to imagine how anyone could have had sufficiently good eyesight to have pieced them together.

The museum organises special holiday activities for over-7s based on various exhibits, and quiz trails can be obtained at the information desk. The 'Hunt the Hieroglyphs' trail, for instance, takes older children around the Egyptian Gallery and explains all about the Egyptian alphabet and how to write simple hieroglyphs. The museum is suitable for over-6s, but not for the very young.

Open Mon.–Sat. 10.00a.m.–5.00p.m.; Sun. 2.30p.m.–6.00p.m.
Admission free.
Nearest tubes: Tottenham Court Road, Russell Square.
Nearby buses: 7, 8, 10, 14, 19, 22B, 24, 25, 29, 38, 55, 73, 98, 134, 176.

Cabaret Mechanical Theatre Museum
33–34 The Market, Covent Garden, WC2.
Tel. 071–379 7961.

In the basement of Covent Garden market can be found an intriguing collection of more than seventy automatic models, all of which have been made in the last ten years. In this twilight world of mechanical toys the most surprising things happen. At the touch of a button or the turn of a knob, small, beautifully crafted, hand-made models spring to life – a nickelodeon piano strikes up and plays, ducks take to the air and unexpected objects appear out of nowhere. This is an entertaining place for children of all ages. Take some 10p and 20p pieces with you to try out the coin-operated machines such as Paul Spooner's dream machine and the 'fortune-teller' by Tim Hunkin. The museum is suitable for all ages.

Open Tues.–Sat. 10.00a.m.–6.30p.m.; Sun. 11.00a.m.– 6.30p.m.; Mon. 12.00 noon–6.30p.m.
Admission charge.
Nearest tube: Covent Garden.
Nearby buses: 1, 4, 6, 9, 11, 13, 15, 23, 26, 76, 77A, 168, 171, 176, 188, 196, 501, 505, 521.

Cabinet War Rooms

Clive Steps, King Charles Street, SW1.
Tel. 071–930 6961.

On the eve of the Second World War, an underground warren beneath King Charles Street was converted into safe accommodation, where the prime minister and his aides could work without fear of being bombed. What became known as the Cabinet War Rooms have been preserved exactly as they were when used by Winston Churchill, his war cabinet and the chiefs of staff of Britain's armed forces. There are over twenty rooms on view. They include the desk from which Churchill broadcast his rousing speeches and his 'hot-line' telephone, complete with 'scrambler' device and an antiquated hand-cranked duplicating machine. Wandering through these vast basements where so many life-and-death decisions were made, it is almost possible to imagine a faint whiff of cigar smoke on the wind. This is a tour that would suit older children.

Open daily 10.00a.m.–6.00p.m. (last admission 5.15p.m.). Closed on Bank Holidays.
Admission charge.
Nearest tube: Westminster.
Nearby buses: 3, 11, 12, 24, 53, 77A, 88, 109, 159, 184, 196, 511.

Church Farm House Museum

Greyhound Hill, Hendon, NW4.
Tel. 081–203 0130.

This museum is housed in the oldest building in Hendon, built in the 1600s. A working farm up until the Second World War, it is now a repository of local history, devoted to demonstrating how a typical seventeenth-century farm was run. The kitchen has a huge open fireplace, complete with a bread oven and a weight-operated spit used to turn the roasting meat over the open fire. Some of the exhibitions held here throughout the year are specifically aimed at children. Behind the main building is an orchard with a small pond where you can picnic in summer.

Open Mon.–Thurs. 10.00a.m.–5.00p.m. (closed 1.00p.m.– 2.00p.m.); Sat. 10.00a.m.–5.30p.m. (closed 1.00p.m.–2.00p.m.); Sun. 2.00p.m.–5.30p.m.
Admission free.
Nearest tube: Hendon Central.
Nearby buses: 143, 183, 326.

Clink Exhibition
1 Clink Street, SE1.
Tel. 071–403 6515.

Located on the site of the original Clink prison, this exhibition paints a grim picture of the history of the British penal system. The word 'clink' – still used today to mean prison – seems to have derived from a type of handcuff called 'clenching irons', which were attached to cell walls. This was a relatively harmless device compared to some of the other instruments of torture on show here. Iron collars, manacles, thumb screws, balls and chains constitute a grizzly selection; some of them can be tried on. The museum also incorporates the only working armoury in England, which has expanded since the dismantling of the Tower of London's armoury. There are fine suits of armour from the English Civil War (see page 148) and pieces of armour and weapons collected by King Henry VIII, who built an armoury in the area. This exhibition is not suitable for children younger than 8. You could combine a trip here with a visit to the Shakespeare Globe Museum (see page 70).

Open daily 10.00a.m.–6.00p.m. Closed 24 and 25 Dec. and 1 Jan.
Admission charge; family ticket available.
BR: London Bridge.
Nearest tube: London Bridge.
Nearby buses: 17, 21, 22A, 35, 40, 43, 44, 47, 48, 95, 133, 149, 214.

Commonwealth Institute
Kensington High Street, W8.
Tel. 071–603 4535.

Although the Commonwealth Institute may not seem a likely place to entertain children, there is a surprising amount to see and do here. In the large, multi-level exhibition hall, each Commonwealth country has a gallery in which to display its history, culture, wildlife and natural resources, as well as information on commerce and industry. There are a number of activities to interest children of all ages, including a space-age motorised toboggan ride in the Canadian section. A push-button mechanical see-through cow from New Zealand demonstrates how milk is produced, and among the many wild animals on display a stuffed Royal Bengal tiger prowls around its natural habitat in Bangladesh. The unusual and colourful exhibits give a fascinating insight into the way people in other parts of the world work and live. Special exhibitions are held throughout the year at which individual countries display their arts and crafts. Free films are shown during the school holidays, and there are regular children's workshops. There is plenty of room for younger children to run around and if you feel like a walk after your visit, Holland Park (see page 93) lies just behind the institute. The café on the ground floor is open during museum hours.

Open Mon.–Sat. 10.00a.m.–5.00p.m.; Sun. 2.30p.m.– 5.00p.m.
Admission free.
Nearest tube: High Street Kensington.
Nearby buses: 9, 9A, 10, 27, 28, 31, 49.

Design Museum
Butlers Wharf, SE1.
Tel. 071–403 6933.

How much do the goods we buy reflect the type of people we are? When Sir Terence Conran opened the first Habitat shop in Britain, he started a revolution in functional design which responded to the growing aspirations of the average consumer and shaped attitudes to the purchasing of household goods. This museum, funded by the Conran Foundation, explains and examines the role of design in daily life and looks at the way in which mass-produced goods affect everybody. Regularly changing displays on topics as varied as cameras, cars, graphics and ceramics give a worthwhile introduction to consumer culture. The museum is more suitable for older children. The Blueprint Café on the first floor sells Mediterranean-style food and can provide smaller portions for children (tel. 071–378 7031).

Open Tues.–Sun. 10.30a.m.–5.30p.m. Blueprint Café open daily 12 noon–3.00p.m., Mon.–Sat. 7.00p.m.–11.00p.m.
Admission free.
Nearest tubes: London Bridge, Tower Hill.
Nearby buses: 42, 47, 78, 188, P11.

Florence Nightingale Museum
2 Lambeth Palace Road, SE1.
Tel. 071–620 0374.

Florence Nightingale campaigned ceaselessly for improved health care, and her considerable achievements paved the way for better hospital conditions throughout the world. Her campaigns for medical reform, her sterling work in taking care of soldiers during the Crimean War and the enormous influence she brought to bear on nursing and modern health in general are all highlighted at the Florence Nightingale Museum. Exhibits include a life-size recreation of a hospital scene during the Crimean War and a reconstruction of a room in Nightingale's house at South Street, Mayfair, W1. Personal mementoes, including her private letters and childhood books, help to create a clearer picture of this unique woman. Professional nurses give talks here about their working lives. Located on the site of St Thomas's Hospital, where the first nursing school opened, the museum is suitable for children of 8 years old and upwards.

Open Tues.–Sun. 10.00a.m.–4.00p.m.
Admission charge.
BR: Waterloo.
Nearest tubes: Lambeth North, Waterloo.
Nearby buses: 12, 53, 109.

Funland and Lazer Bowl

The Trocadero, 13 Coventry Street, Piccadilly, W1.
Tel. 071–734 3859.

Britain's newest hi-tech games centre is a dream come true for arcade enthusiasts. Like a vast futuristic fairground, it is packed full of games and rides, some of which are linked to a redemption system

that allows players to exchange points for prizes. There are no
down-market fruit machines in Funland and smoking is banned. The
Dodgems and virtual-reality games such as Flying Aces, where
players become First World War pilots shooting the infamous Red
Baron, and Driver's Eyes, the world's first three-screen racing-car
game, are excellent. Lazer Bowl's biggest attraction is Bowlingo, a
fast, scaled-down version of ten-pin bowling, which can be played by
up to four people. It is easier than regular bowling and great fun for
children. Charges for games start at 50p. The busiest times are during
the evenings and at weekends; like most arcades, it can be a bit grim
when empty. This venue is not suitable for the very young.

Open daily, including Bank Holidays, 10.00a.m.– 1.00a.m.
Nearest tube: Piccadilly Circus.
Nearby buses: 3, 6, 9, 12, 13, 14, 15, 19, 22, 23, 38, 53, 88, 94, 139,
159.
See also Virtual Quest, page 75.

Geffrye Museum
Kingsland Road, Shoreditch, E2.
Tel. 071–739 9893.

This charming little museum in London's East End illustrates the
changing styles in furniture and domestic equipment from Elizabethan times until the 1950s. A series of period 'sets' focus on how
people lived at different periods in history. There is a marvellous
eighteenth-century woodworker's shop, an open-range kitchen and a
splendid Art Deco sitting-room. Although you cannot go inside the
rooms, they provide an intriguing insight into family life over the
centuries. Although there are no 'hands-on' displays, there is a
children's studio in the east part of the museum where over-6s can
paint and draw under supervision. Workshops take place at weekends
and half-terms and during school holidays. Under-8s must be accompanied by an adult. Activities range from making outlandish Easter
bonnets or Hallowe'en costumes to treasure hunts and quizzes. The
museum has a coffee bar and you can also picnic in the grounds.

Open Tues.–Sat. 10.00a.m.–5.00p.m.; Sun. 2.00p.m.– 5.00p.m.
Admission free.
BR: Dalston Kingsland, Liverpool Street.
Nearby buses: 22A, 67, 149, 243, 243A.

Guinness World of Records
The Trocadero, 13 Coventry Street, Piccadilly Circus, W1.
Tel. 071–439 7331.

Superlative is the watchword at this exhibition. Incredible feats from
around the globe are recreated in six different 'worlds' – human,
animal, planet earth, sport, entertainment and structures and
machines. You can see life-size models of the tallest man and the
smallest woman, compare your weight on the scales with one of the

world's heaviest men, or watch Henri La Mothe as he dives 28 feet (8.5 metres) into a foot of water. The entrance to the animal world is through the lifesize jaws of a blue whale (the tongue of this mammal can weigh up to 4.22 tons). Once inside this cornucopia of extremes, you can enjoy the 'greatest leaps' display or pull up special flaps to see some of the largest insects in the world. Memorable sporting achievements are recaptured on video, and databanks enable you to discover other world records. Look out for the summer events' programme and half-term competitions, when children can themselves have a go at breaking a world record. Children of all ages should enjoy a trip here.

Open daily 10.00a.m.–10.00p.m.
Admission charge; good-value family ticket.
Nearest tube: Piccadilly Circus.
Nearby buses: 3, 6, 9, 12, 13, 14, 15, 19, 22, 23, 38, 53, 88, 94, 139, 159.

Geological Museum
Exhibition Road, SW7.
Tel. 071–938 8000.

No rock is left unturned in this museum. Rubies as large as gobstoppers, sparkling emeralds, slabs of jade, gold, silver and diamonds gleam in their glass cases. In the Story of the Earth section a chunk of rock brought back from man's first voyage to the moon sits encased in a glass pyramid. One of the best exhibits in the museum is called Earthquake. Here, in a small, darkened room, a video explains what happens during an earthquake and a simulator platform enables you to experience the sensations of the real thing. For those who want to find out more about the origins of the earth, there is a surprisingly short video covering the 4500 million years of its history. This museum is more suited to older children.

Open Mon.–Sat. 10.00a.m.–6.00p.m.; Sun. 1.00p.m.– 6.00p.m.
Admission charge; free Mon.–Fri. after 4.30p.m.
Nearest tube: South Kensington.
Nearby buses: 14, 45A, 49, 74, 249, 349, C1.

Gunnersbury Park Museum
Gunnersbury Park, Pope's Lane, W5.
Tel. 081–992 1612.

Gunnersbury Park is a local history museum which also houses a collection of dolls and dolls' houses, plus a number of transport exhibits, including two carriages, a pony trap, tandem, penny farthing and a small fire engine. The newly reconstructed Victorian kitchens, looking very much as they must have done when the Rothschild family lived here, are also open to the public. It is a good place to take the family before visiting the park which has a boating lake and café.

Open Mon.–Fri. 1.00p.m.–5.00p.m.; Sat.–Sun. 2.00p.m.– 6.00p.m.
Admission free.
Nearest tube: Acton Town.
Nearby bus: E3.

Horniman Museum
100 London Road, SE23.
Tel. 081–699 2339.

Founded just over a century ago by a travelling tea merchant who was also a keen collector, the Horniman is home to all kinds of strange and wonderful objects, many of which represent the various cultures the collector experienced during his travels around the world. A 100-year-old stuffed walrus holds centre stage in the natural history section, and there is an extraordinary collection of tents from places as far apart as North America and India. The most popular items, however, are the exotic masks and gruesome shrunken heads from Africa and some assorted musical instruments from the Far East. The museum puts on a number of exhibitions and concerts throughout the year and runs an excellent educational programme. The extensive grounds, which were once part of Horniman's home, are open to the public. There are walks and trails to follow, as well as a formal sunken garden and animal and bird enclosures. The museum is suitable for all ages. It has a café which opens in the afternoons and you can picnic in the gardens.

Open Mon.–Sat. 10.30a.m.–6.00p.m.; Sun. 2.00p.m.– 6.00p.m.
Admission free.
BR: Forest Hill.
Nearby buses: 63, 171, 176, 185, 194.

Imperial War Museum
Lambeth Road, SE1.
Tel. 071–416 5000.

Two powerful naval guns mark the entrance to the Imperial War Museum and set the scene for a fascinating journey of exploration through all the military campaigns in which Britain and the Commonwealth have been involved since the First World War. A life-size exhibit called the Trench Experience, complete with dug-out and first-aid post, shows First World War soldiers going over the top to fight the enemy, while an authentic reconstruction of a London street in the 1940s evokes the sounds and smells of life in the city during the Blitz, complete with bomb blasts. Guns, tanks, models of battle campaigns, a one-man German submarine and numerous aircraft – from a Battle of Britain Spitfire to a V2 rocket – are on view, as well as more personal items such as ration books and diaries. One of the highlights of a visit to the museum is a simulated plane ride: authentic archive film makes the past come alive as you join Operation Jericho and experience the excitement of flying with the Royal Air Force on a

secret mission. A museum leaflet gives details of temporary exhibitions and outlines children's activities during the school holidays. There are free quiz sheets available at weekends. This museum is not suitable for the very young. A café provides snacks and lunch.

Open daily 10.00a.m.–6.00p.m. Closed 24–26 Dec. and 1 Jan.
Admission charge; free after 4.30p.m.
BR: Waterloo.
Nearest tubes: Lambeth North, Elephant and Castle.
Nearby buses: 1, 3, 12, 53, 63, 68, 109, 159, 171, 184, 188, 344.

Kew Bridge Engines
Green Dragon Lane (off Kew Bridge Road), Brentford, Middlesex.
Tel. 081–568 4757.

This small steam-engine museum, situated in a nineteenth-century water-pumping station in Kew Bridge Road, reflects half a century of steam-engine development. The arrival of electric pumps in 1944 made the steam-pumping engines redundant. It is soothing and reassuring to hear these great old water giants at work – four have been restored by the museum and are set in motion at various times during weekends. This museum is suitable for all ages.

Open Sat.–Sun. 11.00a.m.–5.00p.m.
Admission charge.
BR: Kew Bridge.
Nearest tube: Gunnersbury.
Nearby buses: 65, 237, 267.

The London Canal Museum
12–13 New Wharf Road, King's Cross, N1.
Tel. 071–713 0836.

This museum is housed in an old warehouse built in the mid-nineteenth century for Carlo Gatti, a famous ice-cream manufacturer. Huge blocks of ice imported from Norway were brought here from the dock at Limehouse via the Regent's Canal. Beneath the warehouse are two vast ice wells, one of which has been excavated and is now on show to the public. The exhibitions in the museum trace the development of London's canals from early times when they were important trade routes to the more leisurely activities of today (see also page 130). Children will enjoy exploring the replica of a boat cabin and there is a video showing a barge trip down the Regent's Canal in the 1920s. Temporary exhibitions and special events are put on throughout the year. The museum is suitable for 7-year-olds upwards.

Open Tues.–Sun. 10.00a.m.–4.30p.m. Closed 24–26 Dec. and 1, 2 Jan. Last admission 45 minutes before closing time.
Admission charge.
BR: King's Cross, St Pancras.
Nearest tubes: King's Cross, St Pancras.
Nearby buses: 10, 14, 14A, 17, 18, 30, 45, 46, 63, 73, 74, 214, 221, 259, C12.

London Dungeon
34 Tooley Street, SE1.
Tel. 071–403 0606.

The London Dungeon is an eerie, bloodcurdling place situated under the arches by London Bridge. The exhibition area embraces a dark, damp network of cellars and reconstructs scenes from Britain's pagan past, drawing on various legends and myths and showing life-like tableaux of the plague and torture victims strung up on the 'rack'. As part of a £1 million facelift, the museum has opened a new exhibition – the Jack the Ripper Experience. Visitors are guided around carefully reconstructed scenes of the Ripper's brutal murders. They can also eavesdrop on a conversation between the police inspector and doctor who were working on the case as they examine a body and discuss the suspects. A fine place for resilient older children, but unsuitable for under-8s.

Open Mon.–Sat. 10.00a.m.–5.00p.m.; Sun. 2.00p.m.– 5.00p.m.
Admission charge.
Nearest tube: London Bridge.
Nearby buses: 4, 17, 21, 22A, 35, 40, 43, 47, 48, 133, 214.

London Fire Brigade Museum
Winchester House, Southwark Bridge Road, SE1.
Tel. 071–587 4273.

A great place for fire-engine fanatics, this museum houses one of the most comprehensive collections of firefighting equipment and veteran fire engines in the country. There are some interesting memorabilia, including a firefighter's leather helmet thought to date from the early 1700s, and fascinating information is provided about how firefighters managed to get water to a fire before the advent of the modern fire hydrant. Tours are arranged by appointment only. Children over 10 years old are welcome.

Admission free.
Nearest tube: Borough.
Nearby bus: 344.

London Planetarium
Marylebone Road, NW1.
Tel. 071–486 1121.

Next door to Madame Tussaud's (see page 60), in the mighty dome of the London Planetarium, the heavens are brought down to earth in spectacular fashion. From the comfort and safety of an armchair you can scour the universe in a simulated journey through space. Far-off constellations come to life and new galaxies open up before your eyes. Large models of the planets are set against a perfect sky, and interactive video monitors give up-to-date information as your travels progress. The constellation of Orion is stunningly reproduced in three dimensions, and special effects make it possible to feel the effects of gravity in a 'black hole'. The Planetarium provides a Spacetrail guide to set children on their way. A new show starts every 40 minutes. The Planetarium is suitable for children over 6.

Open Mon.–Fri. 12.00 noon–5.00p.m.; Sat.–Sun. 10.00a.m.– 5.00p.m.
Admission charge which can be combined with a visit to Madame Tussaud's.
Nearest tube: Baker Street.
Nearby buses: 2A, 2B, 13, 18, 27, 74, 82, 113, 139, 159, 274.

London Toy and Model Museum
21–23 Craven Hill, W2.
Tel. 071–262 9450.

This museum, tucked away behind the Bayswater Road, has something to interest children of all ages. The collection includes tin toys and toy robots, model aeroplanes and motorcycles, as well as a marvellous selection of dolls, ranging from an ancient Roman gladiator doll to Victorian dolls to a Bette Davies lookalike. The museum's newest exhibit is a magnificent model of a fairground, built in 1925. At the press of a button the music strikes up, 10,000 coloured lights blaze out and the fair, peopled by numerous doll figures, swings into action. Best of all, the unique collection of penny slot-machines actually work: simply buy an old penny from the museum shop, insert it in a machine and let Madame Zelda read your fortune or see what happens when a grizzly bear pours wine into a goblet and tries to drink it. For older children who are able to see through the viewfinder, What the Butler Saw mutoscopes show short extracts from old movies – nothing shocking, of course, except perhaps for the fact that they were filmed in black and white. At the back of the museum is a large garden where children can let off steam or ride on a miniature train. There are also some '2½' gauge miniature railways which journey around the garden and a 1920s juvenile roundabout which rotates to the strains of well-known nursery rhymes. There is a party area inside the museum where food is served. Look out for the special 'steam-up' sessions at weekends.

Open Tues.–Sat. 10.00a.m.–5.00p.m.; Sun. 11.00a.m.– 5.00p.m.
Admission charge.
Nearest tubes: Queensway, Paddington.
Nearby buses: 12, 94.

London Transport Museum
Covent Garden Piazza, WC2.
Tel. 071–379 6344.

This museum, devoted to the comprehensive history of London's transport, is tucked away in the south-eastern corner of Covent Garden Piazza. Covering the various phases of technological development during the past 150 years, it is crammed full of trams, horse buses and trolley buses, as well as ultra-modern railway locomotives. There are trains for children to clamber on and pretend to drive, signals to fiddle with and a collection of splendid posters from the vintage years of travel and transport. This is a marvellous place for train enthusiasts and for younger children who appreciate a 'hands-on' approach. Exhibitions and special holiday activities for children include treasure hunts, quizzes and rides on a miniature steam train. Recent alterations to the museum include the addition of three extra galleries which tell the history of the transport system in a new and exciting way.

Open daily 10.00a.m.–6.00p.m.
Admission charge.
Nearest tube: Covent Garden.
Nearby buses: 1, 4, 6, 9, 11, 13, 15, 23, 26, 76, 77A, 176, 188, 196, 501, 505, 521.

Madame Tussaud's
Marylebone Road, NW1.
Tel. 071–935 6861.

They say that you have definitely 'made it' when you are cast in wax for this world-famous exhibition, which comprises hundreds of effigies of well-known people, ranging from leading politicians and members of the royal family to artists and popstars, with a few criminals thrown in. Marie Tussaud (1760–1850) learnt the art of wax modelling as a young woman and went to Versailles to teach King Louis XVI's sister. Caught in the crossfire during the French Revolution, she was saved from the guillotine when anti-royalists employed her skills to make death masks of their enemies, some of whom had been her friends. When she came to England at the beginning of the eighteenth century, she brought with her a collection of masks and opened her first exhibition. Some of the originals can be seen in the Chamber of Horrors, along with a gallows, a guillotine and a selection of England's more notorious murderers. There is a convincing reconstruction of a gas-lit cobbled street, shadowy and dank, similar to the streets that might have been stalked by Jack the Ripper, who is among the characters on show. (Younger children might find this section frightening.) On a lighter note, the new Garden Party exhibit is full of celebrities who appear to be enjoying themselves. Dudley Moore plays the piano, Paul Daniels performs a party trick, Lenny Henry chats to himself, while Dame Edna Everage is seen in a stunning outfit, complete with a koala emblem and her favourite gladioli! Tussaud's spends a great deal of time and care dressing the waxworks. Each new celebrity is photographed and precise measurements are taken from every possible angle before the sculptor sets to work. Tradition dictates that the famous donate a personal set of clothes to the exhibition to make their effigy complete, and in some cases, as celebrities change over the years, so do their wax figures. Using sophisticated computer technology, Tussaud's has moved into the world of animated models that 'move' and 'talk' to you – a major development that Madame Tussaud herself would doubtless have enjoyed. The recently opened Spirit of London is the most ambitious project ever undertaken by the museum. This new, spectacular, £10 million ride in the dark carries visitors in a time-taxi through 400 years of London's history, recreating the sights, sounds and smells of days gone by. Famous figures who have played an important part in shaping the nation's heritage are portrayed in wax and fitted with audio-animatronic devices, so you can see Shakespeare quoting lines from one of his plays and join craftsmen working on St Paul's Cathedral. Unless you are prepared to endure exceptionally long queues, it is advisable to avoid a visit here in summer. Suitable for children over 7.

Open Mon.–Fri. 10.00a.m.–5.30p.m.; Sat.–Sun. 9.30a.m.–5.30p.m. *Admission charge;* joint tickets can be bought for Madame Tussaud's

and the Planetarium (see page 58).
Nearest tube: Baker Street.
Nearby buses: 2A, 2B, 13, 18, 27, 74, 82, 113, 139, 159, 274.

Madame Tussaud's Rock Circus
The London Pavilion, Piccadilly Circus, W1.
Tel. 071–734 8025.

The Rock Circus offers a jump-thumping tour, complete with personal stereo sound system, through the history of rock and pop music. More than fifty waxworks of stars, ranging from the Beatles and Prince to Madonna and Phil Collins, 'sing' their greatest hits as they 'move' to the music. If you like the 'gottle of gear' approach to the fab sixties and seventies, this is definitely the place to go. Not for the faint-hearted or the very young, but older children might find it amusing.

Open Sun.–Mon. and Wed.–Thurs. 11.00a.m.–9.00p.m.; Tues. 12.00 noon–9.00p.m.; Fri.–Sat. 11.00a.m.–10.00p.m.
Admission charge.
Nearest tube: Piccadilly Circus.
Nearby buses: 3, 6, 9, 12, 13, 14, 15, 19, 22, 23, 38, 53, 88, 94, 139, 159.

The Museum of Artillery in the Rotunda
Repository Road, Woolwich, SE18.
Tel. 081–316 5402.

John Nash built the Rotunda as a pavilion for the Prince Regent for the gardens at Carlton House. It was transported to Woolwich in 1819 and became home to the Royal Artillery's fine collection of fighting equipment. Some rare pieces include experimental guns and anti-aircraft guns which were eventually replaced by missile systems. There are also many items of foreign equipment such as multi-barrel cannons and a superb 12-pounder gun presented by the Emperor Louis Napoleon to Queen Victoria. In the grounds of the Rotunda are many guns from both World Wars as well as more modern items. Children may be interested in a sound tour which tells the story of the gun in a simple, concise way. It is possible to combine a visit to the Rotunda with the Royal Artillery Regimental Museum, a mile away in the Old Royal Military Academy (see page 69). The museum is suitable for children over 5, but younger children will enjoy looking at the giant guns outside.

Open Mon.–Fri. 12.00 noon–5.00p.m. (4.00p.m. from Nov. to March), Sat. and Sun. 1.00p.m.–5.00p.m. (4.00p.m. from Nov. to March).
Free admission.
BR: Woolwich Arsenal then bus 53.

Museum of Garden History
Lambeth Palace Road, SE1.
Tel. 071–261 1891.

This museum, owned by the Tradescant Trust, is situated in St Mary at Lambeth Church, just beside the entrance to Lambeth Palace. John Tradescant and his son were gardeners to the Duke of Buckingham and Charles I, and brought back from their travels in America and Europe many of the flowers and shrubs we take for granted today. The ground floor is usually taken up with exhibitions, lectures, plant fairs and numerous other events which are held throughout the year. For a family visit, go inside the Tradescant Garden at the far end of the museum and relax in the beautiful walled cottage garden full of seventeenth-century plants. We owe a great deal to the Tradescants, both of whom are buried in the churchyard. There is an excellent café in the museum and the picture postcard view of the Houses of Parliament from Lambeth Pier across the road is second to none.

Open Mon.–Fri. 11.00a.m.–3.00p.m. Sat. closed. Sun. 10.30a.m.–5.00p.m. Closed from the second Sunday in Dec. to the first Sunday in March.
Admission free.
BR: Victoria, Waterloo.
Nearest tubes: Victoria, Waterloo.
Nearby buses: 3, 77, 159, 344, 507, C10.

Museum of London
London Wall, EC2.
Tel. 071–600 3699.

Situated in the heart of the City, the Museum of London is reached by a high pedestrian walkway from the Barbican. The displays are arranged in chronological order, telling the story of London from pre-Roman times until the present day. The carefully reconstructed period tableaux provide fascinating insights as they take you step by step through the various stages of the City's development. You can go inside a Roman house and inspect Roman armour, as well as magnificent Tudor jewellery and Victorian shops, complete with penny-farthing bicycles. On the podium level, the Great Fire Experience shows a detailed model of London as it was in 1666, when Fire destroyed a large part of the City. Authentic sound effects and realistic atmosphere give a vivid impression of what it must have been like to have been in London at the time. Each show lasts only 5 minutes, so it is suitable for younger children. Before you leave, visit the basement for a look at the Lord Mayor's coach. More than 200 years old, this splendid ceremonial carriage encrusted in fine gold leaf is still functional today – when not in use, it is surrounded by a trough of water to prevent the wood from warping. The museum organises some excellent events at half-terms and during school holidays, and many of its exhibitions are suitable for schoolchildren. For details of current programmes, ring the education department on extension 239. There is a good coffee shop at the museum.

Open Tues.–Sat. 10.00a.m.–6.00p.m.; Sun. 2.00p.m.–6.00p.m.;

closed Monday except Bank Holidays.
Nearest tubes: Barbican, St Paul's, Moorgate, Bank.
Nearby buses: 4, 8, 11, 15, 22B, 23, 25, 26, 172, 279A, 501.

Museum of Mankind
6 Burlington Gardens, W1.
Tel. 071–437 2224.

The Museum of Mankind illuminates styles of life in non-western cultures by focusing on homes, clothes and local arts and crafts. Comprising one of the greatest collections of its kind in the world, the exhibits belong to the British Museum's own anthropological store. General exhibitions, which last up to eighteen months, might include, for example, an intricately carved rice barn from Indonesia or an Indian log cabin. There are free film shows during the week. This museum is not suitable for very young children.

Open Mon.–Sat. 10.00a.m.–5.00p.m.; Sun. 2.00p.m.– 6.00p.m.
Admission free.
Nearest tube: Green Park.
Nearby buses: 8, 9, 14, 19, 22, 38.

Museum of the Moving Image
South Bank, SE1.
Tel. 071–401 2636.

This exciting and comparatively new museum is the first of its kind dedicated to the history of cinema and television. Fifty exhibition areas cover the period since the first black and white flickerings to clips from some of the grand epics and the latest in satellite television. As you progress around the museum, children can participate in various events – they can draw a Disney-type cartoon, for instance, and find out what it feels like to be a newsreader or audition for a part in a Hollywood movie. Actor-guides help to bring the experiences to life. It usually takes a couple of hours to tour the exhibits and there is a great deal to see, but look out for Marilyn Monroe's memorable dress from *Some Like It Hot* and Boris Karloff's stand-in model from the 1935 film *The Bride of Frankenstein*. Although the museum's education courses are aimed primarily at schools, special events are held throughout the year for sixth-form students, covering such subjects as pop videos, animation and photography. To obtain more details, join the museum's free mailing list. The museum is suitable for children over 5. Allow over an hour for your visit.

Open daily 10.00a.m.–6.00p.m.; closed 24–26 Dec.
Admission charge; family ticket available for up to two adults and four children.
Nearest tubes: Embankment, Waterloo.
Nearby buses: 1, 5, 68, 70, 171, 171A, 177, 188, 502, 507.

Musical Museum
368 High Street, Brentford, Middlesex.
Tel. 081–560 8108.

The 90-minute tour of this museum provides a fascinating introduction to a unique collection of automatic musical instruments and offers a golden opportunity to hear everything from the mighty Wurlitzer cinema organ to the dulcet tones of Steinway's Duo-Art piano, which can automatically and accurately reproduce the performance of pianists such as George Gershwin. Other instruments reproduce the rhythms and sounds of racy ragtime, classical concertos or church organ music. Some of the most impressive exhibits have tortoiseshell and ivory keys encased in beautifully hand-carved cases. These are of the type favoured by private owners, for many of whom size was obviously no object. The Wurlitzer, for example, which covers more than 400 square feet (37 square metres) of floor space, was specifically built for an American who wanted it for his home in Chicago; it eventually came to Britain and was installed at the Regal Theatre in Kingston. The tour is not suitable for under-6s.

Open April–Oct. Sat.–Sun. 2.00p.m.–5.00p.m.; also July–Aug. Wed.–Fri. 2.00p.m.–5.00p.m.
Admission charge.
Nearest tubes: South Ealing, then 65 bus; Gunnersbury, then 237 or 267 bus.
Nearby buses: 65, 237, 267.

National Army Museum
Royal Hospital Road, Chelsea, SW3.
Tel. 071–730 0717.

One of the few free museums left in London, the National Army covers five centuries of army history, illustrating the lives of British soldiers not only at war but also at home. The Weapons Gallery has a fine collection of equipment, tracing the development of fighting machines from the longbow to the present day. Army uniforms from as far away as India, medals, paintings and an outstanding model of the Battle of Waterloo, complete with 70,000 soldiers, are just some of the exhibits that can be found here. Additional activities include workshops, trails, videos and competitions organised at half-terms and during school holidays. The museum is not suitable for children under 5.

Open daily 10.00a.m.–5.30p.m.
Admission free.
BR: Victoria.
Nearest tube: Sloane Square.
Nearby buses: 11, 19.

National Maritime Museum
Romney Road, Greenwich, SE10.
Tel. 081–858 4422.

In 1933 the two buildings at Greenwich either side of the Queen's House (see below) were given over to the National Maritime Museum. This houses a collection of maritime treasures unrivalled anywhere in the world. It includes gilded royal barges, dramatic seascapes, ship's models, unusual crafts from foreign countries, weapons and uniforms, including Nelson's own. Detailed displays such as Man's Encounter with the Sea further illuminate British maritime history from the eighth century onwards. The Navigation Room is full of globes, sea charts and maritime instruments. A twentieth-century Seapower Gallery opened in 1992, featuring ships involved in battle, trade and life-saving convoys. There are themed areas covering an operations room, battlefleets and submarines. In the hands-on section, you can try out a modern Marconi missile-control system and experience the Kelvin Hughes radar link from the Channel.

The small seventeenth-century palace known as the Queen's House is also part of the Maritime Museum. This was the first Palladian-style villa to be built in this country, designed by Inigo Jones for Queen Anne of Denmark, the wife of King James I of England and VI of Scotland. She died before building work was completed, but the house enjoyed great popularity with King Charles I's wife, Henrietta Maria, who lived here for some time. As well as a collection of fine seventeenth-century paintings, there is a treasury in the original brick

vaults. A short way up the hill, and also part of the National Maritime Museum, is Sir Christopher Wren's 300-year-old Royal Observatory, which has many important associations. From here Edmund Halley (1656– 1742) recorded a sighting of the famous comet that bears his name; the first nautical almanac was compiled inside these walls; and this is the place where world time is set. The Royal Observatory has recently undergone a dramatic overhaul. Twelve new galleries exploring time and space, astronomy, the meridian and the history of the Observatory are now open to the public, complete with interactive science stations and a sound–light show in the dome which houses a 28-inch telescope, the largest refracting telescope in the UK. A giant digital clock shows Greenwich Mean Time to the nearest tenth of a second, and the Observatory's collection of precision clocks and scientific instruments is one of the finest in the world. Stand with a foot either side of the Prime Meridian Line situated in the Observatory courtyard and you will straddle both halves of the world at the same time. Fibre optics run through and illuminate this famous line which separates the eastern and western hemispheres. A machine nearby issues certificates giving the exact time (GMT) and date you were there. The famous Observatory timeball rises to its full height at 12.58p.m. and moves down again at 1.00p.m. – a movement it has been making daily since 1833. The Observatory is suitable for children over 8. The Bosun's Whistle café restaurant situated behind the museum serves hot and cold snacks throughout the day. Outside terrace seating and a children's play area are available. Open daily 10.30a.m.– 5.00p.m.

Open April–Sept. Mon.–Sat. 10.00a.m.–6.00p.m.; Sun. 12.00 noon– 6.00p.m. Also open in winter but closes an hour earlier.
Admission charge; a good-value Passport Ticket covers entry to four historic maritime sites, including the National Maritime Museum, the Old Royal Observatory, the Queen's House and the *Cutty Sark* (see page 129).
BR: Greenwich.
DLR: Island Gardens, then Greenwich foot tunnel.
Nearby buses: 47, 53, 177, 188, 199.
River boats from Charing Cross, Tower Pier and Westminster.

National Postal Museum
King Edward Building, King Edward Street, EC1.
Tel. 071–239 5420.

Keen stamp collectors will love this museum. It came into being in 1965, when one of the leading philatelists in the world, Reginald Phillips, gave his magnificent collection of Victorian stamps to the nation. Later additions have included stamps from the Post Office's own archives, all of which put this among the world's best philatelic collections. There are millions of stamps in the museum, although not all of them are on display. Those you can see include special-issue nineteenth-century Valentine stamps, rare Penny Blacks, Twopenny Blues, Coronation sets and proof sheets of nearly every British postage stamp issued since 1840. On display are Rowland Hill's famous letters leading up to the introduction of the penny post service on 6 May 1840, the story of the Penny Black, nineteenth-century postal dies, franking machines, postal stationery and stamp designs that, for one reason or another, never saw the light of day. You can also inspect the Post Office's interesting collection of letterboxes, which include some rare examples of pillar-boxes and wall-boxes dating from early Victorian times. The museum shop is a good hunting ground for new stamps and first-day cover albums.

Open Mon.–Fri. 9.30a.m.–4.30p.m.
Admission free.
Nearest tubes: Barbican, St Paul's.
Nearby buses: 4, 8, 22, 25, 141, 501, 509.

Natural History Museum
Cromwell Road, SW7.
Tel. 071–938 9123.

It is easy to be put off by the sheer size of the Natural History Museum. There are thousands of exhibits on display, far too many to see in a single visit. An imposing, life-size replica of a 135-million-year-old Diplodocus stands in the museum's entrance hall and the Ronson Gallery, to the left, is given over entirely to dinosaurs, some of which make startling noises and movements. For a look at more contemporary animal life, you could start at the Whale Hall, which has a full-size, 26-metre-long model of a blue whale suspended in mid-air. Over-hunting through the centuries has brought the world's largest mammal close to extinction and the chances of seeing one in its natural environment are remote. The first floor is full of all kinds of stuffed creatures from different parts of the world. Bears, bats, bush-babies and large animals such as bisons, lions, tigers and panthers look out from glass cages. Alternatively, you could head for the Creepie Crawlies exhibition, where children can test their natural history knowledge and try some of the quizzes. The Hall of Human Biology explains the workings of the human body. Hands-on activities include a demonstration of how blood circulates and a do-it-yourself heart-beat test. The discovery centre in the basement of the museum is a mixed bag of tricks, packed full of objects to examine. There are microscopes to peer through, 'feelie' boxes to stick your hands in and guess what's inside, and a python skin to touch and a tortoise shell to hold. Children can also play detectives by finding out what trails animals leave. Activity sheets test children's knowledge and there are tables to sit at for those who want to draw. Before you leave, have a look at the dinosaur footprints in the museum garden;

discovered near Swanage, they are 60 million years old and were made by a dinosaur which walked on its hind legs. There is a snack bar on the ground floor and a museum restaurant. A museum for all ages.

Open Mon.–Fri. 10.00a.m.–6.00p.m.; Sun. 1.00p.m.– 6.00p.m.
Admission charge includes entry to the Geological Museum; free entry after 4.30p.m. during the week.
Nearest tube: South Kensington.
Nearby buses: 14, 45A, 49, 74, 249, 349, C1.

Pollock's Toy Museum
1 Scala Street, W1.
Tel. 071–636 3452.

To wander through this tiny, old-fashioned museum is like entering a time-warp. It occupies two adjoining houses off Tottenham Court Road, and the steeply winding staircase takes you to various rooms, each with its own theme. One is devoted to toys, another to toy theatres and dolls' houses. Sooty has his own corner, and there are musical bears and Edward Bears more than a hundred years old. Toy theatre performances are given during the school holidays. For children who like a hands-on approach, the museum toyshop with its wonderful collection of Pollock's own toy theatres, is hard to resist.

Open Mon.–Sat. 10.00a.m.–5.00p.m.
Admission charge.
Nearest tube: Goodge Street.
Nearby buses: 14, 24, 29, 73.

Quasar
1st Floor, The Trocadero, Coventry Street, W1.
Tel. 071–734 8151.

It's all systems go at the Quasar Centre, home to London's only live-action laser game. Children and adults enter a space-age fantasy world in which laser beams race through the dim light and survival depends on quick thinking and clever tactics. After a thorough briefing, players are divided into two teams. Each team scores points by 'de-activating' their opponents. The game arena is like a scene from a science-fiction film. For 20 minutes you can stalk the enemy with a specially designed Quasar-gun linked to a chest pack which keeps track of your score. As the players move across the battle zones, they fire through mesh floors and at strategically placed mirrors, while loud music reverberates and coloured lights flash. At the end of the game players are given a data sheet showing how they performed. A visit to Quasar would be fun as a party treat for over-8s.

Open daily 10.00a.m.–12.00 midnight.
Admission charge.
Nearest tube: Piccadilly Circus.
Nearby buses: 3, 6, 9, 12, 13, 14, 15, 19, 22, 23, 38, 53, 88, 94, 139, 159.

Royal Air Force Museum
Grahame Park Way, London NW9.
Tel. 081–205 9191, 081–205 2266.

The Royal Air Force Museum, Britain's national museum of aviation, is home to one of the world's finest collections of aircraft. The museum takes you through the fascinating history of aviation, highlighting the people and the different aeroplanes they flew. The aircraft, over 70 in all, are housed in enormous hangars sited on an old airfield. You can walk under the wings of the mighty Vulcan V-bomber or take a look inside the famous Spitfire and relive history's most famous air battles in the incredible 'Battle of Britain Experience'. One of the most exciting 'hands-on' features is the museum's amazing flight simulator, in which you can ride in an RAF Tornado and find out what pilots experience when they take off. One of the newest exhibits is the Jet Provost trainer in which Prince Charles trained as a pilot, and it is possible to climb inside the cockpit to see what it is like inside. The museum holds a variety of special children's events throughout the school holidays ranging from Easter art sessions to model aircraft workshops. Other attractions include 'Plane and Simple' demonstrations which go some way to explain to children the mystery of flight, and there is a free, all-day cinema. There is so much to see here that the chances are you'll want to come back at a later date. The museum ticket allows a free return visit for up to six months. The museum is suitable for all ages.

Open daily 10.00a.m.–6.00p.m.
Admission charge.
BR: Mill Hill Broadway.
Nearest tube: Colindale.
Nearby bus: 303.
Car access from A5 and via A41 from M1.

The Royal Artillery Regimental Museum
Royal Military Academy, Woolwich, SE18.
Tel. 081–854 2242.

This museum tells the story of the Royal Artillery Regiment from its formation in 1716 to the present day. The museum is housed in the Old Royal Military Academy central block and is full of pictures, models, tableaux, uniforms and many other exhibits covering the Regiment's long history. There is a short video presentation at the entrance giving a brief history of the Regiment and explaining the layout of the museum. Because the museum is housed in Ministry of Defence property it is not always open at the advertised times so please ring to check before you set out. Suitable for 7-year-olds upwards. See also the Museum of Artillery in the Rotunda page 61.

Open Mon.–Fri. 12.30p.m.–4.30p.m.
Admission free.

BR: Woolwich Arsenal.
Nearby buses: 161, 166.

Royal Mews
Buckingham Palace Road, SW1.
Tel. 071–930 4832.

Just around the corner from Buckingham Palace a heraldic lion and unicorn sit either side of a gateway. This is the entrance to the Royal Mews, where you can see the splendid eighteenth-century gold state coach, which has been used for every coronation since that of George IV, as well as other royal carriages and the Queen's horses themselves, the famous Windsor Greys. Hundreds of years ago the monarch kept his falcons in the mews, where they would remain until their 'mewing' or plumage change had taken place. The mews is suitable for all ages.

Open Wed.–Thurs. 2.00p.m.–4.00p.m.
Admission charge.
Nearest tube: Piccadilly Circus.
Nearby buses: 3, 6, 9, 12, 13, 14, 15, 19, 22, 23, 38, 53, 88, 94, 139, 159.

Science Museum
Exhibition Road, SW7.
Tel. 071–589 3456.

This museum, one of the best in London, imaginatively brings to life the various aspects of science. It not only makes science interesting and comprehensible for the non-technically minded, but also demonstrates its relevance to daily life. You cannot cover everything in one visit and some galleries have less appeal to children than others. Pick a few subjects at a time to concentrate on. An entire trip could be devoted to the Launch Pad on the first floor, where numerous hands-on experiments allow children to find out for themselves how glass affects light, for example, or how pedalling a bicycle can generate electricity, or what problems arise from building bridges with lopsided bricks. A finger-painting machine works simply by pressing gently onto a screen, while the Grain Pit shows grain being lifted up inside a tube according to the corkscrew principle devised by Archimedes more than 2000 years ago. On the ground floor is a wonderful life-size exhibit of man's first landing on the moon. The lunar module Apollo 10 looks as though it were made for a science-fiction film and it is hard to imagine the American astronauts travelling in such a craft. The Children's Gallery on the lower ground floor is full of simple scientific tasks that can be performed by twiddling buttons or turning handles. Films and lectures are arranged during the school holidays. There is a museum café.

Open Mon.–Sat. 10.00a.m.–6.00p.m.; Sun. 2.30p.m.– 6.00p.m.
Admission charge; free entry on weekdays after 4.30p.m.
Nearest tube: South Kensington.
Nearby buses: 14, 45A, 49, 74, 249, 349, C1.

Shakespeare Globe Museum
Bear Gardens, Bankside, SE1.
Tel. 071–620 0202.

In the seventeenth century, Bankside, on the south bank of the Thames close to Southwark Bridge, was London's theatreland. The Swan, the Rose and the Globe theatres regularly staged popular plays. For those who wanted more grisly entertainment, the bear-baiting arena, which later became known as the Bear Gardens, provided an alternative diversion. The museum reflects the development of the Elizabethan stage from 1576 to 1642. Models, archaeological finds and photographs recreate William Shakespeare's London and illuminate his career as a popular playwright and actor-manager. Upstairs is a replica of a seventeenth-century indoor playhouse, which is regularly used by professional and amateur companies. This is a good museum for older children, as it demystifies Shakespeare and brings to life the times in which he worked. A few minutes' walk away, close to Cardinal's Wharf, is the site of the new Globe theatre, a unique reconstruction of the original playhouse, due to be completed in 1994. Combine a visit here with a trip to the George Inn (see page 112).

Open Mon.–Sat. 10.00a.m.–5.00p.m.; Sun. 2.00p.m.– 5.30p.m.
Admission charge.
BR: London Bridge.
Nearest tube: London Bridge.
Nearby buses: 17, 149, 344, P11.

Sir John Soane's Museum
13 Lincoln's Inn Fields, WC2.
Tel. 071–405 2107.

All the contents of this museum were collected by the man who gave it its name. The house designed by Sir John Soane in 1812, where he lived until his death in 1837, has been modified and rearranged to accommodate his extraordinary collection and is full of all sorts of rare and wonderful things. Paintings by Hogarth jostle with such items as the sturdy-looking coffin of an Egyptian king who died more than 1000 years before the birth of Christ. Strategically placed mirrors give a deceptive sense of space, and the many busts, vases and statues indicate a wonderfully eclectic taste. Soane is famous for designing the Bank of England. What is not generally known, however, is that he also designed the most elaborate kennel in the world. His plans for the kennel show a palatial residence, built in the classic style and surrounded by fountains and a hunting frieze; intended for the bishop of Derry's dog, it was never completed. This museum is suitable for over-10s.

Open Tues.–Sat. 10.00a.m.–5.00p.m.
Admission free.
Nearest tube: Holborn.
Nearby buses: 8, 25, 168, 188.

Spitting Image Rubberworks
Cubitts Yard, James Street, Covent Garden, WC2.
Tel. 071–240 0393.

A 40-minute tour of the Rubberworks reveals how the computer-controlled puppets from the popular television series *Spitting Image* are made and operated. Puppet politicians, show-business personalities and members of the royal family perform a hectic drama in cramped conditions, presided over by a puppet of the Conservative politician Norman Tebbit, who keeps a strict eye on proceedings. The show is not quite as realistic as the television programme because nearly all the puppets consist of heads without bodies, but an illuminating video explains how the puppets are assembled. Sketches are made of the characters to be featured, which are then sculpted in clay; after firing, the models are painted ready to perform – a process which takes up to six weeks. Children can participate in the show by pressing buttons and bringing the various characters to life. Tours, which start every half an hour, are not suitable for the very young.

Open Mon.–Fri. 11.00a.m.–5.30p.m.; Sun. 11.00a.m.– 6.30p.m.
Admission charge.
Nearest tube: Covent Garden.
Nearby buses: 1, 4, 6, 9, 11, 13, 15, 23, 26, 76, 77A, 168, 171, 171A, 176, 188, 196, 501, 505, 521.

Telecom Technology Showcase
135 Queen Victoria Street, London EC4.
Tel. 071–248 7444 (for free information, telephone 0800–289689).

Bleeps and buzzers of all descriptions make themselves heard at this museum. Exhibits include a replica of Bell's original telephone, high-speed Morse transmitters and receivers and a telephone operator's gas mask from the Second World War, as well as examples of sophisticated new developments in the telecommunications industry. Among the many fascinating innovations on show is the 'thinking' telephone with built-in microprocessors. There are also microwave radios, satellites and even a fax machine which can be used to send messages from one part of the museum to another. A good activity book for over-6s is available in the museum shop. There is no café in the museum, but you can take a picnic to the gardens in front of Baynard House, about a minute's walk away. Combine a trip here with a visit to St Paul's Cathedral, see page 101.

Open Mon.–Fri. 10.00a.m.–5.00p.m. Closed Sat. and Sun.
Admission free.
BR: Blackfriars.
Nearest tube: Blackfriars.
Nearby buses: 45, 59, 63.

Theatre Museum/National Museum of the Performing Arts
Russell Street, Covent Garden, WC2.
Tel. 071–836 7891.

Covent Garden, in the heart of theatreland, is an appropriate setting for the Theatre Museum or the National Museum of the Performing Arts, the aim of which is to increase awareness and knowledge of live entertainment in Britain. The museum deals with the development of theatre, ballet, opera and pop music and has a wonderful collection of photographs, costumes and designs. Its Slap Studio shows how stage make-up has kept pace with increasingly sophisticated lighting techniques, and there are excellent photographs of famous actors at work. Children who want to look like the Wicked Witch of the North or the Phantom of the Opera can be expertly transformed by the museum's resident make-up artist. There are exhibitions that look behind the scenes of successful productions, such as that which examined how the National Theatre's adaptation of Kenneth Grahame's classic tale *The Wind in the Willows* became a smash hit. Other events for children include special plays and musicals. A Saturday Children's Theatre Club has recently been formed. The idea is to have fun and create a play. Sessions for 10–12s are from 11.15a.m.–12.45p.m., and for 7–9s from 1.15p.m.–2.45p.m.; there is a small charge. The museum has a café.

Open Tues.–Sat. 11.00a.m.–7.00p.m.
Admission charge.
Nearest tube: Covent Garden.
Nearby buses: 1, 4, 6, 9, 11, 13, 15, 23, 26, 76, 77A, 168, 171, 171A, 176, 188, 196, 501, 505, 521.

Tower Hill Pageant
1 Tower Hill Terrace, EC3.
Tel. 071–709 0081.

The Tower Hill Pageant is London's first 'dark-ride' museum. With the help of a computer-controlled car you are taken back in time through a 2000-year historical journey passing through life-like scenes of London from the Roman invasion to the present day. Atmospheric sound effects and spicy Elizabethan smells bring the capital's history into sharp focus and show what an important part the river played in London's development. Children of all ages will enjoy the novel feeling of being catapulted back over the centuries while learning a bit of history as they go. The upper level of Tower Hill has a good café selling such things as baked potatoes and hot dogs.

Open daily April–Oct. 9.30a.m.–5.30p.m.; Nov.–March 9.30a.m.–4.30p.m.
Admission charge.
Nearest tube: Tower Hill.
Nearby buses: 15, 25, 42, 78, 100, D1, D9, D11.

Victoria and Albert Museum

Cromwell Road, SW7.
Tel. 071–938 8500 (for 24-hour recorded information, telephone 071–938 8441).

The Victoria and Albert Museum houses a superlative collection of fine arts and crafts from all over the world. The man behind the scheme was Queen Victoria's husband, Prince Albert, who, keen to improve the public's taste in design, provided the museum with furniture, porcelain, glass and other objects that had been shown at the Great Exhibition of 1851. Picking out what to see in a grand collection like this can be daunting, especially if you have children to amuse, so get hold of a copy of the short guide called *Introducing the Victoria and Albert*, which divides the museum into five easy walks, focusing on the most popular areas. Raphael's giant cartoons (walk 1) must be one of the most famous exhibits in the museum. Nowadays we associate cartoons with jokes, but the word comes from the Italian *cartone*, meaning a large sheet of paper. These cartoons were preliminary designs for a set of paintings commissioned by the pope. Walk 3 takes you to the new Nehru Gallery, where Tipu's Tiger, an unlikely mechanical organ, is in the process of savaging a surprised-looking gentleman in a hat. A mechanism to make the man shout and the tiger roar is set in motion by pressing a button; this cannot be activated by

the public, but a video shows the toy in action. The Great Bed of Ware in the Tudor Galleries (walk 2) once slept six couples end to end. Carved out of oak and decorated with odd-looking bearded men, it appears to be extremely comfortable. Shakespeare, who may himself have slept in the bed, mentions it in his play *Twelfth Night*. Fashion has always played an important part at the museum. The Victoria and Albert's wide-ranging Dress Collection (walk 4) highlights the changes in English style, while the 20th-Century Gallery shows all the latest in consumer design, from a Mackintosh fireplace to Swatch watches. Daily guided tours last about an hour. The museum's New Restaurant sells hot and cold food; high chairs are available.

Open Mon.–Sat. 10.00a.m.–5.30p.m.; Sun. 2.30p.m.– 5.30p.m.
Admission free, but donations welcome. The museum's family season ticket includes admission to both the Natural History and Science Museums.
Nearest tube: South Kensington.
Nearby buses: 14, 45A, 49, 74, 249, 349, C1.

Virtual Quest
2 Tower Hill Terrace, Tower Hill, EC3.
Tel. 071–488 2808.

Anyone hooked on Dungeons and Dragons computer games will no doubt enjoy Legend Quest, the 'virtuality' experience available here, in which players battle against extraordinary odds in a three-dimensional, computer-generated world. The object is to overcome outrageous obstacles in the shape of ravenous wolves, lethal spiders and excitable goblins, and thereby gain access to a merrier land beyond. Wearing special helmets and weapons, players assume the guise of different characters, and have precisely 4 minutes to complete the game. Other games at Virtual Quest include a high-powered driving race which tests nerve, concentration and daring, plus a good selection of video games with charges starting at 50p. Decide in advance how much money you want to spend, otherwise this could prove a very expensive outing. It is suitable for over-7s.

Open daily 10.00a.m.–10.00p.m., including Bank Holidays.
Nearest tube: Tower Hill.
Nearby buses: 15, 25, 42, 78, 100, D1, D9, D11.
See also Funland and Lazer Bowl (page 52).

Winston Churchill's Britain at War Museum
Churchill House, 64–66 Tooley Street, London Bridge, SE1.
Tel. 071–403 3171.

Surprisingly, tanks and guns play no part in London's newest war museum. Instead, by means of an authentic Second World War lift, the visitor is taken back to the early 1940s to experience how ordinary people coped when electricity was switched off at 11.00p.m., women took over men's jobs in factories, and clothes and food were rationed.

The museum brings to life many fascinating aspects of survival in war-torn London by recreating the sights, sounds and smells of the Blitz, such as air-raid warnings, the whine of falling bombs, all-clear signals and even a faint whiff of burning. A mock-up of part of the London underground, where hundreds of people sheltered during bombing raids, has been constructed, complete with bunks, blankets, canteen and miniature library. A commentary explains that gas masks for children had coloured Mickey Mouse faces to make them more attractive to wear, and that babies were protected by covered cradles which had air pumped into them by hand. Stepping inside an Anderson shelter, you can hear the V1 flying-bombs, or 'doodlebugs', approaching overhead, and in the BBC Listening Room you can listen to Hitler's declaration of war and Churchill's famous speech to the nation in 1942. At the end of the tour you walk into a London street minutes after a bomb blast. This detailed reconstruction is so realistic that it might be frightening for younger children. Smoke, flames, a burst water main and crashing debris leave little to the imagination.

Open daily 10.00a.m.–5.00p.m.
Admission charge.
Nearest tube: London Bridge.
Nearby buses: 21, 35, 40, 43, 47, 48, 133, P11.

10

Palaces

British kings and queens have left London a rich architectural legacy including many fine palaces and monuments. Not all monarchs lived in opulent style – for example, King William III (of Orange) preferred the simplicity of a smaller residence like Kew Palace – but some, like Queen Victoria, wanted grand houses in the centre of town. Several of London's palaces are still home to royalty, while others are open to the public. Older children will appreciate the pomp and splendour of London's royal residences, younger ones might enjoy the gardens more, but all the family will have a fun day out.

Buckingham Palace
St James's Park, SW1.

Queen Victoria was the first monarch to make Buckingham Palace a permanent royal residence. Buckingham House, as the building was then known, was bought by King George III in 1762 and taken over by his son the Prince Regent who became King George IV. Lack of funds prevented George IV from completing extensive reconstruction work on the building which was finally finished in Victoria's reign. The severe façade was added in 1913, but what the palace lacks in beauty it makes up for in size. There are over 600 rooms, and the 40-acre private garden to the back of the palace has a large lake and some glorious trees including an unusual mulberry tree, the only remaining legacy of King James I's unsuccessful attempt at creating a British silk industry. Under the misguided belief that silk weaving would prevent his subjects from becoming idle he decided to plant several acres of mulberry plants on what was, in those days, crown land. Unfortunately he imported the wrong strain of mulberry and the silk worms refused to eat.

   The annual garden party, held each summer by the Queen, is a chance for invited guests to visit parts of the palace normally only open to heads of state. In August and September 1993, Buckingham Palace opened its doors for the first time to raise money for fire-damaged Windsor Castle. Nineteen rooms were opened to the general public including the Grand Hall, Throne Room, Green Drawing Room, State Dining Room, Music Room and the Silk Tapestry Room as well as several galleries which house part of the Queen's fine art collection. It is hoped that the scheme, which gives a rare opportunity to wander through what is, after all, the residence of the most famous

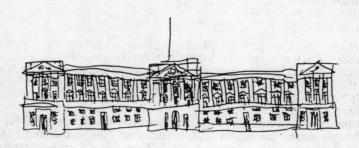

head of state of all, will continue after the Windsor restoration is complete. The Queen is in residence at Buckingham Palace when her personal flag, the royal standard, is flying. For details of changing the guard see page 22.

Admittance by invitation only except during the months of August and September when the palace is open daily 9.30a.m.– 5.30p.m.

Admission charge. Tickets are on sale from 9.00a.m. and as this is the height of the tourist season, it is essential to arrive as early as possible. The majority of tickets are sold by midday.
BR: Victoria.
Nearest tubes: Hyde Park Corner, St James's Park, Victoria.
Nearby buses: 2A, 2B, 8, 9, 10, 14, 16, 19, 22, 36, 38, 52, 73, 74, 82, 137.

Eltham Palace
Eltham, SE9.
Tel. 081–854 2242.

Originally built for the bishop of Durham, Eltham Palace fell into the hands of the crown in the thirteenth century and became the favourite country residence of King Henry III. Little is left of the medieval building apart from its magnificent Banqueting Hall, which is still used for private functions. Extensive renovation in the 1930s included the restoration of the minstrels' gallery and the spectacular hammerbeam roof. The site is approached by means of a fourteenth-century stone bridge which crosses the old moat to the Great Hall. The palace is a fascinating place to visit, giving as it does an unexpected glimpse of medieval England in the midst of bustling suburban London.

Open Thurs. and Sun. 10.00a.m.–4.00p.m.
Admission free.
BR: Eltham.
Nearby buses: 126, 132, 161.

Fulham Palace
Bishop's Avenue, SW6.
Tel. 071–736 3233.

Fulham Palace enjoys an unlikely setting, tucked away behind Bishop's Park and surrounded by Edwardian mansions. It is one of the oldest buildings in Fulham and has been for many years home to the bishops of London. The small museum in Fulham Palace tells the history of the building and its garden and there are free guided tours around the palace, normally on the second Sunday of the month. Both the museum and palace tours are more suitable for older children. The gardens are full of unusual trees and plants from different parts of the world, and the slightly run-down herb garden has large bushes of thyme and lavender. You can picnic in the grounds.

Open Tues.–Sun. 2.00p.m.–5.00p.m.; museum open Wed.– Sun. 2.00p.m.–5.00p.m.; gardens open daily.
Admission free (except for museum).
Nearest tube: Putney Bridge.
Nearby buses: 11, 74, 190, 220, 295, C4.

Hampton Court Palace
Hampton Court, East Molesey, Surrey.
Tel. 081–781 9500.

Originally the residence of Cardinal Thomas Wolsey, Hampton Court was long coveted by King Henry VIII – with its piped water and sanitation, it was far more modern than any property the king possessed – and in 1528 he acquired it, even though he already had more than fifty houses at his disposal. Hampton Court Palace became one of Henry VIII's favourite retreats; five of his wives also stayed here, although for some of them the visits were not long enough. More than a century later King William III and Queen Mary II commissioned Christopher Wren to rebuild the Royal Apartments, and he, with the help of fine craftsmen such as Grinling Gibbons and Antonio Verrio, created some of the most sumptuous state rooms to be found in any palace in Britain. But Hampton Court fell out of favour. George II rarely used the palace, and after Queen Victoria came to the throne it was opened to the public. Today you can wander around the enormous Tudor kitchens, which look as they did when Henry VIII entertained his court here in 1542. For the first time in more than 200 years a fire burns in the fireplace, a wild boar rotates on a spit and the tables are covered with 'sweetmeats' and other sixteenth-century foods. Following a disastrous fire in 1986, the King's Apartments have been meticulously restored to the style in which they appeared in the 1700s. Guides dressed in appropriate period costume bring the eighteenth century to life with the assistance of musicians and dancers, who make daily appearances in many parts of the palace. Among the numerous treasures at Hampton Court is a priceless collection of tapestries and paintings, which includes seventeenth-century copies of Raphael cartoons and paintings by famous artists such as Van Dyck, Titian and Veronese. The indoor tennis court created for Henry VIII, where he heard the news of Anne Boleyn's death, was rebuilt by William III and is still in use. The splendid palace gardens cover more than 60 acres, including a fine walk along the Thames. The Great Vine, planted in 1786 and still producing a fine crop of grapes each year, is the largest vine in Britain, and the unusual Tudor Knot Garden, where Queen Elizabeth I once grew herbs and imported plants, has remained virtually unaltered. One of the most intriguing features of the gardens is the famous maze, established in William III's reign, which is large enough to get lost in. Special children's activities throughout the year include treasure hunts, trails and quizzes. Hampton Court can be very crowded during the summer holidays.

Open mid-March to mid-October daily 9.30a.m.–6.00p.m.; mid-October to mid-March daily 9.30a.m.–4.30p.m. (Opens Mon. at 10.15a.m. throughout the year).
Admission charge includes price of tour (daily at 11.15a.m., 1.45p.m. and 2.15p.m.); good-value family ticket.
BR: Hampton Court.
Nearby buses: 111, 216, 461, 513, R68.
River buses from Kingston, Richmond and Westminster.

Kensington Palace
The Broadwalk, Kensington, W8.
Tel. 071–937 9561.

Some of London's palaces, including Kensington, were originally houses belonging to noblemen which were later acquired by royalty. Preferring the Kensington countryside to the lower reaches of the Thames William III bought Nottingham House, as it was then called, soon after becoming king. Barely six months later the architect Christopher Wren had transformed Kensington into the cosiest palace in the city. Today the State Apartments are open to the public, and you can inspect the rooms Queen Victoria lived in as a young princess. Mementoes of her childhood, her nursery, dolls' house, clothes and jewellery, and even the cradle she slept in, are all on view. It was while living at Kensington Palace that Victoria was woken in the middle of the night to hear of her accession to the throne. Kensington Palace also houses the Royal Ceremonial Dress Collection. The Princess of Wales's fabulous wedding dress is there, along with many other costumes, some of which date back to the seventeenth century. The entrance to the palace is through an archway of limes known as the Sunken Garden. Close by is the Orangery, a fine example of an early eighteenth-century conservatory, hardly altered since it was built in 1704, but easily overlooked unless you know where to find it.

Kensington is one of the few palaces in London lived in by members of the royal family. Princess Margaret, the Duke and Duchess of Gloucester and Prince and Princess Michael of Kent all have private apartments in the palace. The Prince and Princess of Wales also lived here before their separation.

Open Mon.–Sat. 9.00a.m.–5.00p.m.; Sun. 1.00p.m.– 5.00p.m. Admission charge.
Nearest tubes: High Street Kensington, Queensway.
Nearby buses: 9, 9A, 10, 12, 49, 52, 70, 94, C1.

Kew Palace
Kew, Surrey.
Tel. 081–940 3321.

Once inside the main entrance to Kew Gardens (see page 93), you are only a short walk from Kew Palace, a small red-brick building which has an unexpectedly homely appearance for a former royal residence. Rebuilt by a merchant from the Netherlands in the early seventeenth century, the palace – formerly known as the Dutch House – was bought by King George III as a home for some of his fifteen children. The neatly laid-out, seventeenth-century-style gardens planted with herbs and flowers grown at that time are visible from an upstairs window. The palace itself contains unusual pieces of royal paraphernalia, including ivory counters and some silver filigree rattles which look far too elegant to have been chewed on, even by royal teeth.

Open April–Sept. Mon.–Sat. 11.00a.m.–5.30p.m.; Sun. 2.00p.m.–5.30p.m.
Admission charge.
BR: Kew Gardens.
Nearest tube: Kew Gardens.
Nearby buses: 65, 391.

Lambeth Palace
Lambeth Palace Road, SE1.
Tel. 071–928 8282.

Lambeth Palace has been the official home of the archbishops of Canterbury since the twelfth century, when early incumbents of the office were ferried across the Thames to meet the king at the Old Palace of Westminster (which stood on the site of the present Houses of Parliament). The oldest part of the building is the crypt under the chapel, which dates from 1220; the picturesque Tudor gatehouse entrance, Morton's Tower, was built in 1486. A fig tree has flourished in the palace courtyard since 1556; it was planted by Archbishop Cardinal Pole, a cousin of Queen Mary I. Tour groups are taken through the main parts of the palace to the state rooms and to the famous library, which contains Queen Elizabeth I's prayerbook. The Banqueting Hall has some fine old paintings of sixteenth- and seventeenth-century archbishops. When the present archbishop is in residence, his personal flag flies over the building. Parts of the palace grounds were opened to the public at the beginning of this century and some of the best views of the Houses of Parliament can be enjoyed from here. If you would like to be included in one of the palace tours – which take place on Wednesdays and Thursdays at 2.15p.m. – you must apply to the booking secretary in writing. Tours are not suitable for under-12s.

BR: Victoria, Waterloo.
Nearest tubes: Victoria, Waterloo.
Nearby buses: 3, 77, 159, 344, 507, C10.

St James's Palace
Pall Mall, SW1.

Nestling unobtrusively in a corner at the western end of Pall Mall, St James's Palace has been considerably altered and added to over the centuries. However, the fine red-brick clock tower and gatehouse are authentic enough, as is the sentry, whose very stillness might lead you to believe otherwise. Built by King Henry VIII, St James's came into its own after the disastrous fire at Whitehall Palace in 1698, when it was chosen as the official royal residence. So began the tradition of the famous court of St James. Although the palace lost favour during the reign of Queen Victoria, who moved down the road to Buckingham Palace, it is from one of the balconies of St James's that the death of a reigning monarch is formally announced and foreign ambassadors are still officially accredited to the court of St James. The stately white building next door to the palace is Clarence House, home of the Queen Mother, who moved here from Buckingham Palace after the coronation of the present Queen in 1953.

The palace is not open to the public.
Nearest tubes: Green Park, St James's Park.
Nearby buses: 8, 9, 14, 19, 22, 38.

11

Parks, gardens and open spaces

Even in the heart of London it is possible to walk into a park and feel a million miles away from the turmoil of urban life. In fact, more than 10 per cent of the city is given over to 'public open land' and you can walk through almost unbroken parkland all the way from Kensington Palace to Admiralty Arch. It costs nothing to enter London's parks, but there may be charges for the facilities inside. Most parks are open by 7.00a.m., often earlier, and they generally close at dusk. There are seasonal variations, so telephone to find out before you go.

ROYAL PARKS

Although not consistently blessed with brains, Britain's kings and queens have always been blessed with land – and plenty of it. Originally all London's parkland was owned by the monarch but gradually whole areas were given over to the public; they are still known today as the Royal Parks. Summer entertainments such as puppet and band shows are listed in a leaflet called *Royal Parks Band Performances*, available from main libraries and tourist offices.

Green Park
SE1.
Tel. 071–930 1793.

Green Park, one of the smaller Royal Parks, dates from the reign of King Charles II and was long a popular site for violent duels. It has few statues or formal flowerbeds, but the daffodils make a glorious display in spring. Walking through the park from Piccadilly to Buckingham Palace is a good way to avoid traffic and fumes. Exhibitions are sometimes held in the park, and on Sundays artists show their works on the railings along the Piccadilly side. At Hyde Park Corner there is the famous Hard Rock café, the first hamburger restaurant to open in London. Deckchairs are available for hire in the summer.

Nearest tube: Green Park.
Nearby buses: 2A, 2B, 8, 9, 10, 14, 16, 19, 22, 36, 38, 52, 73, 74, 82, 137, 137A.

Greenwich Park
SE10.
Tel. 081–858 2608.

The Italian painter Canaletto (1697–1768) had the right idea when he painted Greenwich from the Thames, capturing a marvellous view with a distinctly Mediterranean feel. Little has changed over the years and the river remains the best place from which to appreciate Greenwich. Close to the National Maritime Museum (see page 64) is Greenwich Park. The oldest of the Royal Parks, it was enclosed by the Duke of Gloucester as a hunting ground in 1433 and there are still deer here today. In the seventeenth century King Charles II brought in a landscape gardener to redesign the park; some of its fine old trees date from that period. At the northern end of the park is a boating lake, playground and sandpit. Greenwich Park tea pavilion is open daily from 10.00a.m.–7.00p.m. during the summer months and from 10.00a.m.–4.00p.m. in winter. The bandstand is 200 yards (180 metres) from Blackheath Gate and to the right of Blackheath Avenue.

BR: Greenwich.
Nearest tube: Island Gardens DLR, then Greenwich foot tunnel.
Nearby buses: 47, 53, 177, 188, 199.

Hyde Park
W1.
Tel. 071–298 2100.

It is rare to find over 300 acres of parkland in the centre of a city. In fact, if a plan by Oliver Cromwell had succeeded, the whole area of Hyde Park would probably have been sold for development. Fortunately for London, King Charles II returned it to public use after the Restoration in 1660. Covering a vast expanse of open space from Marble Arch to Kensington, Hyde Park has become a traditional place for rallies and demonstrations. Speaker's Corner, just inside the park by Marble Arch, is a famous location for outspoken orators to air their views on a whole variety of subjects, attracting great crowds at weekends. The Serpentine lake has boats and pedalos for hire Alternatively, you can swim in the Lido or watch riders exercising their horses in Rotten Row. On the south-west side of the park, not far from the Albert Memorial, there is a playground with swings and slides, and a bar and restaurant can be found by the Lido. The bandstand is 200 yards (180 metres) away from the Hyde Park Corner entrance to the park, to the right of the Serpentine Road. At Hyde Park Corner, near Apsley House, you cannot fail to notice the flamboyant Queen Elizabeth Gate which was commissioned by Prince Michael of Kent to commemorate the Queen Mother's ninetieth birthday in 1990. This fanciful structure has been described by critics as 'three-dimensional knitwear', a 'chocolate box' and 'My Little Pony'. It took 3 years to build and cost £2 million, all of which was raised by public subscription. At night it is floodlit.

Nearest tubes: Hyde Park Corner, Knightsbridge, Lancaster Gate, Marble Arch.
Nearby buses: 2A, 2B, 6, 7, 10, 12, 15, 16, 23, 36, 73, 74, 82, 88, 94, 98, 135, 137, 274.

Kensington Gardens
W8.
Tel. 071–724 3104.

King George II's wife, Caroline, loved parks. In fact she loved them so much that she decided to enlarge her own grounds at Kensington Palace by slicing off a part of Hyde Park and renaming it Kensington Gardens. Out of this grand idea emerged not only the Long Water and the Round Pond but also areas of garden which created a totally different atmosphere from that of the rest of Hyde Park. After Queen Caroline's death the public were allowed in, but only on certain days. Later, during the reign of Queen Victoria, the gardens were opened on a daily basis – a practice that continues. A walk from Hyde Park allows you to enjoy the variety of open parkland, and among the trees can be found flower walks and fountains, as well as the more formal flower gardens. On the west bank of the Long Water, close to the author J.M. Barrie's house stands the statue of his most famous character, Peter Pan. Immortalised in bronze and accompanied by Wendy, Peter is surrounded by squirrels, mice and fairies. Further north, close to the Bayswater Road, is a large playground. Just outside this is the Elfin Oak, an unusual-looking tree stump covered with carved goblins, elves and other fairytale characters. A little further up the Broad Walk is the Round Pond, where you can sail model boats and feed the ducks and geese. When there is enough wind, this is a good place to fly a kite.

Nearest tubes: High Street Kensington, Lancaster Gate, Queensway.
Nearby buses: 9, 9A, 10, 12, 49, 52, 70, 94, C1.

Regent's Park
NW1.
Tel. 071–486 7905.

In the sixteenth century the area of Regent's Park formed one of King Henry VIII's many hunting grounds. It continued to be used for hunting until Oliver Cromwell came to power and sold it to finance his debts. The new leaseholders, aware no doubt of the insecurity of their position, set about making a quick profit; with undignified haste, they chopped down over 15,000 trees, selling off the timber at a premium. After the Restoration, King Charles II decided to resell the land – presumably the existing tenants had to waive their rights – and from then on the area was used for dairy farming. In the nineteenth century the park was revamped for the Prince Regent (later George IV) by John Nash and opened to the public in 1838. Nash did an excellent job. His elegant terraces still flank the park and roses flourish in his secluded Queen Mary's Gardens, in the park's inner circle. The Regent's Park Open Air Theatre puts on productions here during the summer, when actors compete against low-flying jets and the vagaries of the English weather. Both Shakespearean and modern plays are shown. If you are lucky enough to catch a performance on a fine balmy evening, the park makes a perfect theatrical backdrop. Tennis courts and cricket, baseball and football pitches make the park an excellent centre for sporting activities. For younger children there are four separate playgrounds, and the lake has boats for hire and lots of different types of waterbirds to feed. There is a concert bandstand to the north of Regent's College, between the boating lake and the inner circle; free puppet shows are held here in the summer. London Zoo (see page 145) is situated on the north side of the park, and at Easter the popular Harness Horse Parade takes place around the inner circle (see page 13). There is a café in Queen Mary's Gardens.

Nearest tubes: Baker Street, Camden Town, Great Portland Street, Regent's Park.
Nearby buses: 2A, 2B, 13, 18, 27, 74, 82, 113, 139, 159, 274.

Richmond Park
Richmond, Surrey.
Tel. 081–948 3209.

Unlike the more sophisticated central London parks, Richmond is an enormous area of unspoilt country covering more than 10 square miles. Once a hunting ground of King Charles I, the park is still famous for its herds of red and fallow deer, which, although placid by nature, are by no means tame and can be dangerous during the early autumn mating season. Activities inside the park include riding, golf, football, fishing in Pen Ponds (by permit) and birdwatching, and it is a great place for tobogganing. The Woodland Garden in the southern corner (Ham Gate entrance) has a marvellous display of rhododendrons and azaleas in spring and early summer. There is a children's playground close to Ham Gate. White Lodge, originally a hunting lodge, was Queen Elizabeth the Queen Mother's first home after her marriage to the future King George VI; it is now occupied by the Royal Ballet School and opens to the public during August (afternoons only). A short distance from the main Richmond Gate entrance is the Pembroke tea house and gardens. There is access to the park on all sides and ample parking.

BR: Richmond.
Nearest tube: Richmond.
Nearby buses: 65, 371.

St James's Park
SW1.
Tel. 071–930 1793.

It is almost impossible to imagine St James's Park as a stretch of marshy ground, but that is indeed what it once was. Today it is one of the most glorious parks in London, thanks to King Charles II, who decided to create here a miniature version of the gardens at Versailles. Overlooked by Buckingham Palace and secluded enough to resemble the grounds of a stately home, St James's is unique. From the rangy pelicans standing in their sanctuary by the lake to the thousands of ducks and geese on Duck Island, the park is teeming with wildlife, some of which is tame enough to eat out of your hand. For a more organised approach to feeding, watch the pelicans having their daily tea at 3.00p.m. on the eastern side of the lake. Trees and shrubs now line the famous Birdcage Walk, named after the aviaries that were here in Charles II's day. It was customary in that period for foreign dignitaries to give gifts of animals and birds, and the park benefited from this practice on a number of occasions. The first pair of pelicans to nest here were a present to the king from the Russian ambassador; the strangest member of this royal menagerie was a pelican with a wooden leg. One of the best views of the park is from the little bridge over the centre of the lake. Looking south towards the Thames, you can glimpse the turrets, towers and spires of London rising above the trees, and to the west is the imposing façade of Buckingham Palace. There are no organised games in the park today, but it was once the king's favourite place for playing the popular French game of *palle maille*, or croquet – from which the Mall, which borders the north side of the park, takes its name. There is a small playground at the western end and a bandstand for summer lunchtime concerts 100 yards (90 metres) south of Marlborough Gate. The Cake House café and restaurant is open all year round.

Nearest tubes: St James's Park, Westminster.
Nearby buses: 3, 6, 9, 11, 12, 13, 15, 23, 24, 29, 30, 53, 77A, 88, 94, 109, 139, 159, 176, 184, 196.

OTHER PARKS AND GARDENS

Alexandra Palace and Park
Muswell Hill, N22.
Tel. 081–365 2121.

Situated in over 400 acres of parkland and 300 feet (90 metres) above sea-level, 'Ally Pally' was built in 1873, during Queen Victoria's reign, to emulate the Crystal Palace in Sydenham (see page 90). Unfortunately, it burnt down soon after completion and, although partially restored, did not come into its own until 1936, when the BBC made its first live broadcast from the television studios here. In those early days few people had television and transmission covered a radius of only 30 miles. During the succeeding years, however, the vast transmitters became a well-known landmark, until 1956, when the BBC began to broadcast from the television centre at Shepherd's Bush. Today Alexandra Palace is a major exhibition centre hosting a variety of events, including car and motorbike shows, antique and craft fairs, as well as occasional concerts. In front of Alexandra Palace, overlooking central London, is an extensive park with a children's play area, boating lakes, paddling pool, indoor ice rink and ski centre (tel. 081–888 2284). There is always something going on here during the holidays; telephone the park for details of current events.

Nearest tube: Wood Green.
Nearby bus: W3.

Battersea Park
Battersea Park Road, SW11.
Tel. 081–871 7530.

Even though the permanent funfair that used to be here closed down in the 1970s, there is still a lot to do in this large park overlooking the Thames. It has a sizeable boating lake, a paddling pool, a sandpit, a one o'clock club for pre-school children, a deer enclosure, a running track and tennis courts. There are plenty of activities for children during the summer holidays, including pony rides and puppet shows. The colourful annual Easter Parade also takes place here (see page 13).

BR: Battersea Park.
Nearest tube: Sloane Square.
Nearby buses: 19, 37.

Blackheath
SE3.
Tel. 081–305 1807.

Once the haunt of highwaymen, this wide open space is now the home of travelling shows and fairs. It is also one of the best places to fly a kite. There is a pond for sailing model boats and funfairs are held at Bank Holidays (see page 13).

BR: Blackheath.
Nearby buses: 54, 89, 108, 178, 202.

Brent Lodge Park
Church Road, Hanwell, W7.
Tel. 081–566 1929.

Affectionately known as 'the bunny park' because of its once huge rabbit population, Brent Lodge, a large area of land surrounded by dense trees, is one of London's liveliest open spaces. Guinea pigs, squirrels and rabbits all congregate in the 'big pen'. Donkeys, sheep and wallabies wander freely, and a small section inside the main building has been set aside for frogs, spiders, lizards, toads, scorpions and a piranha tank. Two families of marmosets also live here, and a pair of capuchin monkeys entertain visitors with tricks.

BR: Hanwell.
Nearby buses: 207, 232.

Clissold Park
Green Lanes, N4.
Tel. 081–800 1021.

There is an animal enclosure in the park with deer, peacocks, cranes and a small aviary filled with tropical birds. The playground has a paddling pool.

Nearest tube: Manor House.
Nearby buses: 141, 171A.

Chelsea Physic Garden
66 Royal Hospital Road, SW3.
Tel. 071–352 5646.

This beautiful garden was created in the seventeenth century by the Worshipful Company of Apothecaries to promote the study of the healing properties of plants. As you wander through 4 acres of some of the most intensively cultivated ground in the country, you will see not only herbs but also plants from as far afield as South America, southern Europe and Australia. During the eighteenth century cotton seeds grown in the Physic Garden were sent to America to establish what became the staple crop of the new colony of Georgia. The garden tea room sells a delicious selection of cakes.

Open April–Oct. Wed. and Sun. 2.00p.m.–5.00p.m.
Admission charge.
Nearest tube: Sloane Square.
Nearby buses: 11, 137, 239.

Crystal Palace and Park
Crystal Palace Park Road, SE20.
Tel. 081–778 7148.

Crystal Palace was the name given to Joseph Paxton's magnificent conservatory, made entirely of iron and glass, built for the Great Exhibition of 1851, on the prompting of the Prince Consort, Albert. Albert's grand idea was to create a giant showcase for exhibits that would demonstrate to the world Britain's industrial supremacy. Originally sited in Hyde Park, the palace was transported to Sydenham in 1854, where it became a popular attraction, but it burnt down in 1936 and now only the foundations remain. The site has been transformed into a national sports stadium and park. In the park, the islands in the lake are occupied by twenty enormous plaster dinosaurs dating from the Great Exhibition of 1951. There are plenty of live animals here too, including Shire horses, goats, pigs and cows in the park's urban farm. This is situated in the top western corner of the park above the dinosaurs. There is also boating and fishing in the lake (by permit), a miniature railway track (Sundays only) and a small fairground, as well as a playground and one o'clock club for under-5s, a ski centre (tel. 081–778 0131) and, of course, the sports centre. Look out for the unusual T maze in the park, the biggest circular maze in the south of England, which has been redesigned to exactly the same specifications as the original, planted in 1864. A series of 'buzz' events are held during the Easter and summer holidays, when special activities such as egg hunts, puppet shows and modelling sessions are arranged for younger children. There is a café in the park.

Open April–Sept., Mon.–Fri. 11.00a.m.–5.00p.m., Sat. and Sun. 11.00a.m.–5.30p.m.; Oct.–March, Mon.–Fri. 11.00a.m.–3.30p.m., Sat. and Sun. 11.00a.m.–4.00p.m.
BR: Crystal Palace, Penge West.
Nearest tube: Brixton.
Nearby buses: 2B, 3, 63, 122, 137, 154, 157, 176, 202, 227, 249, 351, 358.

Dulwich Park
College Road, SE21.
Tel. 081–693 5737.

Dulwich Park consists of 72 acres of parkland, including an aviary, a boating lake and tennis courts. There is a full programme of children's entertainment in the summer. The park has a café.

BR: North Dulwich, West Dulwich.
Nearest tube: Brixton.
Nearby buses: 12, 63, 78, 176, 185.

Finsbury Park
Endymion Road, N4.
Tel. 071–263 5001.

One of north London's smaller parks, Finsbury is nevertheless good fun for a day out. It has a boating lake, travelling puppet shows in summer and roller-skating sessions at weekends (see page 187).

Nearest tubes: Finsbury Park, Manor House.
Nearby buses: 4, 19, 29, 106, 141, 171, 210, 221, 230, 279, W2, W3, W7.

Hampstead Heath
NW3.
Tel. 071–485 4491.

This 800-acre stretch of open heathland embraces Parliament Hill, Golders Hill and Kenwood House and grounds. A sanctuary for wildlife, it is a wonderfully unspoilt area to explore, and there is so much going on that you could easily spend a whole day here and not see it all. Activities include fishing, boating, dry skiing, horse riding and tennis; the open spaces attract informal games of football and rounders. Whitestone Pond, one of three ponds on the heath, is a favourite spot for testing model sailing boats, and swimming is allowed in the ponds (see page 183). Parliament Hill – named after the Guy Fawkes conspirators, who were rumoured to have planned to meet here to watch the Houses of Parliament burn – is popular for kite flying and offers one of the best views over London. Bank Holiday fairs are held in the Vale of Health at the top of Heath Street, and outdoor painting exhibitions take place here in summer beside the railings. Free musical events are staged on the bandstands at Golders Hill and Parliament Hill on Sunday afternoons in summer. Programmes include light orchestral pieces and works by brass bands and jazz bands. A varied programme of free children's events is organised during the summer holidays on the Parliament Hill and Golders Hill bandstands, including puppet shows, magicians and clowns. For up-to-the-minute details of the heath's many activities, telephone 081–348 9908 for a free copy of the Hampstead Heath diary.

A short distance away from the main heath, down North End Road, is Golders Hill Park (West Heath). It has a pretty lake and a small zoo with deer, goats and various birds. Touring puppet shows visit here in the summer, and during the school holidays brightly coloured inflatables are set up for younger children to play on. Bands perform concerts on Sunday afternoons in summer. This is a good place for a picnic. The café is open April–Oct.

At the north end of the heath, surrounded by acres of parkland, is Kenwood House, a splendid eighteenth-century building given to the nation by the Earl of Iveagh. Also on view is his famous collection of paintings, many of which feature women and children, by such masters as Rembrandt, Vermeer and Reynolds. The gardens are particularly lovely in spring and early summer, and the sloping lawns leading down to the lake form a natural setting for the popular summer concerts held here. There is a café in the Coach House.

Kenwood House open daily 10.00a.m.–6.00p.m. in summer (closes 4.00p.m. in winter).
Admission free.

For Parliament Hill
BR: Gospel Oak.
Nearest tube: Kentish Town.
Nearby buses: 46, 214, C2, C11, C12.

For Golders Hill
Nearest tube: Golders Green.
Nearby buses: 210, 268.

For Kenwood
Nearest tubes: Archway, Golders Green.
Nearby buses: 210, 271.

Holland Park
W8.
Tel. 071–602 2226.

Famous for its peacocks and colourful formal gardens, Holland Park originally formed the grounds of the eighteenth-century Holland House. It became a public park in the 1950s after the house had been badly bombed during the Second World War. One of London's most attractive open spaces, Holland Park includes an extensive area of woodland that is full of wildlife. The old Orangery is often used for art exhibitions, and in the restored east wing of the house there is an open-air theatre offering a variety of events. An adventure playground and a one o'clock club can be found near the main entrance, and there is a café near the Orangery.

Nearest tubes: Holland Park, High Street Kensington.
Nearby buses: 9, 9A, 10, 27, 28, 49.

Kew Gardens
Kew Road, Richmond.
Tel. 081–940 1171.

Kew Gardens is the world's leading centre for botanical research. Nearly 300 acres are devoted to the cultivation and protection of numerous species of plants and trees, and the whole area is open to the public. You can explore the stunning glass-houses, picnic near the Pagoda, visit Queen Charlotte's Cottage (in the south-west corner), wander around Kew Palace (see page 82), or simply walk by the river and enjoy the views. A recent addition to the gardens is the Princess of Wales Conservatory, where different extremes of climate are simulated by computer within one enormous greenhouse. Tropical vegetation thrives not far from gaily coloured cactuses, tall banana trees with clusters of green fruits grow a few yards from carnivorous plants; and heated pools are full of glorious giant water lilies which look firm enough to lie on. Nearby and not easily overlooked is Decimus Burton's gigantic glass Palm House, dating from 1845. Recently restored, it must rank as one of the finest tropical greenhouses ever built. The eighteenth-century Orangery, one of the loveliest buildings in the gardens, is now an exhibition centre and café. Although Kew is open all year round, one of the best times to visit is in spring, when the lawns are carpeted with crocuses and daffodils, followed a few weeks later by magnificent displays of rhododendrons and azaleas. The visitor centre at the Victoria Gate entrance has a bookshop, gift shop and a video presentation explaining Kew's role as a scientific establishment.

The Orangery self-service restaurant (main entrance) is open from 12 noon to one hour before the gardens close. They serve excellent cream teas in summer. The Bakery (main entrance) has covered seating and sells everything from pizzas and sausage rolls to doughnuts and pastries. It is open from Easter to the end of October 10.00a.m.–5.30p.m. weekdays, Sunday 10.00a.m.– 7.00p.m.; open on Sundays only November to Easter. Closes one hour before gardens. The Pavilion snack bar (Victoria or Lion Gate entrance) is open from 10.00a.m.–5.30p.m. Monday to Saturday Easter to mid-October. Maps of the gardens are available at the entrance gates.

Open daily 9.30a.m.–6.00p.m. in summer (closes 4.00p.m. in winter).
Admission charge; Good-value family ticket.
BR: Kew Bridge.
Nearest tube: Kew Gardens.
Nearby buses: 65, 391.

Millbank Gardens
John Islip Street, SW1.

Directly behind the Tate Gallery, Millbank Gardens with their neat lawns and pretty flower beds make an ideal picnic place after visiting the gallery. The gardens close at the end of British Summer Time and reopen at the end of February.

Nearest tube: Pimlico.
Nearby buses: 2, 3, 36, 77, 88.

Postman's Park
King Edward Street, EC1.

Known as Postman's Park because of its proximity to the General Post Office, the delightful gardens here are only a short walk from St Paul's Cathedral and provide an unexpectedly peaceful oasis in the heart of the City.

Nearest tube: St Paul's.
Nearby buses: 11, 25, 172, 501, 521.

Primrose Hill
NW8.
Tel. 071–486 7905.

The views from the top of Primrose Hill are some of the finest in

London. There is a small playground at the bottom of the hill. A fine firework display is held here during the week of 5 November (see page 20), and the hill is excellent for tobogganing.

Nearest tubes: Camden Town, Chalk Farm.
Nearby buses: 31, C11, C12.

Ravenscourt Park
Paddenswick Road, W6.
Tel. 081–741 2051.

With its adventure playground, one o'clock club, paddling pool and climbing frames, this park is ideal for children of all ages. There are several tennis courts and a basketball pitch. A café is open during the summer months only.

Nearest tube: Ravenscourt Park.
Nearby buses: 27, 94, 237, 267.

Syon Park
Brentford, Middlesex.
Tel. 081–560 0881.

From a distance, Syon House resembles a cardboard cut-out model, complete with its own toy lion marching along the balustrades. This stately eighteenth-century mansion was designed by the architect Robert Adam and is said to be his finest work. The park was laid out by the famous landscape gardener Capability Brown and the gardens include a magnificent glass conservatory (complete with aquarium), which was the inspiration for the original Crystal Palace. There is also a first-rate garden centre and a butterfly house containing more than a thousand free-flying butterflies, some of which are huge and beautifully marked. During the summer you can see the different stages of the insects' development from caterpillar to pupa to butterfly. A permanent exhibition includes giant spiders, scorpions, stick insects, African tree frogs and a colony of leaf cutting ants. A good self-service restaurant sells snacks and lunches.

House open Wed.–Sun. 11.00a.m.–5.00p.m. April–Sept.; Sun. only during Oct. Other visits by appointment.
Butterfly house open daily 9.00a.m.–5.00p.m.
Gardens open May–Sept. daily 10.00a.m.–6.00p.m.; Oct.–April 10.00a.m.–5.00p.m.
Admission charge.
BR: Kew Bridge then 237 or 267 bus to Brentlea Gate.
Nearest tube: Gunnersbury then bus as above.

Victoria Embankment Gardens
Embankment, SW1.

Beautiful and unexpectedly large, Victoria Embankment Gardens can easily be overlooked. But if you need a break from the hustle and bustle of Covent Garden, then here is where to revive flagging spirits. Bands play in summer, you can see boats plying up and down the river and the flower gardens are splendid. In the section to the east of Charing Cross is a delightful statue of a soldier riding a camel.

Nearest tube: Embankment.
Nearby buses: 3, 6, 9, 11, 12, 13, 15, 23, 53, 77A, 94, 139, 159, 176.

Victoria Park
E2.
Tel. 081–985 1957.

The largest open space in east London, Victoria Park is beautifully laid out, with gardens, a boating lake and a lido. There is a small compound containing guinea pigs, rabbits and chickens, and a separate enclosure which is the permanent home of a small herd of fallow deer.

Nearest tube: Bethnal Green.
Nearby buses: 8, 30, 277.

Victoria Tower Gardens
Millbank, SW1.

The gardens lie a little to the west of the Houses of Parliament and make a perfect stopping off point when visiting the surrounding area. Emmeline Pankhurst, the famous women's suffrage leader, has her statue here as do Rodin's Burghers of Calais who so bravely gave their lives to save the city.

Nearest tube: Westminster.
Nearby buses: 3, 77, 159.

WILDLIFE CENTRES

Apart from London's extensive parklands, there are a number of places in the city which have been set aside to protect nature. Here, frogs flourish, wild flowers bloom and nestboxes are put up for birds to lay their eggs. These safe havens for London's wildlife are not only vitally important for conservation but also enable city children to witness the processes of nature at first-hand. The London Wildlife Trust runs several nature reserves and a great many campaigns. Foxes, hedgehogs, owls, bees and kestrels have all received special attention from the trust, and thousands of people have helped with surveys. The trust has all the latest information on environmental issues. For more details, telephone 071–278 6612 or write to the London Wildlife Trust, 80 York Way, London N1 9AG.

Camley Street Natural Park
12 Camley Street, NW1.
Tel. 071–833 2311.

Camley Street Park is managed by the London Wildlife Trust, with support from Camden Council and local volunteers, who have managed to create a delightful oasis of wildlife in the desolate area behind King's Cross. It covers 2 acres of open space, flanked by the Regent's Canal and busy streets and railway lines. The park has a large pond, which in summer attracts sticklebacks, pond skaters and water boatmen. In springtime, when frogs and newts are about, children can ask for a net and try 'pond dipping'. The bird hide is a great place to watch the comings and goings of various birds in the park without being seen. Mallards and moorhens can be observed nesting on the pond, and herons have also been sighted. Every inch of the nature reserve has been put to good use. The plants in the wildlife garden, for instance, have been carefully chosen to improve the environment and attract wildlife. There are push-button slide shows in the nature centre, and special exhibitions are mounted in the visitor area during the year.

Open Mon.–Thurs. 9.00a.m.–5.00p.m.; Sat.–Sun. 11.00a.m.–5.00p.m. (closes 4.00p.m. in winter).
BR: King's Cross.
Nearest tube: King's Cross.
Nearby buses: 10, 14, 17, 18, 30, 45, 46, 63, 73, 74, 214, 221, 259, C12.

Crane Park Island
Crane Park, Twickenham, Middlesex.
Tel. 081–898 9582.

Gunpowder was manufactured at Crane Park Island until 1926, and the remains of the industry can be seen in the Tower, now a listed building used as a nature centre. Much of the value of Crane Park springs from the variety of habitats in the area. Woodland, scrub and damp ground support many different species of wildlife, including herons, woodpeckers, kestrels and edible frogs.

Open all the time, but if you want to arrange special activities, such as guided walks or river dipping, then ring the warden on the above number.
Admission free.
BR: Whitton.
Nearest tubes: Richmond, Hounslow East.
Nearby buses: 110, 202.

Gunnersbury Triangle Nature Reserve
Bollo Lane, W4.
Tel. 081–747 3881.

At one time orchards flourished here, but in the late nineteenth century a 6-acre triangle was isolated from the surrounding area by railway tracks when the District and Northern tube lines were built. Since the 1950s nature has been left to its own devices and woodland has grown up naturally. Keen birdwatchers will enjoy the 45-minute nature trail around Gunnersbury triangle. There are foxes' paths hollowed out under the fences and blue tits, magpies and robins sheltering in the silver-birch wood. Take wellingtons if the weather is wet, and maybe a camera or tape recorder to record your visit.

Open Mon.–Fri. 8.30a.m.–4.30p.m.; Sun. 2.00p.m.–4.30p.m.
Admission free.
Nearest tube: Chiswick Park.
Nearby buses: 27, E3.

London Ecology Centre
45 Shelton Street, Covent Garden, WC2.
Tel. 071–379 4324.

At London's Ecology Centre you can keep up to date with all the latest information on environmental issues. There is a small shop to browse in and a good café.

Open Mon.–Sat. 10.00a.m.–6.00p.m.
Nearest tubes: Covent Garden, Leicester Square.
Nearby buses: 14, 19, 24, 29, 38, 176.

London Wildlife Garden Centre
28 Marsden Road, Peckham, SE15.
Tel. 071–252 9186.

The centre is a hive of information on anything to do with gardens, and their selection of wildflowers is second to none. The award-winning visitor centre is an amazing self-build construction made entirely of natural materials and the roof, which doubles as a wild flower meadow, has to be seen to be believed. The centre runs a regular children's nature club and puts on a variety of events throughout the year.

Open Tues.–Thurs. and Sun. 11.00a.m.–4.00p.m.
BR: East Dulwich.
Nearby buses: 12, 37, 176, 184, 185, P3.

Sydenham Hill Wood
Crescent Wood Road, SE26.
Tel. 071–278 6612.

The London Wildlife Trust took over Sydenham Wood in 1982, fought off threats from developers and has since made good use of its potential as a valuable urban nature reserve. This is the last remaining section of the ancient Great North Wood, and some of the trees are more than 400 years old. Plants that grow here include wild garlic, wood anemone and barren strawberry, as well as countless fungi, rare insects, woodland mammals and over fifty species of birds.

Open at all times.
Admission free.
BR: Sydenham Hill.
Nearby bus: 63.

CEMETERIES

It is hard to imagine a less likely venue than a cemetery for a jolly day out, but, mainly because of their size and location, a number of London's cemeteries make excellent wildlife sanctuaries, as well as being interesting in their own right. They also have a certain eerie attraction, to which some children seem to respond.

Bunhill Burial Fields
Bunhill Fields, City Road, EC1.

Originally known as Bone Hill Fields, this site holds more than 120,000 bodies, for it was originally a Saxon burial ground. John Bunyan, the author of *Pilgrim's Progress*, is buried here, as is Daniel Defoe of *Robinson Crusoe* fame and the Methodist leader John Wesley.

Open Mon.–Fri. 8.00a.m.–4.00p.m.; Sat. and Sun. 9.30a.m.–4.00p.m.
Nearest tubes: Moorgate, Old Street.
Nearby buses: 5, 43, 55, 76, 141, 214, 243, 271, 505.

Highgate Cemetery
Swains Lane, Highgate, N6.
Tel. 081–340 1834.

Highgate is London's most well-known cemetery. Opened in 1838, it now contains more than 50,000 tombs, as well as some extraordinary memorials and monuments, the largest of which commemorates a Victorian entrepreneur and cost a startling £5000. The giant cedar in the western part of the cemetery, surrounded by catacombs and obelisks, gives the place a sombre, haunted feel, and some of the monuments look as though they might have appeared in the film of Arthur Conan Doyle's *The Hound of the Baskervilles*. Karl Marx's grave can be found on the eastern side of Swains Lane, which bisects the cemetery. His huge figurehead is positioned over a burial chamber on which are written the immortal lines starting 'Workers of the world unite'. Other, less politically minded people are also buried here – the novelist George Eliot, the poet Christina Rossetti and one of Britain's greatest actors of recent times, Sir Ralph Richardson.

East section open daily April–Oct. 10.00a.m.–5.00p.m.; Nov.–March 10.30a.m.–3.00p.m.
West section tours Tues.–Fri. 12.00 noon; 2.00p.m., 3.00p.m.; Sat.–Sun. each hour between 11.00a.m. and 3.00p.m.
Admission charge.
Nearest tube: Archway.
Nearby buses: 143, C10, C11.

Kensal Green Cemetery
Harrow Road, NW10.

Cemeteries only became respectable in the Victorian era. Before then people were buried in a more makeshift fashion, and burial sites posed a serious health hazard. Kensal Green, created in 1833, was inner London's first public cemetery. Many noteworthy people are buried here, including two of King George III's children, novelists Anthony Trollope and William Thackeray, and the daring Emile Blondin, who walked across Niagara Falls on a tightrope. A gentler walk along the Grand Union Canal, which borders the cemetery, leads to Little Venice.

Open April–Sept. Mon.–Sat. 9.00a.m.–6.00p.m.; Sun. 2.00p.m.–6.00p.m. Oct.–March Mon.–Sat. 9.00a.m.–dusk; Sun. 2.00p.m.–dusk.
Nearest tube: Kensal Green.
Nearby buses: 15, 23, 52, 70, 295, 302.

12

Cathedrals and churches

Some of the most intriguing people and stories from the past are found in London's grandest churches. Where else can you find Dick Whittington, a stuffed parrot and where whispering in church is positively encouraged? It is easy to forget that churches are buildings too. Some of them became the life's work of their architects and builders and it is easy to see why. Imagine trying to move tons of stone and wood into a position over 300 feet (100 metres) up in the air without a modern crane! This section does not intend to be a comprehensive listing of cathedrals and churches in London, but a flavour of some of our most glorious ecclesiastical buildings which are well worth a visit.

St Paul's Cathedral
Ludgate Hill, EC4.
Tel. 071–248 2705.

Although it is hemmed in by ugly buildings constructed in the 1960s

and 1970s, St Paul's Cathedral manages to retain an air of lofty calm at the top of Ludgate Hill. Its immediate predecessor was burnt down in the Great Fire of 1666, and the architect Sir Christopher Wren began work on the new St Paul's in 1675. It took over thirty-five years to build. By the time the cathedral was finished and the enormous dome was in place, Wren was an old man. The dome was a revolutionary construction; its inner layers consist of three shells lying one inside the other like a Russian doll. If you climb up to the Whispering Gallery and speak quietly while facing the wall, your voice will be heard on the far side of the dome, over 100 feet (30 metres) away. The fine paintings on the cathedral ceiling by James Thornhill show scenes from the life of St Paul the apostle. These frescoes might have been the last work completed by this painter, had it not been for a quick-thinking assistant. As he was standing on a platform 218 feet (66 metres) in the air, Thornhill decided to step back for a better view of the work on which he was engaged. He was so close to the edge that one more move would have sent him crashing to the stone floor below. The assistant realised that it would be fruitless to reach out for his master, so he calmly walked over to the new painting, grabbed a brush and began to slap paint on it. Furious, Thornhill rushed forward, away from the edge and certain death. Anyone with a head for heights and enough stamina might feel like climbing the 627 steps to the Golden Ball at the very top of St Paul's in order to enjoy the magnificent views of London below. Down on firmer ground in the crypt lies Christopher Wren himself, along with other famous historical figures such as Lord Nelson and the Duke of Wellington. Wren's own epitaph is a fitting one: 'Reader, if you seek his monument, look around you'. St Paul's bell, 'Great Paul', is rung daily at 1.00p.m. for five minutes.

Open Mon.–Sat. 9.15a.m.–4.15p.m.; four tours daily; services on Sunday.
Admission charge; extra charge to go up into the dome.
Nearest tube: St Paul's.
Nearby buses: 4, 11, 15, 17, 23, 26, 76, 172, 521.

Southwark Cathedral
Cathedral Street, SE1.

This fine thirteenth-century cathedral, built on the site of a Norman church destroyed by fire in 1212, is one of England's oldest Gothic church buildings, second only to Westminster Abbey. While parts of the cathedral have survived from the thirteenth century, it has undergone many architectural changes, of which the reconstruction of the Victorian nave is perhaps the most impressive. The cathedral lies in the heart of Shakespeare's London and fittingly has many theatrical links. In the south aisle of the nave there is a memorial to the great bard himself. His brother Edmund is also buried here, along with the dramatist John Fletcher and the poet John Gower, a contemporary of

Chaucer. Another flamboyant character who might well have taken to the stage is a local doctor of sorts called Lionel Lockyer. His fame derived from a pill he claimed to have invented which supposedly cured every known illness. His epitaph includes the lines: 'His virtues and his pills are so well known/That envy can't confine them under stone.' The Harvard Chapel is dedicated to the memory of the founder of one of the top universities in the United States, John Harvard. Born in Southwark and baptised in the cathedral in 1608, he died of consumption a year after emigrating to Massachusetts.

Open daily 9.00a.m.–6.00p.m.
BR: London Bridge.
Nearest tube: London Bridge.
Nearby buses: 4, 17, 21, 22A, 35, 40, 43, 47, 48, 133, 214, 344, 501, 521, D1, D11, P3, P11.

Westminster Abbey
Broad Sanctuary, SW1.
Tel. 071–222 5152.

There is a touch of magic about Westminster Abbey – it is a place that everyone should visit. More than any other building in London, it symbolises the heart and soul of the city; and, with its walls cleaned of

decades of soot and grime, it has never looked finer than it does today. Since Edward the Confessor began building Westminster Abbey nearly 1000 years ago, the coronations of almost all English sovereigns from William the Conqueror to our present Queen have taken place here. The two exceptions were King Edward V, who was murdered, and King Edward VIII, who abdicated before he could be crowned. Many monarchs have also been laid to rest here. Thirteen kings, five queens and many lesser mortals lie inside the abbey, although the grandness of some of their tombs may tell us more about the extent of the occupants' financial resources than any other merits they may have possessed. In fact, the abbey is so crammed with tombs and effigies that one impecunious soul had to be buried standing up. To be buried in the abbey has been the final goal of many an ambitious career. The tomb of the Unknown Warrior, near the west entrance, is a lasting memorial to all the unidentified British soldiers who died in the First World War. In the north aisle, leading to the Royal Chapels, is a small stained-glass window of Dick Whittington and his cat. Whittington, it seems, began to make his fortune when apprenticed to his cousin, a prosperous merchant. He then rose through the ranks to become Lord Mayor of London – a position he held four times. If you continue along the north transept, you reach Statesmen's Aisle, which is full of larger-than-life statues of past prime ministers, including Gladstone, Disraeli and Palmerston. But not everyone in the abbey is so famous. In the east aisle you will come across a striking tomb of the Nightingale family, who seem to be emerging from the stone in which they are carved. A villainous-looking ghost of death is about to carry them off and Mrs Nightingale has fainted into the arms of her husband. There are many children in the abbey, cherubic and otherwise. At the far end of Queen Elizabeth I's tomb lies a monument to the two daughters of King James I of England and VI of Scotland. Princess Sophia, who died when she was three days old, lies forlornly in her stone cot, while her sister, standing nearby, has the appearance of a young girl, although she was only two years old when she died. The urn above them contains the bones of two young boys found in the Tower of London in 1674. King Charles II ordered them to be placed here, believing them to be the skeletons of King Edward V and his brother, the Duke of York, 'the princes in the Tower', who are believed to have been murdered in 1483.

The oldest part of the abbey is Edward the Confessor's Chapel – a lofty, regal place, set apart from the rest by its austerity. Close by the Confessor's tomb stands the battered but glorious Coronation Chair, which has been used in coronation ceremonies since the early fourteenth century. It has left the abbey only once, when Oliver Cromwell removed it to Westminster Hall for his own use. The graffiti on the upper part of the seat demonstrate all too clearly how, even centuries ago, visitors could not resist leaving their marks. The chair is held in position by four golden lions and underneath it lies the ancient Scottish coronation seat, the Stone of Scone. This too has left the abbey only once since its arrival in 1296; it was stolen by Scottish Nationalists in 1950 and returned the following year. The Undercroft Museum, located in the abbey cloisters, is full of unexpected royal treasures, including King Henry V's sword and saddle and the death mask of King Henry VII, made in 1509. An amusing exhibit is the oldest stuffed parrot in England: it is 400 years old (and looks it), but in its heyday it escorted the Duchess of Richmond when she dined with King Charles II. For a quiet breath of fresh air, visit the College Garden (open Thursdays only) at the far end of the cloisters; under cultivation for more than 900 years, it must be one of the oldest gardens in England.

Open Mon.–Fri. 9.20a.m.–4.00p.m.; Sat. 9.00a.m.– 2.00p.m. and 3.45p.m.–5.00p.m.; Services only on Sunday. Museum open daily 10.30a.m.–4.00p.m.
Admission charges to the Royal Chapels, Poet's Corner and Museum, otherwise free; free admission to the entire abbey Wed. 6.00p.m.– 7.45p.m.
Tours: April–Oct. Mon.–Fri. 10.00a.m., 10.30a.m., 11.00a.m., 2.00p.m., 2.30p.m., 3.00p.m.; Sat. 10.00a.m., 11.00a.m., 12.30p.m.; Nov.–March Mon.–Fri. 10.00a.m., 11.00a.m., 2.00p.m., 3.00p.m.; Sat. 10.00a.m., 11.00a.m., 12.30p.m.
Garden: April–Oct. Thurs. 10.00a.m.–6.00p.m.; Nov.–March Thurs. 10.00a.m.–4.00p.m.
Nearest tube: Westminster.
Nearby buses: 3, 11, 12, 24, 53, 77A, 88, 109, 159, 184, 196, 511.

Westminster Cathedral
Ashley Place, Victoria Street, SW1.
Tel. 071–834 7452.

Set back from the bustle of Victoria Street, Westminster Cathedral looms out unexpectedly from a sea of modern office blocks and shops. The most important Catholic church in England, this is the seat of the Cardinal Archbishop of Westminster. Although Byzantine in style, it is in fact a relatively modern building, completed in 1903. With its alternating grey and red rows of brickwork, it presents a faintly eastern image, at odds with the surrounding architecture. Over 12.5 million bricks were used in its construction and the lofty bell-tower, 270 feet (83 metres) high, can be ascended by a lift, which operates between April and September. Inside, the cathedral is richly decorated with marble and mosaics and contains many valuable works of art. The best time to tour the cathedral is between 1.30p.m. and 5.00p.m., when there are no services.

Open daily 7.00a.m.–8.00p.m.
Admission charge for the bell-tower.
BR: Victoria.
Nearest tube: Victoria.
Nearby buses: 11, 24, 507, 511.

13

Monuments and buildings

Whether you walk or drive around any city, its special qualities are found in its monuments and buildings. The skyline is changing all the time, and it can be fun when travelling around town to look up above the level of the pavement and find out what gives London its shape and character and how it has developed into the city we know today.

Bank of England
Threadneedle Street, EC2.
Tel. 071–601 4444.

The Bank of England was founded in 1694 to help King William III raise money for his war against France, and since its very early days it has been known as the government's bank. In 1946 it was nationalised and its capital stock transferred to the Treasury. Not only is the nation's gold reserve stored in the Bank of England's vaults, but it is the only bank that can issue paper money. The museum (see page 46) and entrance hall are the only parts of the building to which the general public is admitted, but from here you can glimpse the central court and the bank's messengers, conspicuous in their pink jackets and scarlet waistcoats. There are several stories about how the bank got its nickname 'the Old Lady of Threadneedle Street'. One concerns a mysterious woman who was said to have made daily visits to the bank asking to see her brother, who had been hanged for printing counterfeit money. The bank was established on its present site in 1788; although most of the seventeenth-century building was revamped in the 1930s, the formidable outside walls designed by Sir John Soane (see page 71) remain. The bank lacks windows for security reasons, and following the riots of the late 1700s, when the bank was under threat, it was assigned its own guards – a practice which continued until 1973, when they were replaced by modern internal security systems.

Open Mon.–Fri. 10.00a.m.–5.00p.m.
Nearest tube: Bank.
Nearby buses: 8, 11, 15B, 21, 22B, 23, 25, 26, 43, 76, 133, 149, 214, 501, D9.

Cleopatra's Needle
Victoria Embankment, SW1.

Although Cleopatra's Needle has little to do with the ancient Egyptian queen, it once stood in front of the palace in which she died. One of a pair – the other stands in New York's Central Park – the monument is more than 3000 years old and was presented to this country by the viceroy of Egypt in 1819. It was another sixty years, however, before it reached London. Not only was the journey a long and difficult one but, at £15,000, extremely costly. The hieroglyphics etched on the side of the monument commemorate two Egyptian rulers; underneath it is buried a mixed bag of Victorian oddities, including a railway guide, a copy of the Bible and some British money.

Nearest tubes: Charing Cross, Embankment.
Nearby buses: 1, 4, 6, 9, 11, 13, 15, 23, 26, 76, 77A, 168, 171, 176, 188, 196, 501, 505, 521.

Duke of York's Column
Waterloo Place, SW1.

The Grand Old Duke of York,
He had ten thousand men;
He marched them up to the top of the hill,
And he marched them down again.
And when they were up they were up,
And when they were down they were down,
And when they were only half way up
They were neither up nor down.

To have a song written about you might have been accolade enough for most people, but in the case of Frederick, Duke of York (1763–1827), he was commemorated in 1834 by what was, at the time, one of the tallest columns in London. When Nelson's column was erected in Trafalgar Square a few years later, it was deliberately made higher to ensure that Nelson was the more visible hero of the day. No doubt the Duke of York would have appreciated the broad sweep of steps leading to his statue, if not the statue itself – for he is placed 124 feet (38 metres) up in the air and cast in solid bronze. A century ago it was possible to climb the stairway to the top and see the panoramic views of London below. Now the onlooker must be content to gaze and reflect on the duke's achievements as a soldier and his flamboyant lifestyle, which often left him in debt. Contemporary humourists argued that the reason he was placed so high off the ground was to protect him from moneylenders. Lack of funds did not detract, however, from his career as a first-rate soldier and staunch military reformer. The cost of the column was paid for by docking a day's pay from every soldier in the army.

Nearest tube: Charing Cross.
Nearby buses: 3, 6, 9, 11, 12, 13, 15, 23, 24, 29, 30, 53, 88, 94, 109, 139, 159, 176, 177E, 184, 196.

Eros
Piccadilly Circus, W1.

Most people who come to London visit Piccadilly Circus. It is one of the best-known city landmarks in the world and certainly one of the most photographed. The word 'piccadilly' comes from a fashion craze in the seventeenth century, when trendy young men took to wearing stiff-necked collars called 'pickadils'. The manufacturer responsible for these uncomfortable-looking garments made a fortune and built a vast mansion in the area, which he named Piccadilly Hall. Today the atmosphere of Piccadilly Circus owes little to its buildings or its history but everything to the star attraction, the Angel of Christian Charity, better known as Eros. For 100 years the statue has maintained its prime position in the heart of London and it continues to draw the crowds. As one tourist remarked, 'I really felt I'd arrived in London when I saw Eros for the first time.' It seems a typically British conundrum that such an unlikely, diminutive sculpture, created in honour of a great nineteenth-century philanthropist, the seventh Earl of Shaftesbury, should be one of the most famous spots in the world.

Nearest tube: Piccadilly Circus.
Nearby buses: 3, 6, 9, 12, 13, 14, 15, 19, 22, 23, 38, 53, 88, 94, 139, 159.

Houses of Parliament (New Palace of Westminster)
St Margaret Street, SW1.
Tel. 071–219 3000.

It is said that King Canute built the first palace on the site of the present Houses of Parliament in the eleventh century. Edward the Confessor followed suit, and succeeding kings often lived at the palace and summoned their councils to meet here. In 1512 the palace was damaged by fire but, although King Henry VIII removed himself and his court to Whitehall Palace, Parliament remained, and from that time onwards Westminster ceased to be a royal residence. In 1834 a small fire quickly took hold and set alight the entire building: the palace burnt to the ground. In the space of a few hours everything except the chapel crypt, Jewel Tower and Westminster Hall had been reduced to ashes. A national competition was held to decide who would design a replacement, and the winner, Charles Barry, helped by Augustus Pugin, set to work to create the new Houses of Parliament. The result was an extraordinary achievement; at dusk, viewed from the other side of the Thames, it looks like a giant, watery, limestone palace emerging from the river depths. For details of tours of the Houses of Parliament, see page 150.

Nearest tube: Westminster.
Nearby buses: 3, 11, 12, 24, 53, 77A, 88, 109, 159, 177E, 184, 196, 511.

Lancaster House
Stable Yard (off St James's Palace), SW1.

One of the most imposing houses lining the Mall, this nineteenth-century extravaganza, on the south side of Stable Yard, was built for the Grand Old Duke of York (see page 107) – but he never lived long enough to enjoy it. Queen Victoria summed up the grandeur of the building when she came to call on her friend the Duchess of Sutherland: 'I have come from my house to your palace,' she said. Her house was, of course, Buckingham Palace. Lancaster House is now used for government hospitality and as a conference centre. Among its notable neighbours are Marlborough House, St James's Palace and the Institute of Contemporary Arts.

Nearest tubes: Green Park, Piccadilly Circus.
Nearby buses: 3, 6, 9, 12, 13, 14, 15, 19, 22, 23, 38, 53, 88, 94, 139, 159.

Lloyd's Building
Lime Street, EC3.
Tel. 071–623 7100.

The new Lloyd's of London building, completed in 1986 to a design by the architect Richard Rogers, houses the world's leading insurance market. It is a spectacular modern construction made entirely of steel and glass. The most striking architectural feature is the placement of all the pipework and ducting on the outside. The lifts are clearly visible as they glide up and down, and the whole impression is of a building that has been turned inside out. Nothing if not controversial, the Lloyd's Building has been unfavourably compared with a mechanical plant and a spaceship, although many believe it to be one of the finest modern buildings in London. The best view of Lloyd's is from the top of the Monument a few minutes' walk away. For details of tours, see page 151.

Nearest tubes: Bank, Liverpool Street.
Nearby buses: 8, 11, 15, 15B, 21, 22B, 23, 25, 26, 43, 76, 149, 501.

Old Bailey
Old Bailey, EC4.
Tel. 071–248 3277.

The notorious Newgate Prison once stood on the site of the Old Bailey; prisoners were kept in appallingly cramped and insanitary conditions, and some died before coming to trial. Until 1868, public executions were carried out at the corner of Newgate Street, but the Victorians stopped the practice, after which hangings took place behind the prison walls. As London's Central Criminal Court, the Old Bailey has been the scene of many of this century's most dramatic trials. Proceedings can be observed from the public galleries. Crowning the building is the famous bronze statue of Justice, standing with her arms outstretched, holding a sword in one hand and scales in the other. Over-13s only are admitted to the Old Bailey and 13–16s must be accompanied by an adult.

Public galleries open Mon.–Fri. 10.30a.m.–1.00p.m. and 2.00p.m.–4.00p.m.
Admission free.
Nearest tube: St Paul's.
Nearby buses: 4, 8, 22B, 25, 56, 172, 501, 521.

Old Curiosity Shop
Portsmouth Street, WC2.

Some historians have said that this Elizabethan building was the shop on which Charles Dickens based his famous novel. Others believe that, at the time when Lincoln's Inn Fields was open pastureland, it was a dairy. Whatever the truth, the shop looks somewhat out of place in its present surroundings, hemmed in on all sides by the office blocks of Portsmouth Street. It has a good selection of knick-knacks, glass and Victorian antiques, and the atmosphere is such that you half expect Mrs Danvers to come in and greet you. You can combine a visit here with one to the Sir John Soane Museum or Covent Garden.

Nearest tube: Holborn.
Nearby buses: 18, 19, 22B, 25, 30, 38, 55, 68, 168, 171, 188, 196, 501, 505, 521.

British Telecom Tower (Post Office Tower)
Maple Street, W1.

It took more than four years to build the Post Office Tower, which is 620 feet (189 metres) high. When it was completed in autumn 1965, it was the tallest building in London and in the process took the national

broadcasting system into a new micro-electronic age. The revolutionary tower is at the heart of a complicated broadcasting and communications network. Satellites beam signals down to a transmitter 39 feet (12 metres) high, which then provides the main link in a nationwide system broadcasting programmes throughout Great Britain on behalf of all the major television channels. Because the sixteen floors of the tower below the aerials house power units and radio equipment, they are protected by special glass which allows light to enter but keeps heat out. Until 1975, the tower's viewing platform and revolving restaurant were open to visitors, but the building was closed to the public after a bomb exploded on the 31st floor; no one was injured, but since then BT (British Telecom), which now operates the tower, has decided that it must remain closed to the public for security reasons.

Nearest tubes: Great Portland Street, Warren Street.
Nearby buses: 10, 14, 18, 24, 27, 29, 73, 74, 134, 135, 253.

George Inn

Borough High Street, SE1.
Tel. 071–407 2056.

The George Inn is one of the few surviving seventeenth-century coaching inns. In the inn's early days plays were sometimes performed in the courtyard, while patrons watched from the galleries above. It remained a major coaching inn until the advent of the railways. The George still operates as a pub and restaurant, and plays are occasionally performed here in summer. Children are welcome in both the wine bar and restaurant and the three-course set menu is excellent value. Reasonable prices are charged for hot and cold food in the wine bar.

Wine bar open daily 12.00 noon–12.00 midnight.
Restaurant open Mon.–Fri. 12.00 noon–12.00 midnight.
BR: London Bridge.
Nearest tube: London Bridge.
Nearby buses: 4, 17, 21, 22A, 35, 40, 43, 47, 48, 133, 214, 344, 501, 505, 521, D1.

Marble Arch

W1.

Marble Arch was designed by John Nash in the early nineteenth century as the principal entrance to Buckingham Palace, but it proved too narrow for the state coach to pass through and in 1851 was removed to its present site at the top of Park Lane. Originally an entrance into the park, it has become increasingly isolated and now stands alone in a sea of roaring traffic. Close by is the site of the old Tyburn Tree, where executions took place from as early as 1196. Later, prisoners were brought here from Newgate Prison and public hangings became a spectator sport. As many as 200,000 people gathered to watch the more notorious criminals 'swing'. This barbaric practice ended in 1783 and now a simple stone marks the spot where so many prisoners met their end.

Nearest tube: Marble Arch.
Nearby buses: 2A, 2B, 6, 7, 10, 12, 15, 16, 16A, 23, 36, 73, 74, 82, 88, 94, 98, 135, 137, 137A, 274.

Royal Albert Hall and Albert Memorial
Kensington Gore, SW7.
Tel. 071–589 8212.

The Albert Hall and the Albert Memorial are both reminders of the great contribution Prince Albert, the Prince Consort, made to art and science during the nineteenth century. The hall seats 8000 people and is home to the largest organ in London, which weighs 150 tonnes. One of London's most popular concert halls, it hosts the famous Promenade Concerts (see page 17), as well as numerous other events, including jazz recitals, folk music and wrestling matches. Overlooking the building, in Kensington Gardens, is the Albert Memorial, erected by Queen Victoria from public funds in memory of her husband, who died of typhoid in 1861. Vast and uncompromising, it cost £12,000 to build and has been called 'the finest monumental structure in Europe'. This splendid piece of Victorian Gothic extravagance, which has recently been renovated, is undoubtedly in a class of its own. The prince is shown sitting under an ample umbrella, a catalogue of the Great Exhibition of 1851 under his arm, surrounded by figures representing the arts and the industrial and scientific achievements of his age.

Nearest tube: High Street Kensington.
Nearby buses: 9, 9A, 10, 52, C1.

Royal Courts of Justice
Strand, WC2.

This romantic-looking building might seem to be better suited to fairytales than justice. It was built at the end of the nineteenth century at a cost of £1,250,000 with the idea of concentrating London's law courts in one central area; most civil cases are tried here, but the final court of appeal remains the House of Lords at Westminster. The main hall is usually open to the public, and you can check the lists of the day's hearings in the central display case. There is also an interesting exhibition of legal costumes in a room off the hall. Over-12s only are admitted to the Royal Courts of Justice.

Open Mon.–Fri. 10.00a.m.–4.30p.m.
Admission free.
Nearest tubes: Covent Garden, Holborn.
Nearby buses: 1, 4, 6, 9, 11, 13, 15, 23, 26, 30, 68, 76, 77A, 168, 171, 171A, 176, 188, 196, 501, 502, 521.

Royal Naval College

Greenwich, SE10.
Tel. 081–858 2154.

The Royal Naval College is built on the site of a royal palace which was once a favourite residence of King Henry VIII. The present buildings were started during the reign of King Charles II, but when William and Mary came to the throne in 1689 they invited Sir Christopher Wren to redevelop the site. The result was the Greenwich Hospital for Seamen, which in 1869 became the home of the Royal Naval College. Members of the public are allowed inside the famous Painted Hall to see James Thornhill's fine ceiling painting, which took more than twenty years to complete; he was paid the princely sum of £6685 for the work. The hall is still in use as an officers' dining room. The chapel, designed by James Stewart in 1789, is also open to the public. Combine a visit here with one to Greenwich Park and the Maritime Museum (see page 64).

Painted Hall and chapel open Fri.–Wed. 2.30p.m.– 4.45p.m.
Admission free.
BR: Greenwich.
Nearest tube: Island Gardens DLR then Greenwich foot tunnel.
Nearby buses: 47, 53, 177, 188, 199.
River boat from Westminster Pier, Charing Cross, Tower Pier and London City Airport.

Mansion House
Walbrook, EC4.

As well as being the Lord Mayor of London's official home, the Mansion House has its own court of justice and prison cells. Each year after the new Lord Mayor has been sworn in (see page 18), he or she arrives at the front entrance in a state coach to assume the reins of an office that dates back to the twelfth century. The most famous man to hold the post was Dick Whittington (see page 104). London's first Lady Mayor was elected in 1983. Tours, suitable for over-11s, take place throughout the week. To apply, write to the secretary at Mansion House, Walbrook, EC4 8BH.

Admission free.
Nearest tubes: Mansion House, Bank.
Nearby buses: 11, 15, 17, 23, 26, 76, 149, 521.

Guildhall
Guildhall Yard, Gresham Street, EC1.
Tel. 071–606 3030.

Guildhall, which stands on the site of a Roman amphitheatre, is the headquarters of the City of London. The medieval structure here was rebuilt in 1411 and, although badly damaged in the Great Fire of 1666 and the Blitz, the building retains some of its medieval features, including the crypt and porch. Today it is the perfect setting for splendid state occasions, and many of the City's ceremonial functions such as the Lord Mayor's Banquet and the election of the Sheriffs are held in the fifteenth-century Great Hall. In the sixteenth century it was also the scene of some famous trials. Fifteen-year-old Lady Jane Grey was tried and condemmed to death here in 1554, as was her husband Lord Guildford Dudley. The banners in the hall represent the twelve original City livery companies – Drapers, Clothworkers, Fishmongers, Goldsmiths, Merchant Taylors, Haberdashers, Salters, Vintners, Skinners, Grocers, Ironmongers and Mercers – which were set up as informal unions to protect their members and look after their interests. Two giants, 9 feet (2.7 metres) tall, the legendary Gog and Magog, guard the musicians' gallery, and the stained-glass window at the south end dates from the fifteenth century. For details of tours, which take place on weekdays when the Guildhall is not in use, write to the Public Relations Department, Guildhall, Guildhall Yard, EC2P 2EJ.

Open Mon.–Sat. 10.00a.m.–5.00p.m.; Sun. 2.00p.m.– 5.00p.m.
Admission free.
Nearest tube: Bank, St Paul's.
Nearby buses: 4, 8, 22B, 25, 172, 501, 521.

Monument
Monument Street, EC3.
Tel. 071–626 2717.

Built by Sir Christopher Wren, the Monument commemorates the Great Fire of 1666, which destroyed most of the City. Described as the 'loftiest stone column in the world', it stands 202 feet tall (62 metres) and precisely 202 feet away from the baker's shop in Pudding Lane where the fire began. A bust of King Charles II should have crowned the top, but the king, preferring a less prominent position, can be seen at the base of the column wearing a Roman outfit and uncharacteristically resembling Julius Caesar. Over 300 steps must be climbed to reach the top, from where you can enjoy magnificent views of London. A recent survey of the building has shown that repairs are needed which will amount to considerably more than the original cost of £13,450. There is no lift to the top of the Monument and the climb is probably too strenuous for young children.

Open Mon.–Fri. 9.00a.m.–4.30p.m.; Sat.–Sun. 2.00p.m.–4.30p.m.
Admission charge.
Nearest tube: Monument.
Nearby buses: 15, 22, 25, 35, 40, 43, 47, 48, 133, 214, 501, 505, 521, D9, D11.

Stock Exchange
Old Broad Street, EC2.
Tel. 071–588 2355.

In a tall tower building sandwiched between the Bank of England and the National Westminster Tower lies the heart of London's financial world. The Stock Exchange is part of a sophisticated global money market where dealers buy and sell shares from dawn to dusk.

Nearest tube: Bank.
Nearby buses: 8, 11, 15B, 21, 22B, 23, 25, 26, 43, 76, 133, 149, 214, 501, D9.

Temple of Mithras
Forecourt of Temple House, Queen Victoria Street, EC4.

The remains of this temple, which dates from the Roman occupation of Britain, were unearthed in 1954, when building work began on nearby Bucklesbury House. Mithras, to whom the temple was dedicated, was a Persian sun-god, fashionable with the Roman army for his outstanding strength and valour. The temple ruins, removed to the forecourt of Temple House, represent a rare opportunity to inspect a complete layout of a Roman building. The marble head of Mithras and other important archaeological finds from the same site can be seen at the Museum of London (see page 62).

Open at all times.
Nearest tube: Bank.
Nearby buses: 21, 43, 76, 133, 141, 214, 271.

Tower of London
Tower Hill, EC3.
Tel. 071–709 0765.

The most important landmark in the City has always been, and still is, the mighty Tower of London. Silhouetted against the evening sky it looks majestic and indestructible, a grand monument to the capital's history. No trip to London would be complete without visiting this famous fortress, the oldest part of which is the White Tower, built by William the Conqueror more than 900 years ago. Later monarchs made various additions, and what is visible today is an imposing collection of buildings from different periods surprisingly untarnished by time. The Tower has fulfilled many different functions during its long history, not only as a palace and fortress, but also as a prison, arsenal, mint and zoo. The only animals left today are the ravens, overfed and larger than life; a curious quirk of tradition dictates that their wings must be clipped – for it is feared that, if they fly away, the Tower will collapse. The best time to visit is in spring or winter, when the queues are less daunting.

Just past the main entrance to the Tower is Traitor's Gate, through which many famous prisoners made their final journey. The quality of life in prison depended largely on the rank of the prisoner and the offence committed. Those too poor to buy privileges fared worst and were sent to the basement of the White Tower and held in a particularly dismal dungeon under the sub-crypt. Most terrifying of all was the cell known as Little Ease; this box-like dungeon was so small that a prisoner was unable to stand up straight in it or lie down. Sir Walter Raleigh spent twelve years in the Bloody Tower, accused of various offences against the crown which he strongly denied. However, as an important knight of the realm, he enjoyed certain privileges. Family and friends were allowed to visit and he had servants to look after him. During captivity Raleigh kept himself busy by writing a lengthy *History of the World*. He also dabbled in medicine using herbs grown in the Tower gardens. Few prisoners escaped from this impregnable fortress, but one who did so was a bishop by the name of Ralph Flambard. Wealthy and powerful, Flambard was placed under guard in the Banqueting Hall of the White Tower. One night he gave a particularly lavish party to which the soldiers on guard were invited. A great deal of wine was consumed and by the end of the evening everyone had become quite drunk and fallen asleep – everyone, that is, except the bishop. With spirited haste, he lowered himself by a strong rope from one of the windows in the keep. Although he had misjudged the distance and had to leap the final 23 feet (7 metres) to the ground, luck was on his side. He managed to flee to the coast and board a boat to France. Kings and queens were also imprisoned in the Tower. While still a princess, Queen Elizabeth I came by river to Traitor's Gate to be kept in custody for over two months. Two of King Henry VIII's wives were executed here. In contrast to others who died on Tower Hill, Anne Boleyn was killed not by an axe but at the hands of a swordsman brought over especially from France. Of all the Tower's memories the saddest must be that of the two young sons of King Edward IV, who may have been murdered in the Bloody Tower in 1483. No one is absolutely sure what happened to them, but some believe that their uncle, the Duke of Gloucester, ordered them to be killed so that he himself could become King Richard III. Many years later, during King Charles II's reign, two small skeletons were found under a staircase by the White Tower. Thought to be the remains of the young princes, the bones were removed to Westminster Abbey and buried there.

It seems fitting that a mighty fortress such as the Tower should house the magnificent Crown Jewels. Most date from Charles II's reign and are closely linked to the coronation ceremony. The Imperial State Crown, made for Queen Victoria, contains more than 3000 jewels, including Edward the Confessor's sapphire and the priceless Prince's Ruby, worn by King Henry V at the Battle of Agincourt. Some of the largest diamonds in the world are also displayed here, including the Star of India and the famous Koh-i-Noor diamond, Mountain of Light, which has been set in Queen Elizabeth the Queen Mother's crown. As much a part of the Tower as its bricks and mortar are the Yeoman Warders – or Beefeaters, as they are popularly known. In their colourful red costumes and Tudor hats, they are a traditional part of Tower life. They have guarded the Tower for hundreds of years and now give guided tours and provide a fund of information.

Open Mon.–Sat. 9.30a.m.–6.30p.m.; Sun. 2.00p.m.–6.00p.m. (closes an hour earlier from Sept. to end March).
Admission charge.
Nearest tube: Tower Hill.
Nearby buses: 15, 25, 42, 78, 100, D1, D9, D11.

14

The river Thames

In the twentieth century the Thames retired. No longer the busy highway of past centuries – the M1 of the waterways, ferrying people and goods from place to place, kings and queens from palace to palace – it was made almost redundant by the huge expansion of travel by road and rail and the growing desire for speed. Today the river thrives on a gentler kind of travel. River launches, pleasure boats, private yachts and rowing boats cruise up and down at a leisurely pace. In Elizabethan times the Thames was London's principal thoroughfare and it was thronged with watermen who earned their living ferrying passengers to and fro. River transport was one of the most convenient ways of getting around and in particular for crossing the Thames, which, until as late as 1729, had only one bridge, London Bridge. Before the arrival of sophisticated vehicles with springs and rubber tyres, it was also much more comfortable to travel by boat, as well as being safer and pleasanter. There are now over twenty bridges spanning the Thames, the most famous of which are London Bridge, Tower Bridge and the newest, the Queen Elizabeth II Bridge.

BRIDGES AND THE THAMES BARRIER

London Bridge

'London Bridge is falling down,' the old song says. Some might remark that it would be no bad thing if the current London Bridge were to go the same way. Of all the bridges to span the Thames since Roman times, this must be the ugliest. By far the most interesting of those bridges must have been the medieval London Bridge, crowded with people, houses, shops and a chapel. A detailed illustration of the bridge at that time can be seen in a painting by William Hogarth from the series *Marriage à la Mode* (plate 6), which hangs in the National Gallery. As one writer described it:

> I well remember the street on London Bridge, narrow, darksome and dangerous to passengers from the multitude of carriages; frequent arches of strong timber crossed the street from the tops of the houses, to keep them together and from falling into the river. Nothing but use could preserve the repose of the inmates, who soon grew deaf to the noise of falling waters, the clamour of waterman and the frequent shrieks of drowning wretches.

In the 1780s, after much deliberation, the bridge was dismantled.

Six hundred years of wear and tear and ever-increasing traffic had taken their toll. The new London Bridge, built by John Rennie and completed in 1831, did not fare so well, and in 1973 it was replaced by a much needed larger bridge. Sold and exported piece by piece to America and faithfully reconstructed in the Arizona desert, the Rennie bridge now carries a six-lane highway.

Nearest tubes: Bank, Monument (north bank); London Bridge, Waterloo (south bank).
Nearby buses: 43, 47, 48, 133 (north bank); P11 (south bank).

The Queen Elizabeth II Bridge
Dartford, Kent.

One of the longest of its kind in the world, the Queen Elizabeth II Bridge took three years to build and was opened by Her Majesty in 1991. As you approach the Dartford river crossing, this £13 million bridge rises dramatically into view, the largest and most dominant feature on the landscape. It is an extraordinary technical achievement, resting on two giant reinforced concrete foundations each weighing 85,000 tonnes. The scale of the bridge is tremendous. It provides a clear span of 450 metres between the two main piers plus a vertical clearance of just under 60 metres to enable shipping to pass safely underneath. From the road, slender steel pylons rise 137 metres into the sky above the river and powerful spiral cables splay out from each.

By car: M25.

Tower Bridge and Exhibition Centre
Tel. 071–407 0922.

This impressive Victorian Gothic structure, completed in 1894 to complement the Tower of London, was the easternmost bridge across the Thames until the Queen Elizabeth II Bridge was built. Thanks to two mighty hydraulic lifting mechanisms, weighing some 1000 tons each, the two halves of the bridge can be levered upwards from the centre to allow large and high-masted ships to pass underneath. An exciting new exhibition centre opened in October 1993. Called the Tower Bridge Celebration Story, it occupies three floors of the north and south towers and tells the history of the bridge and its construction. There is an educational section which includes videos, one of which features a merchant describing busy commercial life on the river at the turn of the century. Another shows the Victorian architect presenting his plans for the bridge's supporting structures, which he eloquently described as 'steel skeletons clothed with stone'. Lifts within the towers operate as time capsules, taking visitors back over the centuries, while a robot called Harry Stoner acts as guide. The pedestrian walkways at the top of the bridge give panoramic views over London and the river, and telescopes linked to interactive

compact-disc systems demonstrate changes and developments over the past century. In the basement there is a small Victorian theatre showing a re-enactment of the bridge's grand inauguration, and visitors can also see the massive boiler and engine room from which the hydraulic lifts are controlled. The entrance to the centre is in the north tower. Allow at least 1½ hours for your visit. Suitable for children over 6 years old. There is a café on the south bank.

Open daily 10.00a.m.–6.30p.m. (closes 4.45p.m. Nov.– March).
Admission charge; good-value family ticket. Last admission 1½ hours before closing.
Nearest tube: Tower Bridge.
Nearby buses: 15, 25, 42, 78, 100, D1, D9, D11 (north bank); 42 47 78 188, P11 (south bank).
River boats from Charing Cross and Westminster.

Thames Barrier
Unity Way, Woolwich, SE18.
Tel. 081–854 1373.

If you travel downriver by boat towards Woolwich, the Thames widens and starts to straighten out. As it does so, you catch a first glimpse of the world's largest flood barrier, rising up from the riverbed like a row of giant, gleaming, silver whales. The Thames has always been susceptible to flooding. The last serious flood took place in 1928, when fourteen people died, but as long ago as 1663 Samuel Pepys wrote in his diary, 'I hear there was last night the greatest tide that ever was remembered in England to have been in this river; all White Hall having been drowned.' Each century water levels rise by over 2 feet (0.6 metres) increasing the possibility of a tidal surge which would cause the Thames to flood. The barrier, opened in 1984, was constructed to combat this hazard. Its movable steel gates close off the upper Thames from the sea and prevents the Thames Basin from flooding. For the annual closing of the barrier, see page 18. At the Thames Barrier Information Centre on the south bank of the river at Woolwich, videos and working models explain how the barrier operates and why it was constructed. The devastating impact a storm and flood might have in the absence of the barrier is shown in graphic detail. You can get a closer view of the giant piers from raised viewing platforms and riverside walks, or – even better – take a round-the-barrier cruise. You can also walk along the river from here to Greenwich, the National Maritime Museum, the *Cutty Sark* and the Royal Observatory. There is a café at the centre and a number of terraces and lawns for picnicking.

Open Mon.–Fri. 10.30a.m.–5.00p.m.; Sat.–Sun. 10.30a.m.–5.30p.m.
Admission charge.
BR: Charlton.
River boats from Greenwich, Tower Pier and Westminster.

DOCKLANDS

London's river trade has played a crucial part in the development of the capital. This trade approached its peak at the beginning of the nineteenth century, when the first commercial dock was built to the east of the City. As one writer noted, dockland was 'a great plain: a plain of enclosed waters . . . holding upon its surface fleet upon fleet . . . Masts to the right, masts to the left, masts in front, masts yonder above the warehouses . . . they wait in stillness the rising of the tide.' By the end of the nineteenth century the romantic days of tea-clippers sailing the high seas had ended. The docks had passed their prime and entered a period of decline. Their revival in the 1980s as a new commercial and residential area was one of the most ambitious development ventures this century. Its immense scope can be best appreciated from the river or from nearby rail routes. If you travel eastwards, Tower Bridge heralds the start of this modern city within a city, where a diversity of architectural styles, using glass, cement, brick and steel, jostle for position in a newly wrought landscape. Warehouses have been transformed into flats, leisure complexes and offices, and skyscrapers loom large and uncompromising. But the development of docklands has not been an unmitigated success story. Since the boom of the late 1980s was overtaken by recession, a large proportion of the new office space has remained empty.

St Katharine's Dock
SE1.

Only a short distance downriver from the Tower of London is St Katharine's Dock, which took on a new lease of life when it was successfully converted into a marina and is a popular venue with Londoners and tourists alike. St Katharine by the Tower is now the home of the World Trade Centre. There are a number of shops in and around the marina, as well as yachts, launches and the famous Norse Lighthouse Ship, the only vessel remaining here from the Maritime Trust's Historic Ships' Collection, disbanded in 1987. At the centre of the marina is the Dickens Inn, a useful stopping-off point for snacks and drinks, although it is doubtful that Charles Dickens himself ever drank here. Parts of the building date from the nineteenth century. One of the oldest warehouses at St Katharine's Dock is the Ivory House, an impressive building which in the 1850s stored thousands of elephants' tusks. It has recently been renovated and converted into a restaurant and shops.

Nearest tube: Tower Hill.
Nearby buses: 15, 25, 42, 78, 100, D1, D9, D11.
River boats from Charing Cross and Westminster.

Tobacco Dock
Wapping, E1.
Tel. 071–702 9681.

A few minutes' walk downriver from St Katharine's Dock is Tobacco Dock. No longer bursting with fine cargoes of tobacco and wine, Tobacco Dock's renovated eighteenth-century ware-house now contains shops, cafés, tearooms and restaurants. Moored alongside the forecourt are two replicas of eighteenth-century sailing clippers. One, *The Three Sisters*, has been trans-formed into a pirate ship and tells the story of piracy from the days of ancient Greece, when by all accounts it was considered quite a dignified profession. For as long as ships have carried cargoes there have been pirates bold enough to raid them and the adventures of the more daring captains, some of them women, are astonishing. The other, an American merchant schooner called *Sea Lark*, has been rigged out to portray Robert Louis Stevenson's adventure story *Treasure Island* in a series of tableaux. On a more sombre note, this is also the site of Execution Dock, where sailors were once hanged; some suffered an even more dreadful fate, being tied to a post and left to drown by the incoming tide. Children under 7 must be accompanied by an adult. Tobacco Dock has recently come under new management and some changes are likely when it reopens in 1994. For details, telephone before you make your visit.

Open daily 10.00a.m. till late April–Sept.; 10.00a.m.–5.00p.m. Oct.–March.
Admission charges to ships; free for under-5s.
DLR: Shadwell.
Nearby buses: 100, D1, D9, D11.

Canary Wharf
E1.

Canary Wharf, where ships once set sail for the Canary Islands, lies at the northern tip of the Isle of Dogs. A major redevelopment has transformed the area from a crumbling expanse of warehouses and river frontage into London's newest commercial centre. It consists of 31 separate sites, the majority of which are located on land adjoining the edge of the old wharf. Centre stage is Cesar Pelli's famous Canada Tower, the tallest building in Britain, rising 800 feet (240 metres) into the sky like a giant cigarette lighter. Canada Square, where the tower is sited, is surrounded by leafy open spaces, and there is no shortage of shops and cafés. A successful community arts and events programme guarantees an exciting calendar of entertainments throughout the year. For details of Canary Wharf's *Arts and Events* leaflet, write to Olympia and York, 1 Canada Square, E14.

Nearest tube: Bank, Tower Gateway then DLR.
DLR: Canary Wharf.
Nearby buses: 277, D1, D3, D5, D7, D8, D9, D11, P14.
River bus.

Mudchute and Island Gardens
E14.

Two stops beyond Canary Wharf on the Docklands Light Railway, you come to Mudchute, an undeveloped rural area with a riding school, allotments, a wetland area and the Mudchute Park and City Farm with its cattle, sheep, pigs, goats and riding school (see page 147). If you carry on to Island Gardens, you can walk under the river by the Greenwich foot tunnel.

Nearest tubes: Bank, Tower Gateway then DLR.
DLR: Mudchute or Island Gardens.
Nearby buses: D8, D9, P14.

BOAT TRIPS ON THE RIVER

The only way fully to appreciate the kaleidoscope of fascinating sights that the Thames has to offer is from the river itself. Well-known sites such as the Tower of London and Hampton Court take on a new perspective when viewed from a boat. It can be fun to take a picnic to sustain you during a boat trip but refreshments are available on all boats except the river bus and the Westminster–Tower service. Make sure you have warm clothes – even on summer days it can be chilly on the river. All scheduled boats from Westminster Pier have guided commentaries highlighting the sites on the waterside and there are lavatories on board. Child rates apply for children under 16 years.

River Thames Boat Services start in early April and run up to the end of October. During the winter season there are usually no upriver services and fewer round trips on the pleasure boats. The changing tides make all timings approximate so contact the relevant boat operator for confirmation of departure.

Discoverer ticket

The Discoverer ticket is a good value offer that gives you discount on entrance fees to four riverside sites. You can buy a one-day Discoverer ticket from Charing Cross, Tower and Greenwich piers. For further details call 071–987 1185.

Downriver services

Westminster to Tower

Westminster Tower Boat Trips.
Tel. 071–515 1415, 071–930 9033.

The trip takes 30 minutes. Boats leave Westminster at 10.20a.m., 10.40a.m., 11.00a.m., 11.30a.m., 12 noon then every 20 minutes until 3.00p.m., then every 30 minutes until 5.00p.m. and 5.30p.m., 6.00p.m. from the end of May to the first week in September.

Tower to Westminster

Tel. 071–488 0344.

Boats leave Tower Pier from the end of May to the first week in September at 11.00a.m., 11.20a.m., 11.40a.m., 12.10p.m., 12.40p.m. and every 20 minutes until 3.40p.m. Then every 30 minutes until 5.40p.m., also 6.10p.m. and 6.40p.m.

Westminster to Greenwich

Westminster Passenger Services Association Ltd.
Tel. 071–930 4097.

The trip takes between 40 and 50 minutes. Boats leave every 30 minutes 10.30a.m.–4.00p.m. (peak season last boat leaves at 5.00p.m.

Greenwich Pier to Westminster

Tel. 081–858 3996.

Boats leave for Westminster every 30 minutes from 11.30a.m.– 5.00p.m. (peak season last boat leaves at 6.00p.m.).

Westminster to the Thames Flood Barrier

London Launches.
Tel. 071–930 3373.

The trips takes 75 minutes each way. Boats leave April–Oct. at 10.00a.m., 11.15a.m., 12.40p.m., 1.45p.m., 3.15p.m. returning from the barrier at 11.15a.m., 12.30p.m., 2.00p.m., 3.00p.m., 4.15p.m. All vessels call at Canary Wharf Pier for London Docklands – 40 minutes from Westminster and 35 minutes from the barrier.

Charing Cross to Greenwich via the Tower

Catamaran Cruises.
Tel. 071–987 1185.

The trip to the Tower takes 20 minutes and to Greenwich between 40–50 minutes. Boats leave for the Tower April–Oct. every 20 minutes from 10.30a.m. and 4.00p.m. returning between 12.25p.m. and 5.55p.m.

Boats leave for Greenwich every 30 minutes between 10.30a.m. and 4.00p.m.; returning to the Tower between 11.00a.m. and 4.30p.m. and to Charing Cross between 11.45a.m. and 5.15p.m.

Greenwich to the Thames Flood Barrier
Campion Launches.
Tel. 081–305 0300.

Boats leave for the barrier from 6 April–12 July and 7 Sept.–25 Oct. at 11.15a.m., 12.30p.m., 2.00p.m. and 3.30p.m. and between 13 July–6 Sept. at 11.00a.m., 12.20p.m., 1.40p.m., 3.00p.m. and 4.20p.m. Return trip from 6 April–12 July and 7 Sept.–25 Oct. at 11.50a.m., 1.05p.m., 2.35p.m., 4.05p.m. Between 13 July–6 Sept. at 11.35a.m., 12.55p.m., 2.15p.m., 3.35p.m. and 4.55p.m.

Ferry from the Tower to HMS Belfast
Livetts Launch.
Tel. 081–468 7201.

Boats leave from 19 March until early November every 15 minutes between 11.00a.m. and 6.00p.m. (see page 128).

Upriver services
Services run from the Monday before Easter until the end of September.

Westminster to Hampton Court (via Putney, Kew and Richmond)
Westminster Passenger Services Association Ltd. (Upriver)
Tel. 071–930 4721, 071–930 2062.

The trip to Hampton Court can take anything between 2½ to 4 hours depending on the tide. Boats leave for Hampton Court at 10.30a.m., 11.15a.m. and 12 noon returning at 3.00p.m., 4.00p.m. and 5.00p.m.

The trip to Kew takes over an hour and boats leave Westminster at 10.15a.m., 10.30a.m., 11.00a.m., 11.15a.m., 12 noon, 2.00p.m. and 3.00p.m. returning at 12.05p.m., 12.50p.m., 3.30p.m., 5.00p.m. and 6.30p.m.

The trip from Westminster to Richmond takes between 2 and 3 hours and boats leave at 10.30a.m., 11.15a.m. and 12 noon returning at 4.00p.m., 5.00p.m. and 6.00p.m.

Boats from Westminster to Kew, Richmond and Hampton Court stop at Putney approximately 30 minutes and at Kew 1½ hours after departure from Westminster. For details, call Putney Pier, tel. 081–788 6822.

Boats leave Richmond for Hampton Court from 17 April to 5 June weekends only at 11.30a.m. and 2.30p.m. and from 25 May to mid-September daily at 11.30a.m. and 2.30p.m. returning at 1.00p.m., 3.00p.m., 4.00p.m. and 5.00p.m.

Round trip cruises

Richmond Circular Cruises
Colliers Launches.
Tel. 081–940 8505, 081–892 0741.

Boats leave Richmond for Teddington Lock for a 45-minute round trip from 17 April–24 May weekends only every hour 11.00a.m.–5.00p.m. and from 25 March to the end of September daily every hour 11.00a.m.–5.00p.m.

Festival South Bank Cruises
Tel. 071–278 6201.

Operate a one-hour trip from Festival Pier daily throughout the year from 12 noon to 9.00p.m. The route takes you upriver as far as Lambeth pier, then the boat heads downriver to Tower Bridge before returning upriver to the Festival pier.

Crown River Cruises
Tel. 071–936 2033 (out of hours tel. 071–839 3424).

Operate a one-hour cruise from Westminster Pier daily March–Nov. between 11.00a.m. and 6.20p.m. The route is the same as the one taken by Festival South Bank Cruises.

Thames Commuter Services Ltd
Tel. 071–537 4111.

Thames Commuter Services Ltd have recently taken over the RiverBus. Unlike other more leisurely services operating on the river, this one, as its name implies, is aimed at commuters and those who want to get from point to point in the quickest time. They operate large passenger boats from two piers across the heart of London: Festival Pier, for Waterloo Station and London Bridge Station, and City Pier which will serve London Bridge Station and Canary Wharf.

Weekday departures are every fifteen minutes from 7.30a.m. to 9.30a.m. and from 5.00p.m. to 7.00p.m. There is no service at other times or at weekends.

Catamaran Cruises
Tel. 071–839 3572.

Catamaran Cruises offer a wide variety of trips on the river Thames. Their new Thames Barrier cruise, running from Charing Cross and Tower Piers (March to November) takes you down river to Greenwich and beyond for a close up view of the famous Thames Barrier. It also gives a 20 per cent discount against entrance to the visitors' centre. Catamaran offer a Discoverer ticket enabling you to travel for a whole day to or from any of the following piers: Charing Cross, Tower Pier and Greenwich. This pass also includes discount vouchers to several riverside attractions.

For a night-time trip on the Thames, Catamaran Cruises operate a floodlit supper cruise from May to September (not Saturdays), departing at 9.00p.m. Their Sunday lunch cruise is available all year round and departs at 12.45p.m. On Saturday nights only they run a disco cruise with hot supper. This starts at 7.00p.m. and ends at 11.00p.m.

BOATS TO BOARD

HMS Belfast
Symons Wharf, Vine Lane, Tooley Street, SE1.
Tel. 071–407 6434.

The only 'big gun' ship surviving from the Second World War, this powerful 102,000-tonne cruiser has found a permanent home on the Thames, close to Tower Bridge. HMS *Belfast* has been converted into a historical museum showing the workings of the ship and how the sailors lived when on active duty. There are lots of interesting things to do on board. Helpful trails make it easy to explore the ship from top to bottom. The boiler and engine rooms are open for inspection, as are the galley and somewhat bleak punishment cells. Two 6-inch gun turrets look out over the river, and you can have a go at defending the ship from a simulated air attack. This is not a trip to be rushed. Very young children who tire easily (there are seven decks and numerous stairs) might find it too much. A visit here could be combined with one to Tower Bridge Walkway.

Open daily 10.00a.m.–5.20p.m. (closes an hour earlier in winter).
Admission charge.
Nearest tubes: London Bridge, Tower Hill.
Nearby buses: 4, 17, 21, 22A, 35, 40, 43, 47, 48, 133, 214, 344, 501, 505, 521, D1, D11, P3, P11.

Kathleen May
St Mary Overy Dock, Cathedral Street, Southwark, SE1.
Tel. 071–403 3965.

Somewhat hidden from the river, the *Kathleen May* was the last three-masted topsail schooner to be built. There is not a great deal to see inside, although you can experience some convincing rough-weather sound-effects. Even if you decide not to go on board, however, it is worth having a look at this lovely coastal trading ship, perhaps while on your way to Hay's Galleria (see page 172) or the London Dungeon (see page 57).

Open Mon.–Fri. 10.00a.m.–4.00p.m.
Admission charge.
Nearest tube: London Bridge.
Nearby buses: 47, P11.

Cutty Sark and Gypsy Moth
Greenwich Pier, SW10.
Tel. 081–858 3445.

The famous tea-clipper *Cutty Sark*, which in its day was one of the fastest vessels travelling between the Far East and Europe with its cargoes of tea, lies a stone's throw from Greenwich Pier. It is now a museum. On deck you can view the tiny galley and crew's quarters, and down in the bows is a selection of fine figureheads.

Moored close by the *Cutty Sark* is the famous *Gypsy Moth IV*, in which Sir Francis Chichester completed a round-the-world voyage in 1967. This small boat appears far too fragile for such a long and arduous journey. The opening hours for *Cutty Sark* and *Gypsy Moth* are the same, except that *Gypsy Moth* is closed in winter.

Open April–Sept. Mon.–Sat. 10.00a.m.–6.00p.m.; Sun. 12 noon–6.00p.m. Oct.–March Mon.–Sat. 10.00a.m.–5.00p.m.; Sun. 12 noon–5.00p.m.
Admission charge.
BR: Greenwich.
Nearest tube: Island Gardens DLR, then Greenwich foot tunnel.
Nearby buses: 177, 180, 188, 286.

Bookboat
Cutty Sark Gardens, Greenwich, SE10.
Tel. 081–853 4383.

London's only floating bookshop is situated in a colourful barge moored alongside *Gypsy Moth IV* (see above). Full to the gunnels with children's literature, it has a cheerful atmosphere and helpful staff, making it one of the nicest bookshops in town.

Open Fri.–Wed. 10.00a.m.–5.00p.m.
BR: Greenwich.
Nearest tube: Island Gardens DLR, then Greenwich foot tunnel.
Nearby buses: 177, 180, 188, 286.

15

Canals

After many years of disuse and decline, London's canals are coming into their own again, but with a strong emphasis on leisure rather than industry. Chugging along at a relaxed pace past colourful houseboats and waterbirds, canal-trip passengers can enjoy the sights of London from a different perspective. Listed below are companies which offer services along the Regent's Canal between Little Venice and Camden Lock.

Canal Cruises
250 Camden High Street, NW1.
Tel. 071–485 4433.

Canal Cruises runs a trip aboard the *Jenny Wren* narrowboat which takes you along the most picturesque part of the Regent's Canal, from Camden Lock, past London Zoo and Regent's Park, then via the canal tunnel to Maida Vale, around the island at Little Venice and back again. The journey takes 1½ hours and includes a commentary on the canal and its history. Trips are available at weekends and during school holidays from March to October, departing at 11.30a.m., 2.00p.m. and 3.30p.m.

The Waterside restaurant at nearby Walker's Quay is run by Canal Cruises and is a good place to have a bite to eat. It also provides picnics to take on board. The restaurant is open Tues.–Fri. 10.00a.m.–10.00p.m. (last orders), and Sat.–Sun. 9.00a.m.–10.00p.m. (last orders). Canal Cruises also offers a more luxurious approach to London's waterways in the shape of a restaurant on board the *My Fair Lady* narrowboat, which cruises through Hampstead Road lock, past London Zoo and Regent's Park to Little Venice and back. The Sunday lunch cruise sails at 1.00p.m. (boarding from 12.30p.m.), and the three-course set menu of traditional English food is good value, with reductions for children. All cruises start from the Garden Jetty, 250 Camden High Street, NW1. Advance booking is essential.

Nearest tube: Camden Town.
Nearby buses: 3, 24, 27, 29, 31, 53, 74, 74B, 134, 137, 168, 214, 253, C2.

Jason's Boat Trip
opposite 60 Blomfield Road, W9.
Tel. 071–286 3428.

Jason is a traditionally painted narrowboat, built in 1906, which travels between Little Venice and Camden Lock along Regent's Canal. The return journey takes about 1½ hours and a simple cold lunch or afternoon tea can be provided if booked in advance. There is a coffee shop at the boarding place. Trips are available from April to October, departing at 10.30a.m., 12.30p.m. and 2.30p.m. From June to August there is an extra daily trip leaving at 4.30p.m.

Nearest tube: Warwick Avenue.
Nearby buses: 6, 46.

London Waterbus Company
Camden Lock, NW1.
Tel. 071–482 2550.

The London Waterbus Company runs a regular boat service between Little Venice and Camden Lock. If you want to stop off along the Regent's Canal to visit London Zoo (and avoid summertime queues at the main gate), you can buy a special ticket that includes entrance to the zoo. From April to October boats leave daily from Camden Lock and Warwick Avenue every hour on the hour from 10.00a.m.– 5.00p.m. In winter boats depart, weekends only, from Camden Lock at 11.15a.m., 12.45p.m., 2.15p.m. and 3.45p.m., and from Little Venice at 10.30a.m., 12.00 noon, 1.30p.m. and 3.00p.m.

Nearest tube: Warwick Avenue.
Nearby buses: 6, 8, 16, 18, 46.

BRITISH WATERWAYS

British Waterways manage over 2000 miles of inland waterway and have lots of useful information on London's canals. Their comprehensive *Canal Walks in London* leaflet lists six different routes along the canals which give walkers an opportunity to see familiar landmarks from an unfamiliar viewpoint. There are also useful hints on cycling, fishing and the opening and closing times of the towpaths. For more information telephone them on the number given below. Useful addresses are:

British Waterways
Melbury House, Melbury Terrace, NW1 6JX.
Tel. 071–262 6711.

Inland Waterways Association
114 Regent's Park Road, NW1 8UQ.
Tel. 071–586 2556.

Regent's Canal Information Centre
289 Camden High Street, NW1 7BX.
Tel. 071–482 0523.

16

Clocks

A hundred years ago watches were a luxury that many people could not afford. Londoners relied heavily on public clocks and in Victorian times there was no lack of them. Sadly, twentieth-century architects seem less inclined to incorporate 'timepieces' in their buildings, feeling perhaps that they have outgrown their usefulness. Listed below are some famous and unusual London clocks. They are not worth making a special trip to see, but they are interesting to note when you are passing by.

Astronomical Clock
Hampton Court Palace, Hampton Court, Surrey.

Flanked by brick columns, King Henry VIII's Astronomical Clock, complete with its bell turret, makes a fitting centre for the entrance to Clock Court. Constructed in 1540 for the king during his marriage to Catherine Howard, it not only tells the time, but calculates how many days have passed since the beginning of the year and what day of the month it is.

BR: Hampton Court.
Nearby buses: 111, 216, 461, 513, R68.
River bus from Westminster, Richmond and Kingston.

Big Ben
Houses of Parliament, Parliament Square, SW1.

Big Ben is arguably the most famous time machine in the world. Named after Sir Benjamin Hall, who first managed the running of the clock, 'Big Ben' refers to the great bell inside the tower which chimes the hours, not to the clock itself. Installed in 1859, it weighs 13 tons and was the heaviest bell to have been cast in Britain. Four smaller bells around it chime the quarter-hours and half-hours. The big hand alone measures 14 feet (4.2 metres), while the numerals are nearly 2 feet (0.6 metre) tall. The clock has always kept excellent time, although an unruly flock of starlings once alighted on its face and caused the mechanics to grind to a halt.

Nearest tube: Westminster.
Nearby buses: 3, 11, 12, 24, 53, 77A, 88, 109, 159, 177E, 184, 196, 511.

Fortnum and Mason Clock
181 Piccadilly, W1.

Unless you happen to be passing at the right moment, you could easily miss one of the merrier tunes to be heard in Piccadilly. For only on the hour does this splendid clock come alive: its doors open, Mr Fortnum and Mr Mason stride out, bow elegantly to one another and go back in again, closing the doors firmly behind them. To complete the picture, the chimes are accompanied by a selection of delicate eighteenth-century tunes played on a series of small bells. If you have time to spare, explore Fortnum and Mason. It is a shoppers' paradise, full of everything from designer clothes and delicate china to unusual pickles and sumptuous fruits. If the food hall fails to make your mouth water, ask one of the assistants, clad in full morning dress, to direct you to the Fountain Bar, where you can sample some delicious ice creams.

Nearest tubes: Green Park, Piccadilly Circus.
Nearby buses: 8, 9, 14, 19, 22, 38.

Liberty Clock
Regent Street, W1.

This splendid art deco clock is set in the archway linking the two halves of Liberty's department store, a mock-Tudor building, totally at odds with the rest of Regent Street. The clock shows St George slaying the dragon – which he does with great aplomb every hour on the hour.

Nearest tube: Oxford Circus.
Nearby buses: 3, 6, 9, 12, 13, 15, 23, 53, 88, 94, 139, 159.

Shell Clock
Shell Building, SE1.

This is the biggest clockface in London. Big Benzene, as it is affectionately known, is just 2 inches (5 centimetres) wider than Big Ben. The large, art deco Shell Building on the South Bank was built in the early 1930s and paved the way for even grander corporate schemes.

BR: Waterloo.
Nearest tubes: Embankment, Waterloo.
Nearby buses: 1, 4, 26, 68, 76, 77, 149, 168, 171, 176, 188, 501, 505, 507, 511, 521, D1, P11.

Shepherd Gate Clock and Time Ball
Old Royal Observatory, Greenwich Park, SE10.
Tel. 081–858 4422.

The fine clock found at the entrance to the Old Royal Observatory was built by a nineteenth-century designer called Charles Shepherd. It is a 'slave' clock and receives signals from a master clock inside the Observatory. Until 1852, it was wound manually, but in that year electricity brought even greater precision to the mechanism. In Victorian times, local shops had miniature versions of this clock on display. At that time the Observatory also provided the commercial telegraph service, which gave the correct time signal. Nearby is the famous Time Ball. Before the days of radio time signals one of the only ways you could get the precise time was by watching this ball. Stand with your back to Greenwich Park facing Flamstead House and you will see a pole on the eastern turret. The red ball rises half way up it at 12.55p.m., reaching the top at 12.58p.m. and falling back down again at 1.00p.m. precisely. Sailors, viewing the Time Ball from their boats on the Thames set their marine chronometers by it.

BR: Greenwich, Maze Hill.
Nearest tube: Island Gardens DLR, then Greenwich foot tunnel.
River boats from Westminster, Charing Cross, Tower Pier.
River buses run from most piers, including London City airport.

Swiss Centre Clock
Swiss Centre, Leicester Square, W1.

Very much at home above the Swiss national tourist office, this brightly decorated glockenspiel, complete with twenty-seven assorted bells, plays a selection of popular alpine tunes while entire herds of model cows and sheep parade around its base, followed by a village band. Milkmaids, farmers in national costume and a couple of cockerels complete the picture. The performance lasts for about 5 minutes. It can be seen Mon.–Fri. 12.00 noon, 6.00p.m., 7.00p.m. and 8.00p.m.; Sat.–Sun. 12.00 noon, 2.00p.m., then on each hour from 4.00p.m.– 8.00p.m.

Nearest tubes: Leicester Square, Piccadilly Circus.
Nearby buses: 14, 19, 24, 29, 38, 176.

17

Markets

MIXED MARKETS AND FLEA MARKETS

Bustling, bright, noisy markets have been an integral part of London life since medieval times. Many of those flourishing today are 'mixed' markets selling fruit and vegetables as well as household goods; while the more general 'flea' markets, as they are sometimes called, deal in everything from second-hand bric-à-brac, coins and jewellery to toys, tools, clothes and three-piece suites. For a successful visit, timing is all-important. There are bargains by the dozen if you arrive early enough and are prepared to haggle, but do not believe everything you hear – or you may suffer the sort of problem faced by one customer who attempted to return a cut-price freezer because it had failed to function, 'Look, mate,' said the stallholder, 'all you've got to do is turn it upside down and 'course it'll work.' Listed below is a selection of the most popular and interesting markets, but many more can be found all over the city.

Covent Garden Market
The Piazza, Covent Garden, WC1.

London's largest fruit and vegetable market moved from Covent Garden to a new location south of the river in the mid-1970s and the original site was redeveloped. Covent Garden retains the lively atmosphere of a busy market, with open stalls in the central hall and all kinds of shops from expensive boutiques and herbal emporiums to those selling children's books and toys. No cars are allowed in or around the piazza, which makes strolling along the paved walkways a more pleasant experience than you would encounter in the average West End street. The market has become famous for its street entertainers. Jugglers, mime artists, musicians, fire-eaters and magicians entertain the crowds – with the best acts performing at weekends. Musicians who use odd household items as instruments draw the biggest audiences; it is not until you hear rock 'n' roll arranged for 'litterbin and bottle' that you can appreciate the true inventiveness of buskers. One of the weirdest places in Covent Garden can be found in the basement of the central covered market building. Here, next to Eric Snook's toyshop, is the Cabaret Mechanical Theatre, a marvellous den full of bizarre oddities. Outside the entrance a life-size model of a chiropodist with dangerously long fingernails massages tired feet, while inside more than seventy mechanical toys spring into action in a noisy, twilight world (for details, see page 48). On the west side of the piazza is St Paul's Church (not to be confused with St Paul's Cathedral), built for the Earl of Bedford by Inigo Jones in 1633. The earl, more concerned with cost than style, suggested that a 'barn of a place' would do. Inigo Jones promised him 'the handsomest barn in England' and created a simple and dignified church, now the sole reminder of Jones's original Covent Garden. Today it is sometimes referred to as the actors' church, for many theatrical personalities are buried here. Another famous double act associated with Covent Garden is Punch and Judy. A plaque marks the spot where Samuel Pepys saw his first Punch and Judy show here, as recorded in his diary of 1661. There are plenty of good places to eat in the area, ranging from street stalls selling hot dogs and baked potatoes to burger bars and restaurants. A favourite is the Rock Garden on the piazza itself, where the food is simple and inexpensive. In summer you can sit outside at several cafés and restaurants. Close by are the London Transport Museum (see page 59), the Spitting Image Rubberworks (see page 72) and the Theatre Museum (see page 73). For Covent Garden's seasonal programme, see page 15. An antiques market is held each Monday in the covered way on the south side of the piazza, and a general crafts market operates from Tuesday to Saturday.

Nearest tube: Covent Garden.
Nearby buses: 1, 4, 6, 9, 11, 13, 15, 23, 26, 76, 77A, 168, 171, 176, 188, 196, 501, 505, 521.

Brick Lane
Shoreditch, E1.
Sunday morning.

A large, rambling market that operates only on Sunday mornings, Brick Lane has enough stalls to keep you browsing for hours. Cheshire Street, to the east of the lane, sells everything from bric-à-brac and nearly new books in mint condition to second-hand records and clocks, clothes, bicycles, household goods, china and silver. Friendly and full of atmosphere, Brick Lane is slightly smaller than its sister market down the road in Petticoat Lane (see page 137), and more fun. Parking restrictions are in force on Sundays so, if you are travelling by car, use a car park (see page 5).

Nearest tubes: Aldgate East, Liverpool Street.
Nearby buses: 25, 67, 253.

Church Street
Lisson Grove, W2.

Just north of Baker Street, off Lisson Grove, Church Street is transformed every Saturday into a small but interesting market, selling everything from clothes and vegetables to bric-à-brac and toys.

Alfie's, at the Lisson Grove end of Church Street, is England's largest covered antiques market. It has over 350 stalls.

Nearest tube: Edgware Road.
Nearby buses: 6, 7, 15, 16, 18, 23, 27, 36, 98.

Camden Lock
Camden Lock Place, NW1.

Situated alongside the Regent's Canal, Camden Lock has developed into one of the most popular markets in London. Open every Saturday and Sunday, it sells both new and second-hand goods. Craft stalls occupy most of the central market area and old warehouses have been converted into craft workshops. Pretty and picturesque with colourful barges cruising up and down, the 'lock' still operates today; boats leave at regular intervals for trips to London Zoo and Little Venice (for details, see page 130). A huge flea market underneath the arches to the north sells second-hand clothes, carpets, bric-à-brac and furniture, and there are a number of good foodstalls in the main area. It can be very busy at Camden Lock; if the crowds seem too pressing, take a gentle walk along the canal path.

Nearest tube: Camden Town.
Nearby buses: 24, 27, 29, 31, 68, 134, 135, 168, 214, 253, 274, C2.

Petticoat Lane
Middlesex Street, E1.

Petticoat Lane market, which embraces a network of neighbouring streets, has been associated with the clothing trade since the seventeenth century. Today it is one of London's most famous markets, selling almost everything. It is practically impossible to explore the entire market in one visit; the main areas to head for are Petticoat Lane, Club Row and Goulston Street. The market is open on Sunday mornings only – when parking restrictions are in operation in the area.

Nearest tubes: Aldgate, Aldgate East, Liverpool Street.
Nearby buses: 8, 15, 25, 40, 67, 158, 253.

Portobello Market
Portobello, W11.

There has been a fruit and vegetable market here since the early nineteenth century, but Portobello became popular in the 1960s for its antiques stalls and remains west London's best-known market. Open from Monday to Saturday, it runs the full length of Portobello Road. On Fridays and Saturdays, when the market is in full swing and the pavements are crammed with stallholders, the atmosphere is buzzing with excitement. At the north end, under the flyover, cheap stalls sell bric-à-brac, second-hand clothes, bicycles and general knick-knacks. Further south, towards Pembridge Road, the more expensive antiques shops take over.

*Nearest tubes:*Ladbroke Grove, Notting Hill Gate.
Nearby buses: 15, 23, 52, 70, 295.

WHOLESALE MARKETS

A few wholesale markets that sell directly to the trade are also open to the public. They are fun to visit if you are prepared to get up in time to catch the early traders at work (see opening times), but they are not suitable for young children.

Billingsgate
North Quay, West India Dock Road, E14.

London's premier fish market moved from its old site in the City to the Isle of Dogs in the East End. It is a good place to wander through and take in the atmosphere (and smells). Look out for the special flat-topped hats that the porters wear to transport huge loads of fish around the market. This is an extremely busy trading centre at any time of the week, so tread carefully.

Open Mon.–Sat. from 5.00a.m.
Nearest tube: Poplar DLR.
Nearby bus: D8.

New Covent Garden
Nine Elms, SW8.

When the famous fruit and vegetable market moved to Nine Elms from its original site in Covent Garden, wholesalers found they had a great deal more room and better facilities in which to operate. New Covent Garden is an enormous area, where trading swings into action before most people are usually awake. Head for the glorious display of colour and smells in the flower market, where friendly stallholders occasionally allow members of the public to buy a few plants.

Open daily from 4.00a.m.
Nearest tube: Vauxhall.
Nearby buses: 44, 77, 77A, 344.

18

Squares

The grand squares of London's West End are a legacy from a bygone age when landowners with money to spare encouraged architects to build expensive houses for the rich. Many of them were laid out during the late eighteenth and early nineteenth century, when smart establishments – large enough to cater for an upstairs-downstairs kind of life, with plenty of room for servants and a mews at the back for horses – sprang up like mushrooms. During the past fifty years a great many such houses have been split up into flats, but to some they still epitomise London life at its most affluent. Many squares have gardens which can provide a welcome respite for tired shoppers or sightseers and their children. Some are accessible only to keyholders, while others are open to the general public – several of the latter are listed below.

Berkeley Square, W1.

Even though the nightingales no longer sing in Berkeley Square, its 200-year-old plane trees make an excellent sanctuary for other birds. West End shoppers can rest their aching feet here and contemplate the day's purchases, while across the way ghosts make ready for a lighter kind of window-gazing – No. 50 is reputed to be the most haunted house in London. At the end of summer the famous Berkeley Square Ball is held here to raise money for charity.

Nearest tubes: Bond Street, Green Park.
Nearby buses: 8, 9, 14, 19, 22, 38.

Bloomsbury Square, WC1.

This site was the first open space to be termed 'a square', but its original seventeenth-century houses have disappeared. The gardens were planted by Humphry Repton, a famous landscape designer of the early nineteenth century.

Nearest tube: Russell Square.
Nearby buses: 30, 68, 168, 188.

Cavendish Square, W1.

This eighteenth-century square is situated behind the John Lewis department store and the gardens are a good place to take a break from Oxford Street, sit down and relax.

Nearest tubes: Bond Street, Oxford Circus.
Nearby buses: 3, 6, 7, 8, 10, 12, 13, 15, 23, 53, 55, 73, 88, 94, 98, 113, 135, 137, 139, 159, 176.

Grosvenor Square, W1.

Purpose-built mansion blocks now flank three sides of this eighteenth-century square, which covers more than 6 acres and is just a short walk from Oxford Street. Although it is not possible to go inside the gardens, as one of London's best-known squares, it deserves to be mentioned. Little remains of the original architecture and the west side is entirely occupied by the vast American Embassy, which is topped by a golden eagle 10 feet (3 metres) tall. Associated with the USA since 1785, the square is affectionately known as 'Little America'. General Eisenhower had his headquarters at No. 20 during the Second World War and there is a statue of President Franklin D. Roosevelt in the gardens.

Nearest tube: Bond Street.
Nearby buses: 6, 7, 10, 12, 13, 15, 16A, 23, 73, 88, 94, 98, 113, 135, 137, 139, 159.

Leicester Square, WC1.

Nowadays the main reason to visit Leicester Square is to see a film or go out for a meal, but it was once famous as a site for fighting duels. Named after Leicester House, which once stood on the site, the square has a small garden adjacent to it which contains sculptures of some notable former residents of the area. There are plenty of places to eat in the square, which is now a pedestrian precinct. For a treat you could visit Baskin Robbins – an American's answer to paradise – or the Häagen-Dazs ice-cream parlour (see also Swiss Centre Clock, page 134).

Nearest tube: Leicester Square.
Nearby buses: 14, 19, 24, 29, 38, 176.

Parliament Square, SW1.

Not an ideal spot for a picnic perhaps, but Parliament Square is overlooked by some of the finest and oldest buildings in London: the Houses of Parliament, St Margaret's Church and Westminster Abbey. The square itself was not laid out until 1926, when it became the first roundabout in London. Around the central gardens are statues of ministers of state, the most recent of which, and probably the most famous, is the bronze of Winston Churchill. This square seems to attract more than its fair share of pigeons who enjoy being fed.

Nearest tube: Westminster.
Nearby buses: 3, 11, 12, 24, 53, 77A, 88, 109, 159, 184, 196, 511.

Queen Square, WC1.

Slightly off the beaten track, behind Southampton Row and a short walk from the British Museum, is one of the prettiest squares in town. It is close by Coram Fields, which boasts a phenomenon unusual in the heart of London – a playground set among classic Georgian colonnades with swings, slides, Wendy houses, sculptures to climb on, and some very noisy cockerels.

Nearest tube: Russell Square.
Nearby buses: 14, 19, 24, 29, 38, 176.

Russell Square, WC1.

A short walk from the British Museum takes you to Russell Square with its shady lawns and glorious displays of roses in the summer. The café in the square is open from 8.00a.m. to 6.30p.m. from April to September.

Nearest tube: Russell Square.
Nearby buses: 30, 68, 168, 188.

Soho Square, W1.

The word 'soho' was a hunting cry used by the huntsmen when sighting the hare. The square, originally named King Square after Charles II, was built in the seventeenth century to try and attract the nobility to what was then an up and coming area. Today, most of the original houses have gone but the slightly battered statue of Charles II in the garden is one of the oldest outdoor monuments in London and dates from the 1680s. It holds centre stage in front of an unusual Tudor-style lodge and the garden is peppered with plane trees.

Nearest tube: Tottenham Court Road.
Nearby buses: 7, 8, 10, 14, 19, 22B, 24, 25, 29, 38, 55, 73, 98, 134, 176.

Trinity Square, EC3.

This is a good place to relax or have a picnic after visiting the Tower of London, despite its gruesome past: the site of Trinity Square was reputedly one of the best spots from which to watch public executions on Tower Hill.

Nearest tube: Tower Hill.
Nearby buses: 15, 25, 42, 78, 100, D1, D9, D11.

Trafalgar Square, WC2.

One of London's most famous landmarks, Trafalgar Square was created to mark Lord Nelson's victory at the Battle of Trafalgar in 1805. Nelson's Column, completed in 1842, was deliberately made taller than that of the Duke of York in what became Waterloo Place (see page 107). It took over three years to build; when it was finished and just before Nelson's statue was hauled into place, a dinner party was held on the top of the column to celebrate the occasion. The guests, none of whom seemed to suffer from vertigo, tucked into a hearty meal 170 feet (52 metres) up in the air. An integral part of the square – and fed to bursting point – are the pigeons, which spend a great deal of time perching on Nelson's hat. (Over half a tonne's worth of their droppings was removed at great cost a few years ago, when the column was cleaned.) The pigeons are remarkably tame and will eat out of your hand. Edwin Landseer's four huge lions, symbolising the courage of the British people, guard the base of the column. Trafalgar Square is at its merriest over Christmas. In early December a giant Norwegian Christmas Tree is erected – a gift from the people of Oslo in appreciation of the help Britain gave them during the Second World War. Christmas carols are sung around the tree each evening until Christmas Eve, and on 31 December traditional celebrations to mark the New Year attract vast crowds.

On the north-east corner of the square is the church of St Martin's-in-the-Fields, where regular lunchtime concerts are held. There is a café in the crypt, and the church is also the home of the London Brassrubbing Centre (see page 158). The National Gallery (see page 41) dominates the north side of the square, and Covent Garden (see page 135) is only a few minutes' walk away. At the head of Whitehall, and easily overlooked, is a splendid seventeenth-century statue of King Charles I on horseback. It stands on the site of Charing Cross, where in 1292 King Edward I stopped on the final stage of his journey to Westminster to bury his wife Eleanor. It is from this point that all distances from central London are now measured.

Nearest tubes: Charing Cross, Leicester Square.
Nearby buses: 3, 6, 9, 11, 12, 13, 15, 23, 24, 29, 30, 53, 77A, 88, 94, 109, 139, 159, 176, 184, 196.

19

City walks

In the City
They sell and buy
And nobody ever
Asks them why.
But since it contents them
To buy and sell
God forgive them
They might as well.

Anon

The City of London, known as 'the square mile', is a metropolitan enclave separate from the rest of the capital. Unlike London's other local authorities, the City has its own government, headed by the Lord Mayor. It even has its own police force, recognisable by their red and white hatbands and armbands and bronze badges. The City has been the nerve-centre of Britain's financial world for hundreds of years. In Roman times it was walled, but today a bronze 'griffin' marks the boundary in Temple Bar where Westminster gives way to the City. Custom dictates that, even when a reigning British monarch wishes to enter the City, he or she must wait at the City boundaries before proceeding. Then, in a ceremony dating from the time of Queen Elizabeth I, the Lord Mayor hands over his sword to the sovereign; this is then returned to him as a symbol of his authority.

The best way to get to know the area is by means of an organised walk. During the week the City is a hive of activity, teeming with bankers, stockbrokers, secretaries and wheeler-dealers, but at weekends it is much less frenetic and full of the unexpected. At these quieter times you can appreciate the history of the City and its wide variety of architecture, from Dickensian alleys and hidden courts to busy markets and modern skyscrapers.

A company called City Walks has professional guides who conduct various tours for small groups. The guides wear identity badges and carry City Walks leaflets. The company also arranges tours to fit in with school or college curriculums. One of its most comprehensive walks, 'London Story – Romans to the Blitz', takes you through the best preserved sections of the old City and to visit, for example, a Victorian market and Dickens's favourite dining rooms; a commentary explains how the Great Fire and Blitz devastated large swathes of the City. Tours meet outside Tower Hill tube station at 10.30a.m. every Sunday, Tuesday, Wednesday, Thursday and Saturday. For more information ring 071–700 6931.

Older children who enjoy a mystery might like to join the 'Trail of Jack the Ripper', which takes you back to nineteenth-century London and, with the help of a Victorian-style policeman, allows you to discover hidden alleys and cobbled streets while tracing the footsteps of the Ripper himself. Tours meet at 7.00p.m. every day at Tower Hill tube station. Each walk lasts about 2 hours. There is a charge, but accompanied children under 12 go free. For more details, telephone Susan Ferguson-Menge on 071– 700 6931.

If organised walks do not appeal to you, strike out on your own and follow the Silver Jubilee Walkway. Paving stones marked with easily identifiable jubilee crowns highlight a 5-mile trail from Leicester Square to Tower Hill. A London Tourist Board booklet gives additional information (see page 6). Alternatively, the Museum of London (see page 62) tells the story of the City and produces an excellent booklet detailing the 'Roman Wall Walk'. This walk lasts about 2 hours and takes you around the old medieval city, whose boundaries have remained very much the same as they were centuries ago. When the wall was first erected, its 2 miles of solid stone were over 20 feet (6 metres) high in places, creating a formidable barrier, the remnants of which are still visible.

For details of other walks in the City and elsewhere in London, consult listings magazines such as *Time Out*.

20

Zoos and city farms

ZOOS

London Zoo
Regent's Park, NW1.
Tel. 071–722 3333.

As zoological societies throughout the world examine the ethics of keeping large wild animals in captivity in major cities, many zoos have had to re-evaluate their position. London Zoo is no exception and this, coupled with serious financial problems, has led the zoo to consider major changes to its structure and role. Situated in Regent's Park only 5 minutes' drive away from the West End, London Zoo is home to one of the most comprehensive collections of animals in the world. Over the past two decades sterling efforts have been made to make life for those in captivity as pleasant as possible, and new houses have been built for the monkeys and big cats, giving them more space in semi-natural surroundings. You can rub noses with the lions through glass barriers or watch the elephants enjoying their daily feast of hay – they consume more than 2 tons a week. In Moonlight Hall an artificial night-time world has been created, where visitors can examine the habits of nocturnal animals. During summer there are camel rides and excursions in pony or llama traps, while the Children's Zoo, set apart from the main zoo, gives younger children an opportunity to meet and stroke farm animals. From the 3-foot (1-metre) high green and brown spotted frog (actually a well-camouflaged dustbin) to some large, fluffy rabbits, all sorts of domesticated animals are here. To find out about new arrivals, feeding times, and so on, check the noticeboard inside the main gate. An interesting way to reach the zoo is by waterbus (see page 131). An all-in ticket is available which includes the canal trip and entrance to the zoo at a reduced price.

Open April–Oct. daily 9.00a.m.–6.00p.m.; Nov.–March daily 10.00a.m.–6.00p.m.
Admission charge; half price on the first Saturday of each month except in June, July and August; season tickets available.
Nearest tubes: Camden Town, Baker Street.
Nearby buses: 274, C2.

Battersea Park Zoo
Albert Bridge Road, SW11.
Tel. 081–871 7530.

Farmyard animals and exotic birds roam freely around Battersea Park Zoo. Pony rides are a popular attraction in summer.

Open April–Sept. daily 11.00a.m.–6.00p.m.; Oct.–March Sat.–Sun. only 10.30a.m.–3.30p.m.
Admission charge.
BR: Battersea Park.
Nearby buses: 44, 137, 137A, 344.

Crystal Palace Zoo
Thicket Road, Penge, SE20.
Tel. 081–778 7148.

Crystal Palace Zoo is in many ways closer to an urban farm than a zoo. A cross-section of animals, ranging from shire horses, goats and cows to penguins, otters and llamas, can be found here, and many domesticated animals wander freely outside their enclosures. After visiting the zoo, you could explore the park, which includes a sports stadium, a maze, a miniature railway and a boating lake (see page 90).

Open daily April–Sept. 11.30a.m.–5.00p.m.; Oct.–March 11.30a.m.–3.30p.m.
Admission charge.
BR: Crystal Palace, Penge West.
Nearby buses: 2A, 3, 63, 122, 137A, 157, 202, 227, 249.

CITY FARMS

The bricks and mortar of Greater London have spread out further and further in recent years. Yet in the middle of all this development the opportunities to see a slice of country life have increased. London is one of the few capitals in the world where a number of active small farms can be found within the city limits. Unlike many country farms, these urban oases welcome visitors. While London Zoo offers a close-up view of creatures from all over the world, city farms give children the chance to see activities that have a relevance closer to home, such as feeding and milking of domesticated animals. Many different kinds of animals can be found at the farms, including goats, pigs, chickens, rabbits and ponies. Most city farms are open daily, but check before you go.

Freightliners Farm
Paradise Park, Sheringham Road, N7.
Tel. 071–609 0467.

Hackney City Farm
1a Goldsmith's Row, E2.
Tel. 071–729 6381.

Mudchute Community Farm
Pier Street, E14.
Tel. 071–515 5901.

Newham City Farm
Stansfield Road, E16.
Tel. 071–476 1170.

Spitalfields Community Farm
Weaver Street, E1.
Tel. 071–247 8762.

Stepney Stepping Stones Farm
Stepney Way, E1.
Tel. 071–790 8204.

Surrey Docks Farm
Rotherhithe Street, SE16.
Tel. 071–231 1010.

Vauxhall City Farm
24 St Oswald's Place, SE11.
Tel. 071–582 4204.

21

Visits behind the scenes

This chapter explains how you can find out about what goes on behind the scenes in a wide variety of activities, from firefighting to glassmaking to rugby-playing, while enjoying yourself at the same time.

Clink Armoury
1 Clink Street, SE1.
Tel. 071–403 6515.

At the Clink Museum you can visit the only working armoury in southern Britain and see armour dating back to medieval times. There are always interesting activities going on here. Craftsmen might be making anything from a replica of Viking armour to Cromwellian helmets and gauntlets to miniature suits and modern-day equipment. Every object is hand-crafted on site and children are allowed to handle the various pieces and find out how they were constructed. High-quality armour was first produced in this country in the sixteenth century. Before then noblemen bought their armour from abroad, particularly from continental Europe, where craftsmen were considered the finest in the world. As weapons of attack became more sophisticated, so did armour, and the techniques required to produce such complicated items are still in demand today. A team from the US Space Agency NASA came to Britain some years ago to research ideas for a space suit for the astronaut John Glen and used designs taken from a suit of armour made for King Henry VIII in 1520.

Open: museum hours (see page 50).
Admission included in museum entrance fee.
Nearest tube: London Bridge.
Nearby buses: 17, 21, 22A, 35, 40, 43, 44, 47, 48, 95, 133, 149, 214.

Fire stations

If you have ever been in a queue of traffic and had to pull over to make way for a fire engine as it screams past sounding its siren, you might wonder how firefighters manage to operate in London. The London Fire Brigade – or, to use its proper title, the London Fire and Civil Defence Authority – seems to take everything in its stride, however, and now deals with more than 190,000 calls annually. Young children who dream of being firefighters when they grow up will enjoy visiting a fire station, where they can climb on gleaming fire-engines and thoroughly inspect the vehicles inside and out; the firemen on duty will be pleased to explain the station drill that has to be followed when they are called to an emergency. Visiting times vary and have to fit in with station duties, so apply in writing to the PR Department, London Fire Brigade, H, Albert Embankment, London SE1 7SD.

Glasshouse
65 Long Acre, WC2.
Tel. 071–836 9785.

The Glasshouse provides an opportunity to watch glassblowers at work. In a studio at the back of the shop, they use giant furnaces to transform raw materials into runny-looking substances which are then blown into glass. The temperatures are high and the craftsmen immensely skilled. Although the final stages of production are carried out elsewhere, the end-products can be admired and purchased at the front of the shop. Not suitable for very young children.

Open Mon.–Sat. 10.00a.m.–1.00p.m. and 2.00p.m.– 6.00p.m.
Admission free.
Nearest tube: Covent Garden.
Nearby buses: 14, 19, 24, 29, 38, 176.

Heathrow airport
Heathrow, Middlesex.
Tel. 081–759 4321.

More than 33,000 aeroplanes a month use the four runways at Heathrow, making it the busiest airport in the world. From the viewing gallery in Terminal 2, plane-spotters can have a field day watching at close quarters all the various aircraft arriving and taking off. Concorde usually lands from New York at 6.10p.m. and 10.25p.m., daily but the flight is occasionally cancelled, so check beforehand by telephoning 081–759 4321. Flight information monitors in the viewing area give details of arrivals and departures, and there is a small covered area to provide shelter, as well as a café and gift shop.

Open daily.
Admission free.
Nearest tube: Heathrow.
Buses: A1 from Victoria station, A2 from Euston.

Houses of Parliament
St Margaret Street, SW1.

Although there is extensive television coverage of MPs at work (and asleep) in the House of Commons, you may be interested to witness parliamentary machinations at first hand. If so, head for St Stephen's Porch, the entrance to the Strangers' Gallery. For a more detailed look at governmental procedures, write to your local MP and ask him or her to organise a tour. For details of admission times, telephone 071–219 3000.

Admission free.
Nearest tube: Westminster.
Nearby buses: 3, 11, 12, 24, 53, 77A, 88, 109, 159, 184, 196, 511.

Lloyd's of London
Lime Street, EC3.
Tel. 071–623 7100.

Visit Richard Rogers' famous 'inside-out' building (see page 110) to observe the London insurance world at work. From the visitors' gallery on the fifth floor, you can look down on the underwriting room and see Lloyd's brokers placing their risks with various syndicates. Nowadays almost anything can be insured, but in 1688, when the idea took root, shipping was the main line of business. Edward Lloyd owned a coffee-house near the Thames where traders and ship-owners would meet to exchange news. From this small start developed *Lloyd's List*, a broadsheet of the latest shipping forecasts – a version of which is still published today. By the mid-1770s Lloyd's had more than seventy members and was installed in the Royal Exchange. On the ground floor of the Lloyd's Building, in the underwriting room, hangs the Lutine Bell, salvaged from the frigate HMS *Lutine*, which sank in 1799 with no survivors. Today it is rung only on ceremonial occasions or as a mark of respect to important visitors, but before the advent of modern technology it was rung once for bad news – for instance, if a ship were overdue; and twice for good news – when the ship arrived in port. The last time the bell was rung to announce an overdue vessel was in November 1981, when the Liberian motor vessel *Gloria* failed to arrive on time. It has also been used to announce many major disasters at sea, including the sinking of the *Titanic* in 1912 and the wrecking of the Norwegian tanker *Berge Istra* in the 1970s. There is a self-explanatory exhibition in the gallery. Groups of four or more should apply in writing to visit. Over-14s only are admitted.

Open Mon.–Fri. 9.30a.m.–4.30p.m.
Admission free.
Nearest tubes: Bank, Liverpool Street.
Nearby buses: 8, 11, 15, 15B, 21, 22B, 23, 25, 26, 43, 76, 149, 501.

London Diamond Centre
10 Hanover Street, W1.

A tour around the London Diamond Centre can be a real gem. Not only is it an eye-opener for anyone lucky enough to be thinking about buying a diamond, but it also demonstrates how skilled craftsmen cut and mount the stones. The first diamond was discovered in Brazil in 1725, and ever since then diamonds have been the most sought-after jewels in the world. Even with modern technology, however, diamond-mining is a painstakingly intricate process, for gravel and sand many million times the diamonds' weight must be sifted through to find the stones. Whatever their size or colour, all diamonds are valuable, and the secret of top-class stones lies in the cutting. One of the most famous diamonds ever to be broken up was the Cullinan, which weighed over 1.25 pounds (0.57 kg). The tour shows how this process works. Write to the centre to arrange a visit. Not suitable for under-7s.

Open Mon.–Sat. 9.30a.m.–5.30p.m.
Nearest tubes: Bond Street, Oxford Circus.
Nearby buses: 6, 7, 8, 10, 12, 13, 15, 16A, 23, 73, 88, 94, 98, 113, 135, 137, 139, 159.

London Glass Blowing Workshop
Hope (Sufferance) Wharf, 109 Rotherhithe Street, SE16.
Tel. 071–237 0394.

The London Glassblowing Workshop, founded in 1976 by Peter Layton, is the oldest of its kind in Britain. Each piece is free-blown, which encourages a rare attention to detail. Unlike factory production, freehand glassblowing under studio conditions allows the artist–craftsman to work by himself in an exacting but exciting medium. Each piece is formed from molten glass and individually coloured, making it unique. Telephone the workshop for an appointment to see the glassblowing process in operation. Not suitable for under-7s.

Admission free.
Nearest tube: Rotherhithe.
Nearby buses: 47, 70, 188.

London International Financial Futures Exchange (LIFFE)
Canon Bridge, EC4.
Tel. 071–623 0444.

In new premises on top of Cannon Bridge station, LIFFE's purpose-built, high-tech building is nearly three times the size of its old headquarters at the Royal Exchange. Formed in 1982, LIFFE is now Europe's leading centre for trading in financial futures and options. The tour takes visitors to the public viewing gallery, where you can look down on the busy trading floor, with its 595 booths. LIFFE's turnover has risen from just over a million contracts in its first year to 38 million in 1991. This is an informative tour for anyone interested in the financial futures market. Apply in writing to arrange a tour. Over-13s only are admitted.

Visitors' gallery open Mon.–Fri. 11.30a.m.–1.30p.m.
Admission free.
BR: Cannon Street.
Nearest tubes: Cannon Street, Bank.
Nearby buses: 15, 21, 25, 35, 40, 43, 47, 48, 133, 214, 501, 505.

Lord's Cricket Tours
Lord's Cricket Ground, St John's Wood Road, NW8.
Tel. 071–266 3825.

You must make an appointment to go around the famous Lord's

pavilion. Except on match days (see page 16), special tours take place twice daily at noon and 2.00p.m. when visitors are taken through the Long Room (normally restricted to members only) and Cricket World Museum which charts the history of cricket from its earliest reference in 1550, to the present day. Different artefacts on display include bats, balls, photographs of great moments and the famous 'Ashes' urn, the prize for the winners of the England v. Australia Test series. Look out for the stuffed sparrow, mounted on the ball that killed it in 1936. The tour takes approximately 1½ hours. Over-8s only are admitted.

Admission charge.
Nearest tube: St John's Wood.
Nearby buses: 13, 82, 113, 274.

Mount Pleasant Royal Mail Sorting Office
Farringdon Road, EC1.
Tel. 071–239 2191.

Britain's largest sorting office offers a tour that demystifies the complicated business of moving mail around the country and abroad. Lasting 2 hours, it shows how letters and parcels are transported by means of a mini underground railway system before distribution. Tours, for over-9s only, are held twice daily Mon.–Thurs., but telephone for details.

Admission free.
BR: Farringdon.
Nearest tube: Farringdon.
Nearby buses: 19, 38, 63, 171A, 196, 259.

Twickenham Rugby Football Ground
Whittin Road, Twickenham, Middlesex.
Tel. 081–892 8161.

Visit Twickenham's famous rugby pitch, watch a video and find out what it feels like to tread the turf where such famous players as Will Carling and Wade Dooley have won glory. Tours can be booked in advance by written application.

Admission charge.
BR: Twickenham.
Nearest tube: Hounslow East then by 281 bus.
Nearby buses: 281.

Wimbledon Lawn Tennis Museum
All England Club, Church Road, SW19.
Tel. 081–946 6131.

The museum has all the inside information on the great tennis stars, as well as a video showing highlights of some of the most memorable matches played over the years at the Wimbledon Championships.

Open Tues.–Sat. 11.00a.m.–5.00p.m.
Admission charge.
BR: Wimbledon.
Nearest tubes: Southfields, Wimbledon.
Nearby buses: 39, 93, 156 only during Wimbledon fortnight (see page 15).

THEATRE AND CONCERT HALL VISITS

Many organisations arrange special tours to show the public what goes on behind the scenes of theatrical productions. These are generally not suitable for the very young.

Barbican Centre
Silk Street, EC2.
Tel. 071–628 3351.

The Barbican Centre (see page 24) runs a number of guided tours each week which take in the theatres, concert hall and conservatory and demonstrate how the arts complex works. Book in advance by writing to Level 5 information desk.

Admission charge for tour.
BR: Blackfriars, City Thameslink, Farringdon, Liverpool Street.
Nearest tubes: Barbican, Moorgate, St Paul's.
Nearby buses: 4, 141, 172.

National Theatre
South Bank, SE1.
Tel. 071–633 0880.

A tour of the National Theatre allows you to enjoy a comprehensive inspection of all three auditoria, as well as a chance to go on stage if rehearsals are not in progress. In the large backstage workshops you can see where scenery is made and stored. Tours are held from Monday to Saturday five times a day. Book in advance by telephone.

Admission charge for tour.
BR: Waterloo.
Nearest tubes: Embankment, Waterloo.
Nearby buses: 1, 4, 26, 68, 76, 77, 149, 168, 171, 176, 188, 501, 505, 507, 511, 521, D1, P11.

Royal Opera House
Covent Garden, WC2.
Tel. 071–240 1200.

Backstage tours of the Royal Opera House give an interesting insight into the operation of one of the most famous opera venues in the world. Visitors can see the rehearsal rooms and workshops, as well as Covent Garden's extensive wardrobe collection. If you wish to join a tour, apply in writing well in advance.

Admission charge for tour.
Nearest tube: Covent Garden.
Nearby buses: 1, 4, 6, 9, 11, 13, 15, 23, 26, 30, 68, 76, 77A, 168, 171, 176, 188, 196, 501, 505, 521.

Sadler's Wells Theatre
Rosebery Avenue, EC1.
Tel. 071–278 6563.

Tours take you behind the scenes at both of Sadler's Wells's auditoria and teach you something about the theatre's colourful history and the various companies that have worked here. Telephone the community and education department to arrange tours for groups of at least ten. Suitable for over-6s.

Nearest tube: Angel.
Nearby buses: 19, 38, 153, 171A, 196, 279.

22

Hands-on activities

ARTS AND CRAFTS

Most London boroughs organise arts and crafts activities for children – contact your local town hall for details. Alternatively, there are a few arts and crafts workshops where children can try their hand at, for example, making pots or creating models out of clay. Telephone the individual centres for details of classes and charges. One of the best places to see the latest in arts and crafts design is the Contemporary Applied Arts Centre, 43 Earlham Street, WC2. The centre's Christmas and summer shows include many weird and wonderful creations made from wood, ceramics, metal, plastic and porcelain.

Camden Arts Centre
Arkwright Road, NW3.
Tel. 081–435 2643.

Camden Arts Centre runs termtime Saturday morning classes in painting and pottery for 7–16s and holiday courses for younger children.

Nearest tubes: Finchley Road, Hampstead.
Nearby buses: 13, 46, 82, 113, 139.

Chelsea Pottery
13 Radnor Walk, SW3.
Tel. 071–352 1366.

Chelsea Pottery offers over-4s a trial three-hour class to find out whether or not they like hand-building in clay. Subsequent lessons take place on Saturdays during termtime. There is an annual club membership. Adult classes are held on Wednesday evenings.

Nearest tube: Sloane Square.
Nearby buses: 11, 19, 22.

Commonwealth Institute
Kensington High Street, W8.
Tel. 071–603 4535.

During the summer holidays the institute runs various workshops for children, some of which include pottery and painting sessions.

Nearest tube: High Street Kensington.
Nearby buses: 9, 9A, 10, 27, 28, 31, 49.

Candle Makers Supplies
28 Blythe Road, W14.
Tel. 071–602 4031.

This marvellous shop is full of everything you could need for making candles, including moulds, dyes and waxes. It also sells videos explaining all about the craft.

Nearest tube: Hammersmith.
Nearby buses: 9, 9A, 10, 27.

Fulham Pottery
8–10 Ingate Place, SW8.
Tel. 071–720 0050.

This well-known pottery shop has been in existence since 1671. If you do not have access to a kiln, its 'cold clay starter kit' is ideal for beginners because it allows the clay to harden without having to be fired.

BR: Queenstown Road (Battersea).
Nearby buses: 44, 137, 137A, 344.

Hackney City Farm
1a Goldsmith's Row, EC2.
Tel. 071–729 6381.

Pottery classes for 5-year-olds and over are held on Sunday afternoons between 2.00p.m. and 4.00p.m. Younger children should be accompanied by an adult. Telephone to book.

The Horniman Museum
100 London Road, Forest Hill, SE23.
Tel. 081–699 1872.

The museum runs a variety of workshops throughout the year ranging from pottery to painting. Aimed at 7-year-olds and over, the places are free but not bookable.

Kidsplay
67 Aveling Park Road, E17.
Tel. 081–523 0478.

Arts and crafts workshops are held here during the summer holidays for 5–14s.

Nearest tube: Walthamstow Central.
Nearby buses: 34, 97, 97A, 215, 257.

Polka Theatre for Children
240 The Broadway, Wimbledon, SW19.
Tel. 081–543 4888.

During the summer holidays Polka run their summer school, a multi-arts programme for children of all ages. This includes a craft week when children can make their own puppets, design jewellery and experiment with tie and dye.

Waterman's Arts Centre
40 High Street, Brentford, Middlesex.
Tel. 081–847 5651.

The Waterman's Arts Club is open each weekday during term time, and a collection run from local schools provides a useful service for working parents and their children. Professional staff involve children in different arts and crafts and sessions continue until 6.00p.m. Subjects range from mask-making to collage and painting. For further details telephone the number above.

BRASS-RUBBING

There are several brass-rubbing centres in London that provide help and advice as well as materials. No previous experience of the craft is necessary. Whether the subject is medieval knights or heraldic beasts, you can produce a glorious picture in about half an hour and discover a little bit about the age of chivalry in the process. Charges vary according to the size of the brass, but start at about 50p.

All Hallows-by-the-Tower
Byward Street, London, EC3.
Tel. 071–481 2928.

Open Mon.–Sat. 11.00a.m.–4.30p.m.; Sun. 1.00p.m.– 4.00p.m.
Nearest tube: Tower Hill.
Nearby buses: 15, 25, 100.

London Brass Rubbing Centre
Church of St Martin-in-the-Fields, Trafalgar Square, WC2.
Tel. 071–437 6023.

Open Mon.–Sat. 10.00a.m.–6.00p.m.; Sun. 12.00 noon– 6.00p.m.
Nearest tube: Charing Cross.
Nearby buses: 3, 6, 9, 11, 12, 13, 15, 23, 24, 29, 53, 77A, 88, 91, 94, 109, 139, 159, 176, 184, 196.

Westminster Abbey Cloisters
London, SW1.
Tel. 071–222 2085.

Open Mon.–Sat. 9.00a.m.–5.30p.m.
Nearest tube: Westminster.
Nearby buses: 3, 11, 12, 24, 53, 77A, 88, 109, 159, 184, 196, 511.

23

Out to lunch

Unlike most other countries in western Europe, Britain remains generally hostile to the presence of children in restaurants. It is not simply a question of children being seen and not heard – but of children not being seen at all. Customers are expected to accept what is on offer while their real needs are ignored. For far too long restaurateurs have been allowed to disregard the fact that eating is as much to do with people as with food. Although pizza and hamburger chains have enabled children to get used to the idea of restaurants, there is still a long way to go before they can be sure of receiving welcoming smiles elsewhere. Fortunately some restaurants have had the foresight to cash in on the need for family lunches, especially at weekends. Those listed below have all been tried and tested, but check prices before you go, as they may vary considerably. Somewhere like Smollensky's on the Strand, for instance, is more suitable for a special birthday treat than a routine Sunday lunch.

Café Pasta
184 Shaftesbury Avenue, WC2. Tel. 071–379 0198.
8 Theberton Street, N1. Tel. 071–226 2211.
179 King Street, W6. Tel. 071–741 0005.
2–4 Garrick Street, WC2. Tel. 071–497 2779.
8 High Street, Wimbledon Village, SW19. Tel. 081–944 6893.
200 Haverstock Hill, NW3. Tel. 071–431 8531.

Café Pasta serves all kinds of delicious pasta dishes in an easy-going family atmosphere. Although there is no children's menu as such, small portions are available at reasonable prices.

Chicago Meatpackers
96 Charing Cross Road, WC2.
Tel. 071–379 3277.

Generous helpings of cartoons plus special children's entertainment on Sundays makes this an excellent restaurant for families. The children's menu is reasonably priced. If you ask the waitress for a dime, you can serve yourself from an old-fashioned Coca Cola machine.

Ed's Easy Diner
Four branches at:

12 Moore Street, W1.
Tel. 071–439 1955.

353 Fulham Road, SW10.
Tel. 071–352 1952.

16 Hampstead High Street, NW3.
Tel. 071–431 1958.

362 King's Road, SW3.
Tel. 071–352 1956.

Ed's Easy Diner specialises in good old-fashioned hot dogs and hamburgers (their 'brat burgers' go down well with children who have smaller appetites) plus American-type cakes and pies.

Glaister's Bistro
4 Hollywood Road, SW10.
Tel. 071–352 0352.

If you like the idea of having the children taken off your hands for Sunday lunch (1.00p.m.–5.00p.m.) then Glaister's Bistro will do just that. The registered crèche next door is run by qualified staff and, although the food is more along the lines of a school packed lunch than a Sunday meal out, the entertainment includes painting sessions and video games with the added bonus of having other children to play with.

Lauderdale House
Waterlow Park, N6.
Tel. 081–348 8716.

On the fourth Sunday of each month (except August) a special cabaret is organised here for children from 12.30p.m.–2.00p.m., with games, music, poetry and competitions. Meanwhile, parents can sit back and enjoy a relatively relaxed meal.

Le Shop
329 King's Road, SW3.
Tel. 071–352 3891.

A good selection of mouth-watering crêpes in delicious combinations.

PJ's Grill
30 Wellington Street, Covent Garden, WC2.
Tel. 071–240 7529.

When you arrive at PJ's Grill on Saturday or Sunday between 11.00a.m. and 5.00p.m., a large area of the restaurant will be separated as a supervised play area for children. There will be slides, climbing frames and cars to play with and a cosy corner for babies and children to relax in. The special children's menu for the under-12s is entirely additive free and includes avocado dips, pasta, small hamburgers and some great puddings. While children are being entertained, parents can sit down and relax over lunch. The menu includes Caesar salad, steaks, clam chowder, fresh pasta and other New York grill-style food.

Planet Hollywood

Trocadero Centre, Coventry and Rupert Street, W1.
Tel. 071–287 1000.

Even though the movie stars are made of cardboard, Planet Hollywood has all the glitz and glamour of California and an atmosphere to guarantee a fun time out for all the family. The restaurant seats 400 and is packed with costumes and objects from well-known Hollywood films – the blue and white check dress Judy Garland wore in *The Wizard of Oz*, the sail boat from *The Princess Bride* and Mel Gibson's bullet-proof vest from *Lethal Weapon*. Giant screens show short compilations of favourite movies while giant portions of food leave little space for delicious puddings like Hollywood Mousse Pie and Ebony and Ivory Brownie. There are no children's portions but 'appetisers' include breaded chicken and simple pizzas and the burgers are excellent. No bookings – Planet Hollywood works on a first come first served basis.

Porter's

17 Henrietta Street, Covent Garden, WC2.
Tel. 071–836 6466.

Good, old-fashioned English Sunday lunches are served here. A children's menu provides miniature helpings of roast beef and Yorkshire pudding.

Rock Island Diner

London Pavilion (2nd floor), 1 Piccadilly Circus, W1.
Tel. 071–287 5500.

The Rock Island Diner offers free meals to under-10s at weekends if they are with an adult who buys a main course. Games and competitions provide added entertainment.

Roxy Café

297 Upper Street, N1.
Tel. 071–226 5746.

If you feel like something slightly out of the ordinary for Sunday lunch, visit the Roxy Café in Islington and sample Tex-Mex food at its best – tacos, tortillas, chimichangas or just plain burgers. Sundays are especially geared to children.

San Martino

103 Walton Street, SW3.
Tel. 071–589 1356.

Magic, games and entertainments are put on each Sunday between 1.00p.m. and 3.30p.m. After food, children can go upstairs and watch a video and leave parents to enjoy their puddings in peace.

Signor Zilli
41 Dean Street, W1.
Tel. 071–734 3924.

Sunday lunch at this well-known Italian restaurant takes on a new dimension when different children's shows are performed each week. It might be a Punch and Judy show, a magician's act or maybe a kids' disco. Telephone for details.

Smollensky's on the Strand
105 Strand, WC2.
Tel. 071–497 2101.

Sunday is Smollensky's special children's day, when no effort is spared to create a party atmosphere. Starting at 12 noon, Punch and Judy, clowns and storytellers entertain the children, and a special play area allows energetic diners to let off steam. The children's menu includes junior hamburgers, steaks, pasta and mouth-watering puddings. This is one of the best family restaurants in town.

CHINESE RESTAURANTS

Children enjoy the novelty of going out to a Chinese restaurant and sampling unusual dishes with unpronounceable names. Listed below are some reasonably priced restaurants that might be fun to visit for a family night out.

Bayee Village
24 High Street, SW19.
Tel. 081–947 3533.

Chuen Cheng Ku
17 Wardour Street, W1.
Tel. 071–437 1398.

Fortune Cookie
1 Queensway, W2.
Tel. 071–727 7260.

Mr Wong
313 King Street, Hammersmith, W6.
Tel. 081–748 6887.

North China Restaurant
305 Uxbridge Road, W3.
Tel. 081–992 9183.

Poons
27 Lisle Street, WC2.
Tel. 071–437 4549.

FISH AND CHIPS

Everyone has their 'local', but here are some others that welcome children and serve smaller-sized portions on request.

Brady's
513 Old York Road, SW18.
Tel. 081–877 9599.

Faulker's Fish Restaurant
424 Kingsland Road, E8.
Tel. 071–254 6152.

Geales
2–4 Farmer Street, Notting Hill Gate, W8.
Tel. 071–727 7969.

Master's Super Fish
191 Waterloo Road, SE1.
Tel. 071–928 6924.

North Sea Fish Bar
8 Leigh Street, WC1.
Tel. 071–387 5892.

The Sea Shell Fish Bar
49 Lisson Grove, NW1.
Tel. 071–723 8703.

The Seafresh Fish Restaurant
80 Wilton Road, SW1.
Tel. 071–828 0747.

Staveley's
642 King's Road, SW6.
Tel. 071–359 1401.

Other good restaurants that welcome children include:

Chicago Rib Shack
1 Raphael Street, SW7.
Tel. 071–581 5595.

Chicago Pizza Pie Factory
17 Hanover Square, W1.
Tel. 071–629 2669.

Mongolian Bar-b-cue
162 The Broadway, Wimbledon, SW19.
Tel. 081–545 0021.

Old Rangoon
210 Castelnau Road, SW13.
Tel. 081–741 9655.

Restaurant Arts Bar
Jason Court, 76 Wigmore Street, W1.
Tel. 071–224 2992.

Sal à Manger
153 Battersea Park Road, SW8.
Tel. 071–720 4457.

Smollensky's Balloon
1 Dover Street, W1.
Tel. 071–491 1199.
(Not for under-5s.

Thank God it's Friday
6 Bedford Street, W2.
Tel. 071–379 0585.
Leicester Square, WC2.
Tel. 071–839 6262.

Certain restaurant chains that welcome children include:

Pizza Express with branches at:

Battersea	230 Lavender Hill, SW11.
	54 Battersea Bridge Road, SW11.
Bayswater	26 Porchester Road, W2.
Blackheath	64 Tranquil Vale, SE3.
Bloomsbury	30 Coptic Street, WC1.
Chelsea	363 Fulham Road, SW10.
Chiswick	252 Chiswick High Road, W4.
Crystal Palace	70 Westow Hill, SE19.
Ealing	23 Bond Street, W5.
Finchley	820 High Road, N12.
Fulham	895 Fulham Road, SW6.
Golders Green	94 Golders Green Road, NW11.
Hyde Park Corner	11 Knightsbridge, SW1.
Islington	335 Upper Street, N1.
Kensington	35 Earls Court Road, W8.
	15 Gloucester Road, SW7.
Notting Hill Gate	137 Notting Hill Gate, W11.
Putney	144 Upper Richmond Road, SW15.
Sheen	305 Upper Richmond Road West, SW14.
Shepherd's Bush	7 Rockley Road, W14.
Southwark	The Chapter House, Southwark Cathedral, SE1.
Streatham	84 High Parade, High Street, SW16.
Swiss Cottage	227 Finchley Road, NW3.
Victoria	154 Victoria Street, SW1.
West End	10 Dean Street, W1.
	29 Wardour Street, W1.

Spaghetti House with branches at:

| Knightsbridge | 77 Knightsbridge, SW1. |

West End   39 Charlotte Street, W1.
                            24 Cranbourn Street, WC2.
                            74–76 Duke Street, W1.
                            15–17 Goodge Street, W1.
                            66 Haymarket, SW1.
                            16–17 Jermyn Street, SW1.
                            30 St Martin's Lane, WC2.
                            20 Sicilian Avenue, WC1.

Certain museums have also made great efforts to cater for younger
members of the community, in particular:

National Gallery
Trafalgar Square, WC2.
Tel. 071–930 5210.

Victoria and Albert Museum
Cromwell Road, SW7.
Tel. 071–938 8358.

(New restaurant in the Henry Cole wing.)

A good range of ice-cream bars can be found across London.

Dayvilles
264 Earls Court Road, SW5.
56 Edgware Road, W2.
62 Gloucester Road, SW7.
2 The Mall, Ealing, W5.
Savacentre, 1 Merton High Street, SW19.

Top of the league among the chains for quality and choice.

Baskin Robbins
Leicester Square, WC2.

Mouthwatering American ices.

Häagen-Dazs Ice Cream Parlour
Leicester Square, WC2.

Sample an 'ice-cream tea', complete with scones, cream and a scoop of
Häagen-Dazs.

Marine Ices
18 Haverstock Hill (opposite the Roundhouse), NW1.

Italian ice-creams – the best in town. You can also buy pizzas here,
and other reasonably priced snacks.

Sweet Factory
London Pavilion, Unit 3, Piccadilly Circus, W1.
Victoria Place, Unit 15, 115 Buckingham Palace Road, SW1.
125 Queensway, Bayswater, W2.

24

Shopping

WEST END

There are so many good places to shop in central London that simply to list them would take a book in itself. Perhaps one of the best-known shopping routes in London is Oxford Street. Famous for its numerous boutiques selling all types of clothing, as well as the huge department stores and chain shops that have found their home here – Selfridges, Marks and Spencer, D.H. Evans, Debenhams – Oxford Street offers a shopping feast. It can also be extremely busy, so true grit and boundless energy are essential if you want to get from one end to the other. Alternatively, leave Oxford Street at the halfway point at Oxford Circus and head south down the broad sweep of Regent Street. This is the royal route designed in the early nineteenth century by the architect John Nash for the Prince Regent, after whom it was named. Largely rebuilt at the beginning of this century, it retains an air of grandeur, helped

by the presence of Liberty's store and Hamleys, the most famous toyshop in London, if not the world. Another shop with a worldwide reputation is Harrods, in Knightsbridge, the quintessential department store. Originally a small grocer's shop built by Charles Henry Harrod in the mid-nineteenth century, it had expanded by the turn of the century to become England's largest shop. Most things can be purchased here and the contents of the food halls and toy department never disappoint – although the prices often do. A view of the building at night, with over 10,000 fairy lights glowing on its exterior, gives you an idea of how enormous the place is. It even has its own power station.

CHILDREN'S CLOTHING

West End stores which stock a good selection of children's clothes include:

Benetton
225 Oxford Street, W1.
Tel. 071–439 6311.

Up-to-the-minute styles at affordable prices for children from 6 months to 14 years. No baby changing facilities.

British Home Stores
252 Oxford Street, W1.
Tel. 071–629 2011.

A good range of practical, inexpensive clothes for 0–14 years. Baby changing facilities at the back of the restaurant on the first floor.

C & A
200 Oxford Street, W1.
Tel. 071–631 4576.

A good range of reasonably priced children's clothes for 0–16 years, plus a wide range of nursery equipment. No baby changing facilities.

Debenhams
334 Oxford Street, W1.
Tel. 071–580 3000.

A wide range of clothes for children from 0–12 years. Baby changing facilities on the third floor.

D.H. Evans
318 Oxford Street, W1.
Tel. 071–629 8800.

A reasonable selection of children's clothes from 0–10 years. No baby changing facilities.

Littlewoods
203–211 Oxford Street, W1.
Tel. 071–434 4301.

A very good choice of inexpensive clothes in their under-5 range, but they cover all ages from 0–16. They also stock a small selection of soft toys and baby play things. Their Index Catalogue shop on the second floor (see also page 170) stocks everything from baby buggies and tricycles to cots and cuddly toys (tel. 071–494 2625). Baby changing facilities on the second floor.

John Lewis
278 Oxford Street, W1.
Tel. 071–629 7711.

A reasonable selection of children's clothes can be found on the fourth floor plus an excellent range of nursery equipment. Baby changing facilities on the fourth floor.

Marks and Spencer
458 Oxford Street, W1.
Tel. 071–935 7954.

Great variety and good quality for children up to 14 years. No baby changing facilities.

Mothercare
461 Oxford Street, W1.
Tel. 071–629 6621.

An excellent selection of reasonably priced clothes and nursery equipment for 0–8-year-olds. Baby changing facilities.

Selfridges
400 Oxford Street, W1.
Tel. 071–629 1234.

Good quality children's clothing and nursery equipment on the third floor. Baby changing facilities are also on the third floor.

Many West End department stores have good family restaurants which provide highchairs. A selection is listed below. (For other restaurants, see page 159).

British Home Stores
252 Oxford Street, W1.
Tel. 071–629 2011.

Self-service restaurant on the first floor.

Debenhams
334 Oxford Street, W1.
Tel. 071–580 3000.

Intermissions self-service restaurant on the second floor.

D.H. Evans
318 Oxford Street, W1.
Tel. 071–629 8800.

Terrace café on the ground floor.

Fenwick
63 New Bond Street, W1.
Tel. 071–629 9161.

Terrace restaurant on the second floor.

Hamleys
186 Regent Street, W1.
Tel. 071–734 8040.

Restaurant in the basement.

Harrods
Knightsbridge, SW1.
Tel. 071–730 1234.

Harrods has several self-service restaurants. The Dress Circle on the first floor and the Upper Circle on the fourth floor provide highchairs.

Liberty
210 Regent Street, W1.
Tel. 071–734 1234.

Coffee shop in the basement.

John Lewis
278 Oxford Street, W1.
Tel. 071–629 7711.

Place to Eat restaurant on the third floor.

Peter Jones
Sloane Square, SW1.
Tel. 071–730 3434.

Fourth-floor restaurant and coffee shop.

Selfridges
400 Oxford Street, W1.
Tel. 071–629 1234.

Food Garden café on the fourth floor.

Tube stations along Oxford Street: Oxford Circus, Tottenham Court Road (east section), Bond Street (middle section), Marble Arch (west section).
Buses: 2, 2B, 6, 7, 8, 10, 12, 13, 15, 16A, 23, 73, 82, 88, 94, 98, 113, 135, 137, 139, 159, 274.
Tube station for Harrods: Knightsbridge.
Buses: 14, 74, C1.

SHOPPING FROM HOME

For those who prefer shopping from home, catalogues provide an ideal opportunity to browse in peace and comfort. Listed below are a number of companies specialising in children's clothing. A few also sell nursery equipment. If unsuitable, items can usually be exchanged, but check when you order.

Blooming Marvellous
PO Box 12F, Chessington, Surrey KT9 2LS.
Tel. 081–391 4822.

A good selection of children's clothes from 0–8 years.

Cotton On Ltd
Monmouth Place, Bath BA1 2NP.
Tel. 0255–461155.

A wide range of children's clothing from new born to 15 years. Everything is made from 100 per cent cotton which is particularly good for anyone suffering from skin allergies.

Empire Stores
18 Canal Road, Bradford BD99 4XB.
Tel. 081–549 6161.

Children's clothes for all ages and every occasion.

Heinz Baby Club
Vinces Road, Diss, Norfolk IP2 3HH.
Tel. 0923–221717.

Attractive clothes for younger children, new born to 2½ years.

Laura Ashley By Post
PO Box 19, Newtown, Powys SY16 1DZ.
Tel. 0800 868 100.

Everything from trendy cotton bikinis to winter leggings. Age range from 6 months to 9 years.

Mothercare Catalogue
Cherry Tree Road, Watford WD2 5SH.
Tel. 0923–210210.

Good quality, durable clothes for 1–10-year-olds. They also sell basic baby equipment.

Next Catalogue Directory
PO Box 299, Leicester LE5 5GH.
Tel. 0345–100500.

A wide range of reasonably priced clothes for 2–8-year-olds.

Nipper Mail Order
Gloucester House, 45 Gloucester Street, Brighton, East Sussex BN1 4EW.
Tel. 0273–693785.

English clothes in high cotton content fabric specialising in unusual prints and weaves. Good play range in denim and fleece for pre-school children. Age range from birth to 9 years.

Snap Dragon
The Glebe, Nash Road, Waddon, Milton Keynes MK17 0NO.
Tel. 0908–501928.

Good, all round clothes for 3 months up to 8 years. Everything is made from 100 per cent cotton. Reversible dresses.

SHOPPING ARCADES

The arcades listed below are not shopping suggestions, but they are fun places to wander through if you happen to be passing by.

Burlington Arcade
Piccadilly, W1.

A prime example of how tasteful and elegant shopping precincts used to be, Burlington Arcade was built at the turn of the nineteenth century by an entrepreneurial landowner, Lord George Cavendish. Motivated partly by a desire to prevent people from throwing rubbish over his garden wall from the street, Cavendish designed this beautiful covered way 'for the gratification of the publick and to give employment to industrious females'. Today the exclusivity of the place is reflected in the astronomical prices asked for some of the goods on sale. But even those who do not want to spend money will enjoy window-shopping here, watched over by officers in fancy dress known as 'beadles', who make a courteous contrast to today's surly store detectives. Visitors are expected to comply with the regency laws still in force here, which include bans on whistling, singing and hurrying.

Nearest tubes: Green Park, Piccadilly Circus.
Nearby buses: 8, 9, 14, 19, 22, 38.

Piccadilly Arcade
Piccadilly, W1.

Somewhat overshadowed by 'big brother' Burlington across the road, the Piccadilly Arcade, with its tiny bowfronted shops brimming with flower baskets, is pure regency chic. Halfway along you will find the Armoury of St James's selling all kinds of army paraphernalia in miniature, including busby hats for people the size of Tom Thumb.

Nearest tubes: Green Park, Piccadilly Circus.
Nearby buses: 8, 9, 14, 19, 22, 38.

Quadrant Arcade
80 Regent Street, W1.

Close to Piccadilly Circus, the Quadrant Arcade is light, airy and full of neat, pocket-sized shops selling everything from postcards and shoes to tweed hats and cashmere sweaters.

Nearest tube: Piccadilly Circus.
Nearby buses: 3, 6, 12, 13, 15, 23, 53, 88, 94, 139, 159.

Hay's Galleria
London Bridge City, Tooley Street, SE1.

Hay's Galleria is one of the newest and most spectacular shopping centres in town. Several Victorian warehouses in the City have been renovated to accommodate shops, restaurants and a mobile sculpture 60 feet (18 metres) high called *The Navigators*. There is a great variety of things to see and do. If you fancy a snack under the high glass-vaulted roof, a taste of French cuisine overlooking the Thames or a leisurely browse around the shops, this is the place to go.

Nearest tube: London Bridge.
Nearby buses: 4, 17, 21, 22A, 35, 40, 43, 47, 48, 133, 214.

25

Day trips out of town

If you wish to spend a day out of town with the children, there are plenty of exciting places to visit within a 30-mile radius of London. Most of those mentioned below can be easily reached from the capital by motorway.

Bekonscot Model Village
Warwick Road, Beaconsfield, Bucks.
Tel. 0494–672919.

Built in the 1930s, Bekonscot is the oldest model village in the world. More than 150 buildings make up this traditional English scene, including shops, a church, a cricket pitch, a forge, houses and a lake – all of which have been created in miniature by skilled craftsmen with amazing attention to detail. One of the earliest exhibits, which expanded and developed as the village grew, is the gauge '1' railway system, which is 440 yards (400 metres) long and operated in the same way as a full-size railway. The rolling stock consists of twenty engines, and more than sixty coaches and goods wagons, and there are some beautifully crafted models of people and animals. It takes a large team of real people to keep the system in good working order, including gardeners, electrical engineers and model-makers. The village has picnic areas, a children's playground and a miniature tramway.

Open 27 Feb.–31 Oct. 10.00a.m.–5.00p.m.
Admission charge.
BR: Beaconsfield.
Buses: 325, 305.
By car: Leave M40 at junction 2 and take A40 to Old Beaconsfield; follow signs to the village, which is off the A355 Amersham–Beaconsfield road.

Birdworld and Underwater World
Holt Pound, Farnham, Surrey.
Tel. 0420–22140.

All nature-lovers should visit Birdworld. Set in extensive gardens, it supports more than 1000 birds, from exotic flamingoes, penguins and parrots to one of the proudest birds of prey, the hawk. Younger children will enjoy the new Jenny Wren Farm. Next door is Underwater World with its vast aquaria full of fascinating and beautiful fish from around the world. There is a 2000-acre forest where you can walk and take a picnic. The Owl's Nest, a natural history bookshop, specialises in books about wildlife and keeping animals. A play area is provided for younger children.

Open daily 9.30a.m.–6.00p.m. (closes 3.45p.m. in winter).
Admission charge.
BR: Aldershot, Farnham or Bentley, then bus to Holt Pound.
By car: Leave M3 at junction 4 and follow A325 through Farnham.

Burnham Beeches
Farnham Common, Slough, Buckinghamshire.

Part of the Open Spaces project of the City of London, these magnificent beech woods are situated close to London and are easily accessible from the M40. This is an ideal outing for families who feel like getting away from town for the afternoon. Burnham Woods is home to the largest collection of old beech trees in the world and at Pumpkin Hill the grand master of them all, called His Majesty, boasts a girth of over 28 feet. You can drive or walk through the area and the foot paths are clearly marked. First-time visitors should head for the Lord Mayor's Drive close to Wingrove's Tea Rooms. During the summer months refreshment stalls are parked in lay-bys in the woods themselves.

Open at all times.
BR: Paddington then Slough, then 441 bus.
Greenline coach: 704, 705 then 441 bus.
By car: Leave M40 at junction 2 and then take the A355.

Chessington World of Adventures
Chessington, Surrey.
Tel. 0372–727227.

Chessington World of Adventures, just 12 miles outside London, must rank as Britain's most spectacular theme park. The old zoo has been imaginatively extended and transformed to create nine fantastic 'mini-worlds'. They include the sinister castle and spine-chilling roller-coaster Vampire ride of Transylvania; a journey to the mysterious orient on the Dragon River Water Ride; the 5th Dimension, an eerie fantasy land of robots, monsters and swamp creatures; and the Wild West of Calamity Canyon, set in the days of the California gold rush, the scene for a terrifying runaway train ride. Chessington's famous zoo continues to thrive and to play an important role in the protection of rare and endangered species. A trip on the Safari Skyway monorail provides the best general view of the zoo, but for a closer inspection visit the Children's Zoo, where you can stroke and pet some of the smaller animals. Nearby, in Circus World, there is the Big Top with its international entertainers and Kiddies' Corner, which has climbing frames and a play area for younger children.

Theme Park, Circus and Zoo open 27 March–31 Oct. 10.00a.m.–
5.00p.m. (last admission 3.00p.m.).
Zoo only open 2 Jan.–26 March and 1 Nov.–23 Dec. 10.00a.m.–
4.00p.m.
Admission charge.
BR: Chessington South, then a 10-minute walk to the main gate.
Buses and coaches: 71, 72, Flightline 777, West Link 468 and London
County 408 and 465 all stop at the main entrance.
By car: A3, then A243; or leave M25 at junction 9.

Chislehurst Caves
Old Hill, Chislehurst, Kent.
Tel. 081–467 3264.

Only 12 miles from Charing Cross, Chislehurst Caves have been hewn
from solid rock over the past 8000 years. There are more than 20 miles of
caverns and passages to explore. Tours take 45 minutes on most days and
guides explain the interesting history of this underground labyrinth. A
90-minute tour on Sundays and Bank Holidays includes parts of the cave
system not otherwise open to the public. Tales of flint-knappers,
Cavaliers and a Druid altar, together with a haunted pool, make
Chislehurst one of the most intriguing places to visit close to the capital.

Open daily Easter-30 Sept. 10.00a.m.–5.00p.m.; 1 Oct.–Easter
11.00a.m.–4.30p.m.
Admission charge.
BR: Chislehurst.
Bus: 161, 269, 725 (Green Line) from Bromley.
By car: A20, then A222 onto the Chislehurst Road.

Chiltern Open Air Museum
Newland Park, Gorelands Lane, Chalfont St Giles, Buckinghamshire.
Tel. 0494–871117.

Historic buildings from the Chiltern area which were due to be
demolished have been re-erected on this glorious 45-acre site. Now
they house permanent exhibitions reflecting the heritage of the
Chiltern region and the lives and work of local people. Visitors can
look inside a 1940s prefab, explore a reconstruction of an Iron Age
house, walk in a Victorian farm yard and even pay a call inside an
Edwardian public lavatory. Throughout the year the museum hosts
special children's days with workshops and exhibitions for children of
all ages. A number of craft events are also held during the summer
months, which highlight the different eras on which the museum
focuses. There is an excellent woodland nature trail, children's
playground and café.

Open April–end Oct. 2.00p.m.–6.00p.m. Wed.–Sun. plus Bank
Holidays.
Admission charge.
By car: From the A413 at Chalfont St Giles and Chalfont St Peter

follow the brown signs with the museum symbol. Or from the A412 at Maple Cross follow the brown signs with the cart symbol.

Cotswold Wildlife Park
Burford, Oxfordshire.
Tel. 0993–823006.

Set in over 100 acres of beautiful gardens and parkland in the heart of the Cotswold Hills, this unusual wildlife park is home to a large and varied collection of mammals, birds, reptiles and fish from all over the world. Enclosures have been carefully sited and designed to accommodate the needs of the particular varieties of animals, and great efforts have been made to help visitors understand what is special about each species. Rhinos, zebras and ostriches roam in large paddocks surrounded by moats, and tigers and leopards can be seen in grassed enclosures. The gardens are put to good use and are home to many tropical birds such as hornbills and penguins as well as smaller mammals including monkeys and otters. The stables have been converted into an aquarium, reptile house and bat belfry. Around the park are a variety of animals which have particular appeal to children. As most of the animals do not enjoy being handled, the park has solved the problem of children wanting to touch and stroke animals by providing a special children's farm yard where pigs, goats, chickens, rabbits and guinea pigs can be petted. Special events held throughout the summer include bird of prey demonstrations and 'Snake Experience Days' when members of the public are given an opportunity to meet a snake and receive expert advice on keeping a reptile.

There is a self-service café at the rear of the Manor House and a large children's adventure playground nearby. There is also a brass-rubbing centre in the old dining-room of the Manor House which is open all year round with a limited service between November and March. For a more leisurely tour around the park, there is a narrow-gauge railway which operates from April to October.

Open daily 10.00a.m.–6.00p.m. or dusk whichever is earlier.
Admission charge.
By car: The park is situated on the A361, two miles south of its junction with the A40.

Losely Park Farm
Losely Park, Guildford, Surrey.
Tel. 0483–304440.

What better way to spend a day out than to sample a slice of farm life on the Losely Park Estate. Among the Surrey woodlands, covering an area of over 1400 acres, some 700 pedigree Jersey cows provide milk and cream for the famous Losely dairy products. Rare breeds of sheep, pigs and poultry also share the farm. 'Trailer rides' (bookable in advance) make it possible to travel around the estate and see the animals and milking. There is a children's play area and picnic spot, and the farm shop sells their delicious ice-creams. Losely House, a magnificent sixteenth-century mansion, is also open to the public as are the splendid gardens and unusual moat walk.

Open: House tours and trailer rides 2.00p.m.–5.00p.m. Wed., Thurs., Fri. and Sat. from late May Bank Holiday to early October. Closed Sun., Mon. and Tues.
Restaurant and shop same dates as house 11.00a.m.–5.00p.m.
Admission charge.
By car: Take the A3 and turn off at the B3000 at Compton.

Thorpe Park
Staines Road, Chertsey, Surrey.
Tel. 0932–562633.

Thorpe Park is one of the country's largest theme parks. Situated in the heart of the Surrey countryside but only 40 minutes' drive from central London, it is a great place to take the family for a day out. There is a huge choice of rides and attractions. Intrepid canoeists can plunge down Logger's Leap and experience the highest water shoot in

Britain; the trip begins with a hair-raising journey through the 'Canadian Rockies' and ends by plummeting down a 50-foot (15-metre) drop into the water below. The less dramatic Flying Fish roller-coaster ride twists and turns at 30 miles an hour through tumbling streams and rockpools, while the Phantom ghost ride takes you through dark caves where skeletons, bats and headless bodies create a spooky atmosphere. Gentler entertainment is provided by the miniature train ride to Thorpe Park's farm and nature world, or the Magic Mill boat trip, a leisurely canal journey through fields and meadows. When you reach dry land, try the family Teacup Ride, a dizzying experience that involves being spun round in a giant teacup. For younger children there is the Carousel Kingdom, a vast, under-cover play area based on a medieval town square and castle. One of its main attractions is the double-decker, traditional hand-painted carou-sel, an exact replica of the steam-powered carousels of the 1890s. The admission charge includes car parking and more than 100 rides, attractions and shows.

Open: April–1 Nov. 10.00a.m.–5.00p.m. (closes 6.00p.m. during summer holidays).
Admission charge; good-value family ticket and group reductions.
BR: Staines, then bus 451 to Thorpe Park.
By car: Leave M25 at junction 11 or 13, then follow A320.

Windsor Castle
Windsor, Berkshire.
Tel. 0753–831118.

This imposing fortress set in over 400 acres of parkland has its origins in the reign of William the Conqueror. Of the many later monarchs to have left their stamp on the building, King George IV was the most influential. Windsor has been lived in continually throughout its long history and remains one of the Queen's favourite residences. The state rooms, recently damaged in a major fire, will not be open to the public again for some years. However eleven of the sixteen are on view, and glass-panelled doors make it possible to see into the burnt rooms that are being refurbished. Some of the Queen's finest treasures are housed at Windsor including Queen Mary's famous Dolls' House, designed by Edwin Lutyens to house her large collection of miniature *objets d'art*. Everything is exquisitely made: there is hot and cold running water in the bathrooms and kitchen, and the tiny paintings displayed throughout the house are by distinguished contemporary artists. St George's Chapel, founded by King Edward IV, is among the most beautiful and perfect examples of fifteenth-century Gothic architec-ture in the world. Many monarchs are buried here, including King Henry VIII and his wife Jane Seymour. The extensive grounds and gardens at Windsor are open to the public, and if the Queen is in residence you may catch a glimpse of her walking the corgis. As at Buckingham Palace, the Changing of the Guard ceremony takes place at 11.00a.m. each day, or on alternate days in winter. Windsor Safari Park has been bought by Legoland and will re-open in 1996.

Open daily except at Christmastime and on certain ceremonial occasions. Check before you go.
Admission charge, although you can visit the grounds free; there is a separate charge for admission to the state apartments, St George's Chapel, Queen Mary's Dolls' House, the Gallery and the Royal Mews.
BR: Windsor.

Whipsnade Wild Animal Park
Near Dunstable, Bedfordshire.
Tel. 0582–872171.

Britain's premier wild animal park is also the country home of the London Zoological Society, famous throughout the world for its conservation and breeding programme. More than 3000 animals live here in over 600 acres of wooded park, including cheetahs, rhinos, elephants, bears, wolves and hippos. The park specialises in breeding animals that have become endangered in their wild habitats. Daily events include flying demonstrations by birds of prey and displays such as the World of Sealions and Elephants at Work. For the 'wildest of all the animals', there is a Run Wild adventure playground. Children's Farm and Bear Maze. Whipsnade arranges special family events throughout the year, including a Spring Bank Holiday Steam Weekend, Easter Egg Hunt, August Bank Holiday Teddy Bears' Party and a visit from Father Christmas and his reindeer.

Open daily 10.00a.m.–6.00p.m. (closed Christmas Day).
Admission charge.
BR: Luton, then Leisure Link coach services.
Coach: Victoria Green Line and Leisure Link from Dunstable and Luton (summer only).

Woburn Abbey
Woburn, Bedfordshire.
Tel. 0525–290666.

For nearly 400 years Woburn Abbey was home to an order of Cistercian monks. In the mid-sixteenth century their abbot was accused of treason and hanged from an oak tree in the abbey grounds, and the monastery was confiscated. King Edward VI then granted Woburn to Sir John Russell, who became the Earl of Bedford, and it has remained with the Bedford family ever since. Most of the present building dates from the mid-eighteenth century. It houses fine art treasures, such as paintings by Canaletto, Reynolds, Rembrandt and Gainsborough, and some exquisite furniture. The house has an outstanding porcelain display which includes a dinner service presented to the fourth Duchess of Bedford by King Louis XV of France – it has 183 pieces, all painted in different designs. Apart from the many splendid state rooms, perhaps the most intriguing room in the house is the Grotto. Probably built between 1619 and 1641, the Grotto has stonework carved to resemble seaweed and stalactites, complete with inlaid sea shells. Even the delicate furniture is carved to resemble shells, with dolphin shapes supporting the table tops. The bookshop provides a good children's trail, which pinpoints interesting things to look out for when going round Woburn. More than 3000 acres of parkland surround the abbey, and many different species of deer have become established here, including red, fallow, Rusa Pere David and Chinese water deer. The Pere David variety originally came from China and were saved from extinction by the eleventh Duke of Bedford. Recently Lord Tavistock returned twenty-two deer to the Chinese government.

Open Jan.–March. Sat.–Sun. 11.00a.m.–4.00p.m.; April–Oct. Mon.–Sat. 11.00a.m.–5.00p.m. (last admission 5.30p.m. Sundays and Bank Holidays).
Admission charge includes entry to park.
BR: Milton Keynes, then taxi.
By car: Leave M1 at junction 13.

Woburn Wild Animal Kingdom
Woburn, Bedfordshire.
Tel. 0525–290407.

More than 350 acres of parkland make up the Woburn Wild Animal Kingdom, Britain's largest safari park. Over thirty species of wild animals live here, including lions, tigers, rhinos, camels and zebras. You can drive through the park and see many of them at close quarters. Indian rhesus monkeys, renowned for their friendliness and fondness for hitching rides on visitors' cars, share a 20-acre wood with some American black bears. Endangered species such as the African white rhino and the bongo antelope have been bred successfully at Woburn; while some are exported to zoos and wildlife parks throughout the world, others have been returned to their homes in the wild. In Pets' Corner there is a large collection of mostly tame small animals. Younger children can stroke llamas, goats and ponies or watch parrot and sealion displays nearby.

Open March–Oct. daily from 10.00a.m. Closed 24, 25, 31 July and 1 August.
Admission charge.
BR: Milton Keynes, then taxi.
By car: Leave M1 at junction 13.

26

Keeping fit

There is no excuse to be unfit if you live in London. The many sports and leisure centres which have opened in recent years run all kinds of different activities for parents and children alike. Although synchronised swimming courses for under-5s may be thin on the ground, there are more opportunities than ever to learn a martial art or to perfect your technique with a longbow. Some sports centres have crèches where children can be left in safe hands while parents exercise. Special events are often organised during school holidays. Swimming pools that provide parent and toddler sessions or duckling classes for under-5s have been marked with an asterisk.

SPORTS AND LEISURE CENTRES

Arches Leisure Centre*
80 Trafalgar Road, Greenwich, SE10.
Tel. 081–858 0159.

Brentford Fountain Leisure Centre*
658 Chiswick High Road, Brentford.
Tel. 081–994 9596.

Britannia Leisure Centre*
40 Hyde Road, N1.
Tel. 081–729 4485.

Central YMCA
112 Great Russell Street, WC1.
Tel. 071–637 8131.

Chelsea Sports Centre
Chelsea Manor Street, SW3.
Tel. 071–352 6985.

Crystal Palace National Sports Centre*
Crystal Palace, SE19.
Tel. 081–778 0131.

Eastway Sports Centre
Quarter Mile Lane, Leyton, E10.
Tel. 081–519 0017.

Elephant and Castle Leisure Centre*
22 Elephant and Castle, SE1.
Tel. 071–582 5505.

Finsbury Leisure Centre
Norman Street, EC1.
Tel. 071–253 4490.

Gurnell Leisure Centre*
Ruislip Road East, W13.
Tel. 081–998 3241.

Ironmonger Row Baths*
Ironmonger Row, EC1.
Tel. 071–253 4011.

John Orwell Sports Centre
Tench Street, Wapping, E1.
Tel. 071–488 9421.

Jubilee Centre*
Caird Street, W10.
Tel. 081–960 9629.

Kensington Sports Centre*
Walmer Road, W11.
Tel. 071–727 9747.

Latchmere Sports Centre*
Latchmere Road, SW11.
Tel. 081–871 7470.

Michael Sobell Sports Centre
Hornsey Road, N7.
Tel. 071–609 2166.

Newham Leisure Centre
281 Prince Regent Lane, E13.
Tel. 071–511 4477.

Pickett's Lock Centre*
Pickett's Lock Lane, Edmonton, N9.
Tel. 081–345 6666.

Queen Mother Sports Centre*
223 Vauxhall Bridge Road, SW1.
Tel. 071–798 2125.

Rotherhithe Leisure Centre
Lower Road, SE16.
Tel. 081–237 3296.

Swiss Cottage Sports Centre*
Winchester Road, NW3.

Tel. 071–413 6490.

Tottenham Green Leisure Centre
1 Philip Lane, N15.
Tel. 081–365 0322.

Wandle Recreation Centre
Mapleton Road, SW18.
Tel. 081–871 7674.

Waterfront Leisure Centre*
High Street, Woolwich, SE18.
Tel. 081–316 6507.

For more details of sports venues and facilities, telephone Sportsline on 071–222 8000.

OPEN-AIR SWIMMING

If you have a strong disposition and appreciate the joys of swimming out of doors, you may wish to try one of the several pools in London which are open to the elements and cost nothing to use. Unsuitable for young children, Hampstead, Highgate and Kenwood Ponds are intended for competent swimmers only. Under-16s must be accompanied by an adult. For more details, telephone 071–485 4491.

Kenwood Pond (women only)

Summer season 7.00a.m.–9.00p.m. (or sunset if earlier).
December and January 7.30a.m.–3.00p.m.
November and February 7.00a.m.–3.00p.m.
Rest of the year: 7.00a.m.–sunset.
BR: Gospel Oak.
Nearby buses: 214, 271, C2.

Highgate Pond (men only)

Summer season 6.00a.m.–9.00p.m. (or sunset if earlier).
December and January 7.30a.m.–3.00p.m.
November and February 7.00a.m.–3.00p.m.
Rest of the year: 7.00a.m.–sunset.
BR: Gospel Oak.
Nearby buses: 214, 271, C2.

Hampstead Pond (mixed bathing)

Summer season only 10.00a.m.–7.00p.m.
Last admission 1 hour before closing time.
BR: Hampstead Heath.
Nearby buses: 24, 46.

Parliament Hill Lido (mixed bathing)
Tel. 071–485 3873.

May–September 7.00a.m.–9.30a.m. and 10.00a.m.– 7.00p.m.
December and January 7.30a.m.–10.00a.m.
Rest of year: 7.00a.m.–10.00a.m.
Free swimming before 10.00a.m.; small charge at other times.
Nearest tube: Kentish Town.
Nearby buses: 214, C2, C11.

Open-air heated pools

Big Splash
Mapleton Road, Wandsworth, SW18.
Tel. 081–871 7618.

There is something for all ages at Big Splash. Toddlers will enjoy the baby pool and there is a big pool for swimmers as well as a diving pool.

Open daily 10.00a.m.–6.00p.m., May–Sept.
Admission charge.

Walford Sports Centre
Bengarth Road, Northolt, Middlesex.
Tel. 081–841 0953.

Open May–Aug. 4.00p.m.–7.00p.m., Mon.–Fri.; 12 noon– 4.00p.m. Sat. and Sun.
Admission charge.

Wandle Recreation Centre
Mapleton Road, off Garrett Lane, SW18.
Tel. 081–871 7674.

Open daily 10.00a.m.–6.00p.m., March to Aug.
Admission charge.

Park Road Pool
Park Road, Crouch End, N8.
Tel. 081–341 3567.

Open weekends 11.00a.m.–7.00p.m. weather permitting, and occasionally during the week if the weather is fine. Telephone and check before you go.
Admission charge.

BASKETBALL

English Basketball Association
Calomax House, Lupton Avenue, Leeds.
Tel. 0532–361166.

The English Basketball Association has up-to-date information of clubs in London and comprehensive literature about the history and development of the game. They also produce a booklet called *Basketball in Greater London*.

BOXING

London Boxing Association
58 Comber Grove, Camberwell, SE5.
Tel. 071–252 7008.

Amateur boxing clubs are run in most London boroughs for children aged 11 years and older. When the coach thinks they are good enough, it is then possible to take it up seriously and become junior boxers. For details of clubs in your area contact the Association at the address above.

CRICKET

MCC Indoor School
Lord's Cricket Ground, St John's Wood Road, NW8.
Tel. 071–289 1611.

Coaching for children of 8 years old and upwards is organised for groups of four to six players. Sessions are conducted weekly on specific days and times between May and August and October to April. For cricket matches see page 16.

CROQUET

The Croquet Association
c/o The Hurlingham Club, Ranelagh Gardens, SW6.
Tel. 071–736 3148.

The Croquet Association will send a list of clubs in your area plus a complimentary copy of the magazine *Croquet*, the official CA magazine.

GYMNASTICS

British Amateur Gymnastics Association
Ford Hall, Lilleshall National Sports Centre, Near Newport, Shropshire.
Tel. 0952–820330.

Gymnastics is open to everyone and the majority of sports centres in London organise classes for all ages including the under-5s. The BAGA organise excellent coaching courses nationwide and nearly 90 per cent of all schools in Great Britain participate in their Awards scheme. The Kitekat awards cover six sets of ten exercises from the simplest Award 6 up to the advanced Award 1.

FOOTBALL

Football Association
16 Lancaster Gate, W2.
Tel. 071–262 4542.

There are over 40 football associations in England, and London, as a county, also has a local football association. Under-18s should get in touch with the London youth section who will give details of relevant clubs in their area. For details telephone 081–980 2460.

ICE SKATING

There are only a handful of ice-skating rinks in London. By far the best is the open arena at Broadgate, next to Liverpool Street station. Here, surrounded by high-tech buildings and cascading greenery, children and adults can glide around a floodlit rink to the music of stars such as Madonna and Prince. Stewards are on the ice at all times and skates from children's size 6 (and bob skates, which tie onto even smaller feet) are available for hire and service is friendly. Lessons are provided, but they are expensive. For details of times and prices, contact Broadgate Ice, Exchange House, 12 Exchange Square, London EC2 (tel. 071–588 6565).

Open Nov.–March.
BR: Liverpool Street.
Nearest tube: Liverpool Street.
Nearby buses: 9, 23.

There are indoor ice rinks at:

Alexandra Palace
Muswell Hill, N22.
Tel. 081–365 2121.

Nearest tube: Wood Green.
Nearby bus: W3.

Streatham Ice Rink
386 Streatham High Road, SW16.
Tel. 081–769 7771.

BR: Streatham.
Nearby buses: 109, 159.

Michael Sobell Ice Rink
Hornsey Road, N7.
Tel. 071–609 2166.
Nearest tube: Finsbury Park.
Nearby bus: 29.

Queens Ice Skating Club
Queensway, W2.
Tel. 071–229 0172.
Nearest tube: Queensway.
Nearby buses: 12, 94.

MARTIAL ARTS

Your local sports centre might run courses in the martial arts. If not, contact the Martial Arts Commission on 081–691 3433. They have all the relevant information on how to begin a martial art and appropriate clubs in the London area.

ORIENTEERING

British Orienteering Federation
Riversdale, Dale Road North, Darley Dale, Matlock, Derbyshire DE4 2HX.

Orienteering is a sport where competitors navigate their way at their own pace between features marked on a special coloured map. You can run, jog or walk and it does not matter how young, old or fit you are. There are about 150 permanent orienteering courses throughout the country and events are usually held on Sunday mornings or summer weekday evenings. To find out about those that are suitable for beginners and information about your local club, send an A5 SAE marked 'GI Pack' to the address above.

ROLLER SKATING

Roller Express
Unit 16, Lee Valley Trading Estate, Angel Road, N18.
Tel. 081–807 7345.

Roller Express, North London's first purpose-built roller rink, has thousands of square feet of skating rink to practise on as well as a café licensed bar, video games area and pool table. It opens from 11.30a.m. to 3.30p.m. every day during the school holidays as well as certain times only during the term. Beginners' sessions take place on Monday evening. Free skate hire is included in the admission charge.

Pickett's Lock Sports Centre (Pickett's Lock Lane, N9) run roller skating sessions during the school holidays between 1.00p.m. and 4.00p.m. Skate hire is available. For more details telephone 081–345 6666.

Supervised skating sessions for all ages take place in Finsbury Park's multi-purpose playground on Saturday mornings between 11.00a.m. and 1.00p.m., May to September. Beginners kick off at 11.00a.m. and the more experienced skaters join later. Free skates and tuition are provided (see page 91).

If you are thinking of buying a pair of roller skates then visit Skate Attack at 95 Highgate Road, Kentish Town, NW5 (tel. 071–267 6961).

ROWING

Amateur Rowing Association
6 Lower Mall, Hammersmith, W6.

Tel. 081–748 3632.

Children of 10 years and over who are keen to participate in the more competitive side of rowing and would like to join a club should contact the Amateur Rowing Association. It is possible to row in central London on the Serpentine (see page 85), Regent's Park lake, Gunnersbury Park lake, Crystal Palace Park and Finsbury Park lake.

RUGBY

The Rugby Football Union (RFU) Handbook which can be bought from the RFU at Whitton Road, Twickenham, Middlesex (tel. 081–892 8161) has up-to-the-minute information of clubs in your area.

SAILING

Royal Yachting Association
Romsey Road, Eastleigh, Hampshire.
Tel. 0703–629962.

If you get in touch with the RYA they will give you an introduction to a sailing club in your area. It is also worth noting that several new sailing centres have recently opened in London Docklands.

Royal Victoria Docks Watersports Centre
Gate 5, Dock Road, off Silvertown Way, E16.
Tel. 071–511 2326.

The Royal Victoria Dock Sports Centre covers 83 acres of calm, sheltered water and is the largest sailing area in inner London. Membership is available to individuals and families and all specialist equipment is provided. Children must be able to swim 100 metres or 50 metres in light clothing and should bring evidence, if under 18, that they can do so. Other centres are:

Docklands Sailing and Watersports Centre
235 West Ferry Road, E14.
Tel. 071–537 2626.

Surrey Docks Watersports Centre
Rope Street, SE16.
Tel. 071–237 4009.

Shadwell Basin Project
Shadwell Pierhead, E1.
Tel. 071–481 4210.

SKIING

Ski Club of Great Britain
118 Eaton Square, SW1W 9AF.
Tel. 071–245 1033.

The Ski Club of Great Britain produce a useful leaflet called *Going Skiing* which lists all the dry ski slopes in London and the United Kingdom. To obtain a copy send an SAE plus a 50p postal order (or 50p piece) to the above address.

There are dry ski runs at:

Alexandra Park
N22.
Tel. 081–888 2284.

Crystal Palace
SE19.
Tel. 081–778 0131.

Hillingdon Ski Centre
Uxbridge, Middlesex.
Tel. 0895–255183.

Mountaintop Ski Village
Becton Alps, Alpine Way, E6.
Tel. 071–511 0351.

TENNIS

Lawn Tennis Association
The Queen's Club, Palliser Road, West Kensington, W14.
Tel. 071–385 4233, 071–385 2366 (information line).

Many public parks in London have tennis courts but if you want to join a club contact the Lawn Tennis Association who will give details. Their information line is open during office hours. Short tennis, a miniature version of the game, is ideal for younger children and was developed specifically for 5-year-olds and over. It has all the fun and excitement of the full-scale game yet it is so easy that anyone can play. For more information contact the Short Tennis Department of the Lawn Tennis Association. See also Wimbledon page 15.

27

Clubs and classes for under-5s

Fewer than four out of ten 3-year-olds in Britain have nursery education. Although we are trailing behind other European countries in providing for the under-5s there is a growing number of alternative facilities available, particularly in London. These help fill the gap especially in areas where nursery schools are scarce.

NURSERY SCHOOLS

Run by the local education authority, nursery schools are staffed by trained teachers and nursery nurses. They encourage children to make use of a wide variety of activities in a positive way and in a stimulating environment. Lessons are very informal and classes are initially for a half-day, morning or afternoon. In the child's last year this is sometimes extended to a full day in preparation for primary school. Your borough's education department at the town hall will have details of nursery schools in your area.

ONE O'CLOCK CLUBS

Whoever came up with the idea of one o'clock clubs deserves a medal. Often based in parks or similar suitable environments, these clubs have been created especially for pre-school children. Their aim is to

give under-5s the chance to get out and about with their parents or minders and enjoy the various activities provided. There is generally a club-house for indoor pursuits such as painting, sticking and looking at picture books, while climbing frames, swings and slides offer more adventurous outdoor play. There is no charge for the clubs, which are run by local authorities and supervised by helpful, experienced staff. However, they are not intended to be a childminding service; children must be accompanied by an adult. For details about one o'clock clubs, contact the information office at your local town hall.

ADVENTURE PLAYGROUNDS

These playgrounds are aimed at older children who want a more challenging type of play. The facilities available vary from borough to borough and from park to park and helpers are often on hand to organise structured activities. For more details, contact the parks and leisure department at your local town hall. There is also a small number of adventure playgrounds in London catering for handi-capped children, such as the Log Cabin, 259 Northfield Avenue, Ealing. For more information, contact the Handicapped Adventure Playground Association at Fulham Palace, Bishop's Avenue, SW6 (tel. 071–731 1435), which runs supervised playgrounds in the Inner London area for children with special needs.

PLAYGROUPS

Pre-School Playgroup Association
314 Vauxhall Bridge Road, SW1V 1AA.
Tel. 071–828 2417.

Playgroups generally cater for 3–5-year-olds, although an increasing number do take younger children. They are unique in that they work very much on the combined efforts of the playleaders, their assistants and voluntary help from parents. Sessions vary and aim to meet the particular needs of children and parents in the community. Some last for two hours, others go on all day. Playgroups are much less makeshift than they used to be and an increasing number are buying their own premises. The equipment provided often comprises a slide, climbing frame, sand and water, paints, books, bricks, assorted toys and games, plus opportunities for imaginary play. These will of course vary to a large extent on the funds available. Although parents are encouraged to attend regularly to help, at the same time they know they can leave their children in the care of the playgroup leaders. The PPA now produces guidelines for sessional playgroups, and give details of full day care, parent and toddler groups (see page 192) and all playgroups, whether the groups take children in their parent's absence, and whether they are registered with the local authority under the Children's Act. To find out where your nearest playgroup is, contact the Pre-School Playgroup Association.

Courses for playgroups
Playgroup leaders have all attended a course or had some form of
suitable training, details of which can be obtained from the PPA.
Colleges who run the Playgroup Practice Diploma course vary from
year to year, but an up-to-date list can be obtained from the PPA.
Anyone interested in working with young children can apply.

PARENT AND TODDLER GROUPS

Parent and toddler groups are organised in a variety of different ways
and each one offers different activities. Some may be affiliated to a
church hall or community centre, while others have been successfully
started and run by parents themselves. Their main value lies in
providing an opportunity for children (and parents) to socialise
together at an early stage. For more details about parent and toddler
groups contact the Pre-School Playgroup Association, 314 Vauxhall
Bridge Road, SW1V 1AA (tel. 071–828 2417).

A number of London boroughs have useful information on activities for pre-school children which cover everything from day nurseries
to swimming pools and sports centres. Look out for the following
booklets: *Under-5s in Barnet, Children's Ealing 135 Group, Hackney
under-8s guide, Under-5s in Camden, Greenwich Under-5s*. Copies can
be obtained from your town hall or main library.

PHYSICAL ACTIVITIES FOR UNDER-5S

Although an increasing number of sports and leisure centres hold
sessions for under-5s (see pages 181–183) there are other groups which
specialise in children's fitness.

Chrechendo
St Luke's Hall, Adrian Mews, Ifield Road, SW10.
Tel. 071–259 2727.

Crechendo run a network of gym play centres aimed at toddlers and
children up to 4½ years old. Separate age group classes make sure
that even the youngest babies (4–9 months) get the most out of
their babyplay sessions. Classes are filled with movement, music,
sights and sounds which children cannot experience at home. A
trial session is available to all newcomers before they join, enabling
them to see how the programme works. Classes are reasonably
priced and run every week of the year closing only over Christmas
and Bank Holidays. They are booked in terms of eight to sixteen
weeks according to the season, although it is possible to join
mid-term if places are available. There are centres at:

Battersea	Lower Hall, Battersea Arts Centre, Town Hall Road, SW11.
Chelsea	St Luke's Hall, Adrian Mews, Ifield Road, SW10.

Chiswick	St Peter's Hall, corner Southfield Road, St Albans Avenue, W4.
Ealing	All Saints Hall, Elm Grove Road, Ealing Common, W5.
Finchley	David Lloyd Club, Glebelands, High Road, Finchley, N12.
Fulham	St Dionis Hall, St Dionis Road, SW6.
Hampstead	St Thomas More Hall, Maresfield Gardens, off Fitzjohns Avenue, NW3.
Islington	Highbury 'Roundhouse', 71 Ronald's Road, N5.
Knightsbridge	St Columba's Hall, Pont Street Lennox Gardens, SW1.
Mortlake	Shoreline Centre, Mortlake High Street, opposite Cowley Road, SW14.
Muswell Hill	St James's Church Hall, Birchwood Avenue, Muswell Hill, N10.
Notting Hill	Tabernacle, Powis Square, W11.
Putney	Putney Leisure Centre, Dryburgh Hall, Dryburgh Road, SW15.
Wimbledon	Trinity Church Hall, Mansel Road, off Wimbledon Hill Road, SW19.

Tumble Tots
Tel. 021–585 7003.

Tumble Tots is an international organisation operating an active physical play programme for young children. The sessions are designed to encourage the development of the main motor skills of climbing, balance, agility and co-ordination in a safe environment with fully trained staff and a strong emphasis on fun. For details of venues in the London area that take part in the programme ring Tumble Tots on the number above.

British Amateur Gymnastics Association
Ford Hall, Lilleshall National Sports Centre, Near Newport, Shropshire.
Tel. 0952–820330.

The BAGA pre-school gymnastics and movement learning programme has no lower age limit and is fun and easy to do. Under-5s learn how to use different objects to make them stretch and curl, roll and jump. They can use balls, hoops, ribbons, bean bags and go on imaginary adventures by pretending to be explorers, fairy-tale characters or super heroes. There is large apparatus to try out and the exercises are challenging but fun. To find out whether there is a BAGA club in your area and for any other information you might need, contact the Lilleshall Sports Centre.

SWIMMING

For most young children, playing in the bath is as much fun as washing is distasteful. In order not to lose this enjoyment an introduction to a swimming pool as early as possible is the best way of preserving their interest in water and eliminating any fear. Listed on pages 181–183 are leisure centres in London. Those marked with an asterisk provide parent and toddler sessions or 'duckling' classes, both of which provide an excellent opportunity for children to play together, learn to swim and feel confident because a parent is there. Instruction is available at some swimming pools.

MUSIC, MOVEMENT AND DANCE

Whatever their age children take great delight in playing and listening to music. Movement and dance are a valuable and natural way to help improve co-ordination, whether through simple songs and nursery rhymes played at home or by taking it a step further and joining one of the classes available in the Greater London area. Telephone to check availability, times and cost.

Amadeus Centre
50 Shirland Road, Maida Vale, W9.
Tel. 071–289 1869.

Susan Zalcman teaches 'pre-ballet' for under-3s as well as ballet classes for 3-year-olds and upwards. Places are limited so book well in advance to guarantee your child a place.

Crackerjack
99 Oaklands Road, Hanwell, W7.
Tel. 081–840 3355.

A series of 40-minute weekly classes for the under-5s from the time they can walk – accompanied by parents or carers – until they are ready to attend on their own. The Crackerjack tumbling programme emphasises the importance of play, parental involvement and fun, and encourages children to sing along and move to music thus experiencing a variety of physical activities like swinging, jumping, climbing and bouncing. Enrolment is for a term but families can try a couple of lessons to begin with and see how they progress.

Dance Works
16 Balderton Street, W1.
Tel. 071–629 6183.

Regular ballet, jive and tap lessons take place for under-5s at the centre. For more information telephone the above.

Ealing Dance Centre
96 Pitshanger Lane, W5.
Tel. 081–998 2283.

Ballet classes for 2-year-olds upwards.

Highgate Newtown Community Centre
25 Bertram Street, N19.
Tel. 071–272 7201.

Weekly music and movement sessions for under-5s during term time only.

Jumpers
Ealing WMCA, 14 Bond Street, Ealing, W5.
Tel. 081–579 1421.

Half-hour sessions of action, songs and rhymes for children aged between 18 months and 2½ years accompanied by a parent or carer.

Kingsgate Community Centre
107 Kingsgate Road, NW6.
Tel. 071–328 9480.

A weekly dance class for 4-year-olds and over.

Pineapple Studio
7 Langley Street, Covent Garden, WC2.
Tel. 071–289 1869.

Susan Zalcman teaches pre-school ballet for under-3s as well as classes for over-3s. Places are limited so book well in advance to guarantee your child a place.

Royal Academy of Dancing
Vicarage Crescent, SW11.
Tel. 071–223 0091.

Classes for 5-year-olds and upwards are held each week with a view to taking the Royal Academy of Dancing exam. Enrolment is for a term.

West London School of Dance
46 Bulwer Street, W12.
Tel. 081–743 3856.

The school operates from four different studios and offers classes in ballet, tap and jazz at all levels for children from 2½ years old. They aim to develop a freedom of movement and self-expression through the enjoyment of dance. All classes except jazz have a pianist.

28

Practical help

Here are a few things you might need to know in order to make your time out in London more trouble free.

PROBLEMS AND EMERGENCIES

Health

If you don't know anyone locally who can recommend a good doctor or dentist, contact your local town hall, which will have up-to-date lists on file. They do not, however, recommend individual people. Libraries also have lists of doctors and dentists; dentists are also listed in the Yellow Pages telephone directory.

The Community Health Council (CHC)

The CHC is a statutory organisation set up by the government to represent your interests in the National Health Service. It will take note of any complaints or criticisms you might have and give advice on all matters relating to health. CHC is drawn from a cross-section of the public, most of whom are voluntary members, and is a valuable watchdog which ensures that the best possible service is given to the public. The CHC publicise their services widely in the local press, libraries, town halls and hospitals.

CHILDCARE

Finding someone to babysit can be a problem, especially if there is no suitable friend or relative close at hand. Fortunately, there are a number of agencies in London who provide babysitters and temporary nannies at short notice. Agencies will probably be more expensive than your regular babysitter, as they charge a fee on top of wages, but they can be useful in a crisis.

Babysitters Unlimited
Tel. 081–892 8888.

Childminders
9 Paddington Street, W1.
Tel. 071–935 2049.

Home Services Agency
5 Cherwell Way, Ruislip, Middlesex.

Tel. 0895–631302.

Just Kidding
250 King's Road, SW3.
Tel. 071–351 5856.

Life Savers
109 Wilkinson Way, W4.
Tel. 081–749 5335.

Universal Aunts
Tel. 071–386 5900.

Pippa Pop-ins
430 Fulham Road, SW6.
Tel. 071–385 2458.

A more luxury approach to childminding can be found at Pippa Pop-ins – opened in 1992 and the first recognised hotel for children in the United Kingdom. It is the brainchild of Pippa Deakin who identified the need for a nursery with overnight accommodation. The idea has proved very successful. Children between the ages of 2 and 12 enjoy the comforts of a four-star hotel while their parents, secure in the knowledge their children are being well cared for, can go out for the evening. Other services include a day nursery school for 2–5-year-olds, excursions during school holidays and a school run service which collects children from seventeen central London schools and supervises high tea, homework and organised activities until children are picked up at 6.00p.m.

The National Association for the Welfare of Children in Hospital
Argyle House, Euston Road, NW1.
Tel. 071–833 2041.

Each year over 900,000 children are admitted to hospital. This can be a distressing experience not only for the child concerned but for parents as well. NAWCH provides a national information and counselling service to encourage parents and help them to cope. It campaigns for all children to be nursed in children's wards with unrestricted visiting for parents and accommodation for mothers who want to stay. Their groups all over the country provide extra facilities, such as hospital playgroups, beds and help with transport.

Accidents

In case of accidents dial 999 and ask for the ambulance service or go to the casualty department of the nearest hospital. The following have 24-hour Accident and Emergency Departments.

North-West Thames:

West Middlesex Hospital
Twickenham Road, Middlesex.

Tel. 081–560 2121.

Ealing Hospital
Uxbridge Road, Southall, Middlesex.
Tel. 081–574 2444.

Royal Free Hospital
(teaching) Pond Street, NW3.
Tel. 071–794 0500.

Hammersmith Hospital
Du Cane Road, W12.
Tel. 081–743 2030.

North-East Thames:

North Middlesex Hospital
Sterling Way, N18.
Tel. 081–887 2000.

Hackney and Homerton Hospital
Homerton Row, E9.
Tel. 081–985 5555.

Whipps Cross Hospital
Whipps Cross Road, E11.
Tel. 081–539 5522.

Whittington Hospital
Highgate Hill, N19.
Tel. 071–272 3070.

University College Hospital
(teaching) Gower Street, WC1.
Tel. 071–387 9300.

St Bartholomew's Hospital
West Smithfield, EC1.
Tel. 071–601 8888.

Queen Elizabeth Hospital for Children
Hackney Road, E2.
Tel. 071–739 8422.

South-West Thames:

Queen Mary's Hospital
Roehampton Lane, SW15.
Tel. 081–789 6611.

St George's Hospital
Blackshaw Road, SW17.
Tel. 081–672 1255.

South-East Thames:

Greenwich District Hospital
Vanburgh Hill, SE10.
Tel. 081–858 8141.

Lewisham Hospital
Lewisham High Street, SE13.
Tel. 081–690 4311.

Guy's Hospital
St Thomas Street, SE1.
Tel. 071–955 5000.

King's College Hospital
Denmark Hill, SE5.
Tel. 071–274 6222.

St Thomas' Hospital
Lambeth Palace Road, SE1.
Tel. 071–928 9292.

Late-night chemists

Doctors will advise on the rota for late-night chemists in your area. Police stations also keep a list of local emergency chemists and doctors.

Boots
Piccadilly Circus, W1.
Tel. 071–734 6126.
Open Mon.–Fri. 8.30a.m.–8.00p.m.; Sat. 9.00a.m.–8.00p.m.; Sun. 12.00 noon–6.00p.m.

75 Queensway, W2.
Tel. 071–229 9266.
Open Mon.–Sat. 9.00a.m.–10.00p.m.

Bliss
50–56 Willesden Lane, NW6.
Tel. 071–624 8000.
Open Mon.–Sun. 9.00a.m.–12.00 midnight.

Warman Freed
45 Golders Green Road, NW11.
Tel. 081–455 4351.
Open Mon.–Sun. 8.30a.m.–12.00 midnight.

Lost Property

To trace lost property first check at your nearest police station. If relevant also try:

London Transport Lost Property Department
200 Baker Street, W1.

Call in person to enquire about lost property left on the underground or buses. It may take a day or two for things to turn up so check again if you're not successful straight away.

Lost Property Office
15 Penton Street, N1.
For possessions left in London taxis.

For property lost on **British Rail** trains, contact the lost property office at the relevant main line terminus at either end of the route.

HAIRDRESSERS

A growing number of salons in London are attempting to take the strain out of children's haircutting sessions. Great efforts go into making the occasion as tear-free as possible by providing diversions such as music, toys, videos and books – with the result that what used to be regarded as a chore can turn into an enjoyable day out. Prices vary considerably so check these before making an appointment. Salons pioneering this approach include:

Nipper Snippers
8 Hollywood Road, SW10.
Tel. 071–351 2329.

Snips
Children's World,
317 Cricklewood Broadway, NW2.
Tel. 081–208 1088.

Snips
The Crypt, St John's Church, West Ealing, W13.
Tel. 081–579 0791.

Open 10.00a.m.–1.00p.m, Tues. Thurs. and first Saturday of the month.

Trotters
34 King's Road, SW3.
Tel. 071–259 9620.

127 Kensington High Street, W8.
Tel. 071–937 9373.

Some large department stores such as D.H. Evans and Selfridges cut children's hair, although only Harrods salon (fourth floor) provides toys and videos to keep the young customers amused.

D.H. Evans
Oxford Street, W1.
Tel. 071–629 8800.

Harrods
Knightsbridge, SW1.
Tel. 071–730 1234.

Selfridges
400 Oxford Street, W1.
Tel. 071–629 1234.

HAND-ME-DOWNS

Exploiting the continuing fashion for 'nearly new' outfits, some enterprising parents have set up shops selling second-hand children's clothes at reduced prices. These shops work on a simple sale-or-return basis. On certain days of the week you can take in the clothes you wish to sell and agree a price for them; then, if they are considered suitable, your clothes are put on sale. After a period of time any items not sold will either be offered back to you or given away to charity. The shop usually takes 30–50 per cent commission. Listed below are some of the shops operating such a system.

Change of Habit
25 Abbeville Road, Clapham Common, SW4.
Tel. 081–675 9475.

Open Mon.–Fri. 11.00a.m.–6.00p.m.; Sat. 10.00a.m.– 6.00p.m.

Just Outgrown
99 Devonshire Road, W4.
Tel. 081–995 5405.

Open Tues.–Fri. 10.00a.m.–4.00p.m.

The Little Trading Company
7 Bedford Corner, The Avenue, W4.
Tel. 081–742 3152.

Open Mon.–Fri. 9.30a.m.–5.00p.m., Thurs. 10.00a.m.– 5.00p.m., Sat. 10.00a.m.–4.00p.m.

One Careful Owner
17a The Burroughs, NW4.
Tel. 081–202 3763.

Open Mon.–Fri. 11.00a.m.–4.00p.m.; Sat. 10.00a.m.– 3.00p.m.

Rainbow
253 Archway Road, N6.
Tel. 081–340 8003.

Open Mon.–Sat. 10.00a.m.–5.00p.m.

Scarecrow
131 Walham Green Court, Moore Park Road, SW6.
Tel. 071–381 1023.

Open Tues.–Fri. 10.00a.m.–5.00p.m.; Sat. 9.30a.m.– 1.00p.m.

Sunflower
36 Union Court, off Sheen Road, Richmond, Surrey.
Tel. 081–948 5792.

Open Tues.–Sat. 10.00a.m.–1.00p.m. and 2.00p.m.– 4.00p.m.

Small Change
Carnegie House, junction of Well Road and New End, NW3.
Tel. 081–794 3043.

Open Mon.–Fri. 9.00a.m.–5.00p.m.; Sat. 10.00a.m.– 5.00p.m.

Totters
57 Tottenham Lane, Crouch End, N8.
Tel. 081–341 0377.

Open Mon.–Sat. 10.00a.m.–5.00p.m.

HIRE SHOPS

There are a number of hire shops that rent out pushchairs. You leave a deposit and hire by the day or week. Check the Yellow Pages for details.

Baby Hire
Tel. 081–870 5846.

Established for over seven years, Baby Hire's impressive selection of equipment includes everything from cots and pushchairs to play pens, Z-beds, potties and breast pumps. They run a delivery and collection service and as the business is home based they are open all hours.

SHOES

Children's feet grow at an alarming rate and shoes can easily become too tight without an adult noticing, so make a point of visiting a good shoe shop at least once every three or four months to have your children's feet measured professionally. The Children's Foot Health Register at Bedford House, 69–79 Fulham High Street, SW6 (tel. 071–371 5185), produces a useful guide to shops which stock shoes in width fittings and where trained staff will measure your child's feet carefully. The health department at Clark's Shoes, 40 High Street, Street, Somerset (tel. 0458–43131), will provide various free leaflets and posters giving lots of useful tips on how to keep your feet in tiptop condition.

PARTY ADVICE

If the idea of giving a children's party fills you with horror, do not despair. Listed below are a number of recommended agencies and entertainers who help take the strain out of party-giving.

Abracadabra Magic
Tel. 081–998 5730.

AM and PM Catering
15–17 Ingate Place, SW8.
Tel. 071–622 6229.

Bob Thingummybob
Tel. 081–907 4606.

Bonzo the Clown
Tel. 081–980 7355.

Crechendo Ltd
St Luke's Hall, Adrian Mews, Ifield Road, SW10.
Tel. 071–259 2727.

Frog Frolicks
123 Ifield Road, SW10.
Tel. 081–370 4358.

Annie Fryer Catering
134 Lots Road, SW10.
Tel. 071–351 4333.

Gorgeous Gourmets
Gresham Way, Wimbledon, SW19.
Tel. 081–944 7771.

Hamlyns
3 Abingdon Road, W8.
Tel. 071–937 3442.

Jolly Roger Entertainments
Tel. 081–902 3373.

Oscar's Party Entertainers
Tel. 081–958 8158.

Peter Pinner
Tel. 081–863 1528.

Smartie Artie
4 New Greens Avenue, St Albans, Herts.
Tel. 0727–50837.

Walligog the Wizard
Tel. 071–624 2287.

Wonderland Puppet Theatre
8 Kempton Avenue, Sunbury, Middlesex.
Tel. 0932–784467.

If you are feeling very rich, telephone I'm a Party Buster on 0753–48822 and arrange to hire a private bus for your children's party, complete with food, puppet show and anything else the little darlings may desire. Alternatively, a directory of professional puppeteers who entertain at parties is obtainable from the Puppet Trust, Battersea Arts Centre, Lavender Hill, SW11. For other ideas, call in at one of the shops listed below that stock party paraphernalia such as jokes, novelties, magic tricks and masks.

Barnums
67 Hammersmith Road, W14.
Tel. 071–602 1211.

Carnival
129 Little Ealing Lane, W5.
Tel. 081–567 3210.

Carnival Store
95 Hammersmith Road, W14.
Tel. 071–603 7824.

Escapade
150 Camden High Street, NW1.
Tel. 071–485 7384.

Knutz
1 Russell Street, WC2.
Tel. 071–836 3117.

Joker
97 Chiswick High Road, W4.
Tel. 081–995 4118.

Lewis Davenport
51 Great Russell Street, W1.
Tel. 071–405 8534.

Non-Stop Party Shop
214–216 Kensington High Street, W8.
Tel. 071–384 1491.

Oscar's Den
127–129 Abbey Road, NW6.
Tel. 071–328 6683.

Partymad
67 Gloucester Avenue, NW1.
Tel. 071–586 0169.

Theatre Zoo
21 Earlham Street, WC2.
Tel. 071–836 3150.

Tridias
25 Bute Street, SW7.
Tel. 071–584 2330.

6 Lichfield Terrace, Sheen Road, Richmond, Surrey.
Tel. 081–948 3459.

CHILDREN'S LIBRARIES

The only qualification required to join your local library is that you live or work in the area. Junior libraries cater for children of all ages. Everyone is welcome and miniature tables and chairs make it easier for small children to sit and enjoy the books available. Three books can usually be borrowed for up to three weeks and no fines are charged, although reminder notices will be sent if books become overdue. Children's libraries can also provide useful information about what's on in the area and many run children's activities during the holidays. Some children's libraries have a mobile bus for those who are unable to get out and about, and certain local authorities arrange storytelling sessions during the holidays. For more details, telephone the Library Association on 071–636 7543. The Yellow Pages include details of local libraries.

The National Resource and Information Centre for Children's Literature at Book House, 45 East Hill, SW18 (tel. 081–870 9055) is a reference library that brings together a selection of the best children's fiction, non-fiction and poetry published over the last two years and which is updated annually. This is not a lending library but visitors can wander around and see all the latest publications and obtain information on authors and illustrators of children's books. The library is open Mon.–Fri. 9.00a.m.–5.00p.m. and admission is free. The centre organises an annual touring exhibition of over 300 titles of children's books, including fiction and non-fiction for all ages. It will visit schools and libraries by arrangement.

USEFUL ADDRESSES

Artsline
5 Crowndale Road, NW1.
Tel. 071–388 2227.

Information and advice for disabled people concerning access to cinemas, theatres, arts centres, musical venues, etc.

Childline
Freephone 0800–1111.

Counselling service for children in need. Adults will be referred elsewhere.

Down's Syndrome Association
155 Mitcham Road, SW17.
Tel. 081–682 4001.

On average, three babies each day are born with Down's Syndrome in the UK. It is a genetic condition caused by the presence of an extra chromosome – the result of a genetic accident at the time of conception or soon after. It is not a disease and cannot be treated. The Association provides immediate vital support and assistance for new parents and gives on-going guidance on a wide range of subjects from early feeding problems, education and adolescence, to life after school.

Gingerbread
35 Wellington Street, WC2.
Tel. 071–240 0953.

A nationally organised self-help association for one-parent families which encourages individuals who face particular problems to get together and provide each other with mutual support.

Invalid Children's Aid Association
126 Buckingham Palace Road, SW1.
Tel. 071–730 9891.

A registered charity running schools for handicapped children. In the Greater London area the association employs a number of social work officers to help parents care for handicapped children.

Kidscape
Tel. 071–731 3300.

A helpline for children who are being bullied at school.

National Asthma Campaign
Providence House, Providence Place, N1.
Tel. 071–226 2260.

The NAC is a medical charity which funds research and provides information and literature about all aspects of living with asthma. The Asthma Helpline (0345–010203, open 1.00p.m.– 9.00p.m. weekdays) is run by nurses with additional asthma training and calls are charged at local rates only. There is also a network of self-help groups run by volunteers.

National Children's Bureau
8 Wakely Street, EC1.
Tel. 071–278 9441.

An independent voluntary organisation concerned with children's needs in the family, school and society in general.

National Council for One-Parent Families
255 Kentish Town Road, NW5.
Tel. 071–267 1361.

Gives help to single parents through its advice and rights department, which is staffed by professional advisers, a welfare rights officer and legal officer. The service is free and confidential.

National Deaf Children's Society
45 Hereford Road, W2.
Tel. 071–229 9272.

Helps deaf children to break through the silence barrier and fights for a better education to suit their needs.

National Society for the Prevention of Cruelty to Children (NSPCC)
67 Saffron Hill, EC1.
Tel. 071–242 1626.

Works to prevent child abuse in all forms, to give practical help to families who are at risk, and to encourage greater public awareness and understanding of child abuse.

Royal National Institute for the Blind
224 Great Portland Street, W1.
Tel. 071–388 1266.

Helps visually handicapped children and young people to take their place in society by supporting children in local schools as well as maintaining their own special schools.

Index